MY CRICKET JOURNEY

Barry Gibbs has a long background in cricket administration at the top level and has written extensively about the game.

He was secretary of the Queensland Cricket Association, Brisbane Cricket Ground Trust and the Queensland Cricketers' Club from 1961 to 1966. Barry was appointed executive manager (later called chief executive) of the South Australian Cricket Association in 1988, and remained in this position until 1997. He was the Australian Cricket Board's Code of Behaviour Commissioner for four years.

In between his time at the QCA and the SACA, Barry Gibbs worked for 22 years as a merchant banker. During that time cricket was still very much a part of his life, as it is now in his retirement in Adelaide where he maintains close contact with the game he loves.

MY CRICKET JOURNEY

Barry Gibbs

Wakefield Press
17 Rundle Street
Kent Town
South Australia 5067

Designed and typeset by Michael Deves
Printed and bound by Hyde Park Press

ISBN 1 86254 569 3

For Peg

AUTHOR'S NOTE

During the three years it has taken me to write this book I have been fortunate enough to receive help from many people.

In the early days the advice and encouragement of a number of journalist friends were crucial in getting me started. In this regard I thank Ian McDonald, Richie Benaud, Alan Shiell, Tom Prior, Robert Craddock and the late Neil Hawke.

When I began to chronicle my journey I didn't know how to turn a computer on. Thanks to the patience of Janet Singh, Colin Park and Michael Hutchesson I was able to complete the manuscript without too many anxious moments.

Along the way many others contributed to the project. In particular I would like to thank Sharene Bowels, Tony Brock, Les Burdett, Bob Carr, Bryan Charlton, Laurie Colliver, Tony Crafter, Mike Deare, Tricia Disbury, Marianne Dunham, Colin Egar, Mark Frankcom, Greg Hobbs, Terry Jenner, Rex Jory, Darren Lehmann, Michael Lovett, Davina Malcolm, Rod Marsh, Tim May, Geoff Macfarlane, Ian McLachlan, Creagh O'Connor, Sharon Polkinghorne, Ray Reynolds, John Schrader, Jeremy Schultz, Joe Scuderi, Nicci Sleep and Richard Watson.

My thanks to Michael Bollen of Wakefield Press who has helped to bring the book to fruition.

Finally, I want to thank my wife Peg. She has been a sounding board, proofreader, creator of ideas, stern critic, motivator and above all, my inspiration. Peg has been on this journey every step of the way. It is hers as much as mine.

CONTENTS

FOREWORD

by Richie Benaud

Barry Gibbs is one of a select band of cricket followers who wasn't at the Gabba on 14 December 1960 for the last day of the 'Tied Test'. Although the crowd was just over the 4000 mark I reckon I've met scores of thousands who claim to have been present, so vividly have the match and the exciting finish been etched in their memories. Mind you, Barry was there shortly after because he had been chosen as the new Secretary of the Queensland Cricket Association and was tidying up a few matters in the southern state of Victoria before taking up a position which he served with dedication and skill, as he did later when he became Chief Executive of the South Australian Cricket Association.

Cricketers, from the time the game began in Australia, have possessed a sixth sense about administrators and the word quickly moved around the players of the various states that Queensland had 'found one' in Gibbs, as indeed was the case, an administrator who, for his employer, did his job with great efficiency, but was also a players' man. The combination is not easily found. As Barry has also been a journalist and has the ability to tell a story, this is a book which will fill in gaps, provide information not readily available to others and, as well, will do so with good humour rather than in heavy-handed fashion, a trait not unknown in administration forty years ago.

In the Queensland teams against which I played there was always a list of players with a rich vein of laconic humour. Ken 'Slasher' Mackay headed that list, Wally Grout was there, Peter Burge and, from the time Barry took over as Secretary, Wesley Hall had the ability to bring down the dressing-room, in lieu of the more traditional house.

The Gabba has been a ground of contrasts for me. It used to be a cricket ground with a dressing-room with a galvanised iron roof and no shortage of splinters on the old wooden floor. Now it is one of the most up to date cricket grounds in the world and through all those eras and earlier it has seen its share of drama. At Test level there was the no-balling of Ian Meckiff in the South Africa–Australia match in 1963, a game preceded by Queensland being beaten on the first innings after making 613; Bob Simpson's 359 was too much for them.

A quarter of a century later Ian Botham played for Queensland and it was a summer with a difference with the extraordinary Flight 55 to Perth. A few months later Barry Gibbs took up the position of Chief Executive of the SACA and his time there was laced with interest in what was one of the most important eras in the history of Australian cricket. The Cricket Academy and the great work done by Rod Marsh, the saga of the lights at the Adelaide Oval and the very close association he had with the late Sir Donald Bradman – all these aspects of cricket history are brought out in delightful and good-humoured fashion, though also with an ability to set out the facts squarely and accurately for history. This book will be successful; it fills a need in Australian cricket literature.

PREFACE

Montgomery Barnes Gibbs, a man I never knew, had a lot to do with this book being written. So did Jack Clarke, lawyer, wine connoisseur, member of the South Australian Cricket Association board and cricket raconteur, who I know very well.

It was Clarke who first put the thought into my mind when I was SACA chief executive. During our countless in-depth discussions on the game Jack would say to me: 'Gibbsy, there has to be a book in you, why don't you write one?'

But I am sure it is the genes of Montgomery Gibbs, my paternal grandfather that gave me the desire to sit down and do it. Anyone who has written a book will tell you that this is not a task to be embarked on lightly. Grandfather Gibbs was an author, and a respected one too. His best-known work was the *Military Career of Napoleon the Great,* first published in the United States of America in 1895. In the preface to that book he said: 'The writing of this anecdotal military history is the result of years of study and careful reading of the subject.'

And so it is with *My Cricket Journey.* The study has been intense during my involvement in the wonderful game of cricket for half a century, the careful reading of the subject an ongoing pleasure to me for even longer. I doubt that Montgomery B. Gibbs ever saw a cricket match, having been born in Chicago in 1858 where he lived most of his life before passing away in 1909. But he had passion for his subject, just as I have a passion for cricket.

This book is intended to provide an insight into the work of a cricket administrator and to highlight how the game has changed over the past four decades. It goes back to 1961, when I became secretary of the Queensland Cricket Association. The Gabba then was a quaint old ground, ringed with giant Moreton Bay and Poinciana trees, and had little more in the way of buildings than a few old wooden grandstands. The permanent staff of the QCA was just two people, one of them me.

The Australian Cricket Board had no staff at all, only a part-time secretary, Alan Barnes, who carried out his duties in conjunction with his job as secretary of the New South Wales Cricket Association.

Cricket at the first-class and international level in Australia has now become a big business with revenue amounting to many millions of dollars annually and employing hundreds of staff.

In my book I take a first-hand look at some of the game's legendary characters, moments of drama and courage, great matches and lighthearted occasions, during a period when Australian cricket was evolving from an amateur game to a full-time professional sport.

I have enjoyed the journey immensely and I thank Montgomery Barnes Gibbs and Jack Clarke for their part in enabling me to share it with others.

1

QUEENSLAND CRICKET CALLS

Cricket has been very much a part of my life for the past 50 years. I played the game with zest from the time I was a very young boarder at Melbourne's Box Hill Grammar School during the dark days of World War II. I loved it as a sport but never in my dreams did I envisage that I would spend most of my working life so deeply involved in the grand old game.

Looking back now, perhaps something that occurred way back in 1947 should have given me an inkling of what the future held. By some minor miracle, I made my way into the grand final of the Victorian Quiz Kids quest – where I felt out of place alongside some seriously brilliant minds, including that of former Federal politician, Labor Party president, historian and Australia's best-ever quiz contestant, the ubiquitous Barry Jones.

It was sport, and cricket in particular, that allowed me to reach the final. For some reason questions kept cropping up on various sports that the other nine finalists, all of who clearly possessed very high IQs, weren't able to answer. This left me, a sports-mad 14 year old who far preferred reading cricket books to history books, with a clear run because I happened to know, for example, that the names of the three Indian-born cricketers who had made centuries for England in their debut Test matches were Ranjitsinhji, Duleepsinhji and the Nawab of Pataudi.

Fast forward to 1960. I was still playing cricket at a modest but respectable level. That was the year when my life, and those of my wife Peg and our three very young daughters, Lyn, Jenny and Sue, took an unexpected turn.

I had a good job as secretary of the Royal Victorian Aero Club at Moorabbin airport and saw the aviation industry as my future career. Cricket was relaxation, a game I enjoyed playing immensely, but I had been immersed in aeroplanes, and the people who fly them, since doing my National Service Training at RAAF Base, East Sale, as an 18 year old in 1951.

For six years in the 1950s I had worked for the Australian Air Pilots Association and its successor, the Australian Federation of Air Pilots, before moving to the Aero Club in 1959. In those days the basic training aircraft were the ageless Tiger Moth and the slightly more modern single-winged Chipmunk, each a delight to fly.

By 1960 I was enjoying life in suburban Melbourne – genuinely engrossed in my work, playing as much cricket as I could and waiting impatiently for the Carlton Football Club to emerge from a VFL premiership drought that eventually stretched to 21 years. Even though we didn't have much in the way of material possessions, my family and I were content with our lot.

Then it happened. I was sitting at the kitchen table one Sunday evening reading the paper and enjoying a cold beer after the domestic mayhem of our youngsters' evening meal and bath time. Suddenly an advertisement in the employment section jumped off the page at me. Why I was reading that part of the paper I do not know, because I certainly wasn't looking for a job.

The advertisement was for a position in Brisbane as Secretary of the Queensland Cricket Association, the Brisbane Cricket Ground Trust and the Queensland Cricketers' Club. I read it through a couple of times and remember thinking, briefly, that working full time in cricket administration would be different, if nothing else.

Half jokingly I showed the advertisement to Peg, expecting that she would tell me to forget all about it. But she surprised me by saying, 'If you really like the look of the position why don't you put in for it?'

That is exactly what I did. As I look back now, it seems an adventurous move. I was only 27, our immediate families lived in Melbourne and we had a close circle of friends. I didn't know much about Brisbane at all, having been there just twice in my life for overnight stops on the way to and from New Guinea in an old Dakota aircraft during my time with the Air Pilots Association. As for Peg, she had never even set foot in Queensland, although she did have a brother who lived there.

On the other hand I felt I had the credentials to do the job. I was honorary secretary of the Burwood & District Cricket Association in Melbourne and was playing sub-district cricket with the Oakleigh Cricket

Club, while my time with the Aero Club and the Air Pilots Association had given me eight years solid experience in association and club management.

I sent off my application as much out of curiosity as genuine interest. A short time later, to my surprise, I received a letter back from the QCA asking if I would be available for an interview in Brisbane. There was nothing to lose, so I accepted the invitation to fly up there in November 1960.

In Brisbane I met the full executive committee of the QCA at the Brisbane Cricket Ground – all 18 of them! I felt that the interview had gone quite well and left feeling mildly optimistic, particularly as one prominent member of the committee had confided to me after the meeting that I had his support (and, as I later discovered, the majority of the numbers around the table which went with that support).

I flew back to Melbourne the next day after having a quick look around Brisbane. During the trip I had plenty of time to think about what I would do if I was offered the position from the field of 80 applicants. I came to the conclusion that while I was very happy in the aviation industry, a full-time role in cricket administration at the top level would be an opportunity that might never come my way again. Besides that, the salary on offer represented a substantial increase over what I was currently earning.

When I got back to Melbourne Peg agreed with my thoughts, so we settled down to an anxious wait for word from the QCA that, thankfully, wasn't long in arriving. A few days later I got a telephone call from Vic Schaefer, the chairman of the executive committee, to tell me that the job was mine if I wanted it at an annual salary of £2000 and that they would like me to start at the beginning of January 1961. I accepted on the spot.

So began my involvement with cricket at the first-class and international level. At the time, although I didn't know until much later, it appears that I was the youngest secretary of a major cricket organisation anywhere in the world. Try that one at your next trivia night.

Before officially starting my new job I was to have gone back up to Brisbane for the first Test of the forthcoming series between Australia and the West Indies so that I could observe first hand the way things were done at the famous old Gabba during a big match. That trip didn't eventuate –

which, at the time, was fine by me as we had so much to do at home in preparation for the big move that lay ahead.

How was I to know that I was about to miss out on that incredible tied Test, the first in cricket history? There I was, the secretary-elect of the QCA, scheduled to be in Brisbane but actually at home in Melbourne and consequently missing out on the greatest Test of all time.

Even now I am occasionally introduced to people as the man in charge at the QCA when the tied Test was played. I then have to go through the business of explaining that, while I had been appointed to the position, I didn't start my new job until three lousy weeks later.

I did, however, spend a few days at the second Test in Melbourne before we headed off to Brisbane. The idea was that I could be shown the ropes by the Victorian Cricket Association secretary, Jack Ledward, whom I had previously met on a few occasions when representing the Burwood and District Cricket Association at meetings of the Victorian Junior Cricket Union held at VCA House in Melbourne.

Jack was a genial man with vast experience. He went out of his way to put me at ease as he showed me the many and varied tasks undertaken by a home State secretary when a Test match was in progress. These included, to list a few, acting as the Australian team manager and dealing with the varying needs of the players, attending to the requirements of the visiting team and its officials, ensuring that the numerous invited guests were well looked after, dealing with the media, attending to urgent items of correspondence and telegrams, liaising with the ground authority (the Melbourne Cricket Club), ensuring that the gate takings tallied up to the attendance figures and that the takings were taken away into secure custody, and handling a constant stream of telephone calls on all sorts of matters, as well as enquiries from spectators.

Initially I found the experience of being exposed to the upper echelons of international cricket an intimidating experience. But, with the help of people like Jack Ledward, it didn't take long for me to feel a lot more comfortable and start to accept the fact that, very soon, I would be directly involved in the running of the game at this elite level.

As Jack Ledward took me around the Melbourne Cricket Ground, I got to meet many past and present players and officials, as well as dignitaries from various walks of life. Among them was Sir Donald Bradman, who was chairman of the Australian Board of Control and the Australian selection panel. It was the first time I had met the greatest cricketer the world has ever known; little did I know then that, in the years ahead, I was to get to know the great man well and have a close working relationship with him.

Like every Test of that unforgettable series, the second at Melbourne had its moments of drama and controversy. The most memorable of these was the Joe Solomon 'hit wicket' incident that occurred early in the West Indies second innings. Jack Ledward and I were working our way through the outer section of the MCG at the time, reading the turnstiles to get the official attendance for the day.

There were more than 60,000 people at the ground when Solomon, the little West Indies opening batsman and one of the heroes of the tied Test, went to pull a ball from Australian captain Richie Benaud only to have his cap fall off and land on the stumps, dislodging the bails in the process. On appeal, Solomon was quite correctly given out hit wicket by umpire Col Hoy.

This was a very unusual type of dismissal at any level of cricket, and especially so in a Test. Many of the spectators were unhappy about the turn of events; the West Indies team by now had become very popular in Australia. They began loudly booing Benaud, largely I believe, as they didn't really understand the reason for Solomon's dismissal.

It was an ugly scene as the Australian captain, for possibly the first time in his career, became the villain in the eyes of the crowd. This was well before the days of large-screen instant replays, so it took some time for it to become clear to spectators just what had occurred. The ABC radio broadcast of the match saved the day when the commentators made it clear that umpire Hoy was absolutely correct in giving Solomon out.

As Jack and I walked back to the official area via the maze of stairs and roads within the MCG, the crowd was stamping and jeering as if this were a football final rather than a cricket match. Fortunately the mood soon changed back again and there were no further incidents.

Two days after that introduction to Test cricket, the Gibbs family flew out of Melbourne full of anticipation about our new life in Brisbane. On arrival at the old Eagle Farm airport Peg, the girls and I were met by a large group of cricket officials and a media contingent.

The print media had shown interest in my appointment when it was announced, running headlines such as 'Cricket Job to Victorian' and 'Victorian Gets Top Job in Queensland Cricket'. At the time I was intrigued about this constant reference to a 'Victorian', as though I was some sort of alien. I soon learned that it took a while to be taken into the fold in the Sunshine State, particularly if you came from down south.

After a warm airport welcome, our adventure started to go downhill. It had been arranged that we would live in a house that was owned by one of the QCA executive committee members, Clarrie Apps, until we located a suitable permanent residence. I had seen the house on an earlier visit and it looked fine but when we arrived there we had a problem. Despite my understanding that the place was vacant and we would have it all to ourselves, we soon found out that Clarrie actually lived there and was still very much in residence.

There we were, a thousand miles from 'home' with three very tired and slightly bewildered children, in a strange house that we found ourselves sharing with a man we really didn't know. By now Peg, understandably, was not at all pleased with the arrangements. Nor was I.

We had to do something in a hurry. Fortunately Peg's brother, Bill Blair, who had been living in Queensland for number of years, had taken over the running of a hotel in a little town called Wooroolin, near Kingaroy up in Joh Bjelke Petersen territory, about 200 kilometres north-west of Brisbane. Bill and his wife, Eunice, were only too pleased to put the family up as they had plenty of spare rooms in the pub.

Within 48 hours of our arrival in Brisbane Peg and the girls had temporarily relocated to Wooroolin, while I went about the business of settling into my job and looking for a home for us to live in. The house-hunting didn't take too long and we were, belatedly, able to start our new life up north – on our own.

In 1961 the QCA offices were located in central Brisbane, about three kilometres by road from the Brisbane Cricket Ground. The staff consisted of just an assistant, Jean Shaw, and me. Having administrative responsibility for the newly opened Queensland Cricketers' Club, a two-storey licensed premises situated about fine leg at the Vulture Street end of the Gabba, in addition to the Brisbane Cricket Ground Trust and the QCA, meant that I had to contend with all sorts of logistical problems in those early days. Being based in an office in the city while the ground-staff and the club were out at Woollongabba was not an ideal situation.

It was obvious to me that the QCA offices would need to be relocated to the Gabba if I was to carry out my three-pronged management role effectively. After a lot of debate, and some opposition, the various committees agreed with me and by 1962 we moved into a newly constructed office building located near the Cricketers' Club with a view straight down the pitch.

My first Sheffield Shield match as QCA secretary was played two weeks after I started in the job. The visiting team was South Australia, captained by Les Favell. I could have never imagined that, 27 years later, I would become chief executive of the South Australian Cricket Association and that four players from that SA team, Ian McLachlan, Rex Sellers, Neil Dansie and Murray Sargent, would be members of the SACA governing body, the Ground and Finance Committee, when I started work at Adelaide Oval in 1988.

That SA team also included John Lill, now retired as secretary of the Melbourne Cricket Club after a long stint in the job; Bob Lloyd, a vice-president of the same club; Barry Jarman, an International Cricket Council referee and a close friend for decades; and the late Neil Hawke, a sporting journalist, who lost his courageous battle against 20 years of illness on Christmas Day, 2000.

This was an exciting time to be involved in the administration of the game, particularly for a young man. After years of mostly boring Test cricket, Australia and the West Indies had breathed new life into it with their entertaining approach. If I ever need reminding of that fact I only have to look at that wonderful photograph of the two Test captains, Richie Benaud and Frank Worrell, being cheered by a massive crowd outside the Melbourne Town Hall in February 1961 following a ticker-tape parade the day after the fifth Test ended.

Some time before that moving occasion Sir Donald Bradman had contacted me with the news that the Board of Control had decided to produce a perpetual trophy for competition in Australia v West Indies Test series, to be named after the West Indies captain. Sir Donald wanted to know if the ball that was being used at the end of the tied Test was available to be mounted on the trophy – if that ball couldn't be located, another one from the box of balls issued for the historic match would be fine.

Unfortunately the actual ball being used when Ian Meckiff was run out by Joe Solomon's direct hit had gone missing in the chaos that followed. We still had the box of Kookaburra 'Turf' cricket balls from the tied Test, so I picked out a couple and sent them to the VCA office in Melbourne, where one of them soon took pride of place atop of the Frank Worrell trophy.

The ball that Wes Hall was bowling at the end of the tied Test was not the only priceless piece of history from that match that disappeared. The official Australian score sheets also went missing. Unlike the ball, which re-appeared out of the blue almost two years later, the score sheets had, unbeknown to me, gone for good.

Some time after the 1961/62 season ended Jean Shaw was checking material for that year's annual report, just as she always had. I was keen to introduce some additional detailed statistical information into the report and asked her casually where the original score sheets from previous seasons were kept.

That was the moment when I learned the awful truth – the score sheets had been destroyed. It turned out that standard procedure in the QCA office for years had been for the scores for each match to be typed up and checked for accuracy, then the typed copies sent off to the printers for inclusion in the annual report. As for the score sheets – I discovered to my absolute disbelief – that they were torn up and discarded after the Annual General Meeting had been held.

It took a while to sink in. The official Australian record of the only tie in Test match history (to that time) had been shredded. Needless to say, the procedure was changed immediately, with all records of this nature being given a 'preserve-at-all-costs' status.

Thirty years later another treasure from that 1960/61 series went missing. The West Indies team had won the series in Australia in 1992/93, retaining the Frank Worrell trophy yet again. It appears that the trophy went back to the West Indies stored away somewhere among the team baggage. The problem was that nobody could recall just where that safe haven was.

Eventually the original trophy was located in time for it to be presented to Mark Taylor following Australia's 2-1 victory in 1995, the first time the trophy had needed to change hands since 1980. A replacement trophy was on hand just in case, but was never needed.

As for the ball from the tied Test, it turned up unexpectedly at the Brisbane Cricket Ground in December 1962 when a chap named Jock Slater, from South Nanango in Queensland, brought it around to my office. Somehow he had finished up with it in the confusion at the end of the match. Jock wanted to get Richie Benaud's autograph on the ball, which I was able to arrange – but despite my attempts to secure the ball for display at the Queensland Cricketers' Club, there was no way Jock was going to part with it.

By the end of March 1961 I had got through my first season as a full-time cricket administrator. Despite a few problems getting the family settled in during those early days I was very happy in my new working environment, Peg had made a number of friends in our newly adopted State and the girls were happy at school. So far, so good, in what would become a long and fascinating journey in the world of cricket.

2

WESLEY WINFIELD HALL: 'THE FASTEST MAN ON EARTH'

At the end of the 1960/61 season, after the West Indies team had flown off to their various destinations, I learned that their giant fast bowler, Wes Hall, was keen to play Sheffield Shield cricket in Australia in 1961/62. By this time Wes was in England playing with Accrington in the Lancashire league. He had asked his good friend and West Indies team mate, Conrad Hunte, who was also a professional in Lancashire, to handle the negotiations for him.

I sent off a cable to Hunte expressing our interest in having Hall play in Brisbane. Conrad replied almost straight away, indicating that Wes was very keen to play the season for Queensland, but that he was also considering an offer to play in Adelaide. Obviously we needed to act quickly to secure Hall's services.

In those days sponsorship was hard to come by. We had the good fortune to secure the financial backing of the Atlantic Union Oil Company, the forerunner to Esso Standard Oil Company in Australia, which agreed to employ Wes for promotional work and to make him available to the QCA whenever required for cricket matches and coaching clinics. We undertook to meet the cost of his airfares and between us were able to submit an attractive offer to Wes that consisted of accommodation and a salary paid by Atlantic Union, plus normal player's match payments and expense allowances. A short while later and much to our delight, Wes cabled back advising that our offer was acceptable and he would arrive in Brisbane in time for the start of the Grade cricket season in September 1961.

This telegram marked the beginning of an outstandingly successful two-season stint by Hall in Queensland both on the cricket field and as a representative of Atlantic Union. It also marked the start of a close friendship between Wes and me, which exists to this day.

The big Barbadian landed in Brisbane to scenes more in keeping with the arrival of a pop star, a thousand people cramming into the old terminal building at Eagle Farm airport to welcome him. It was obvious straight away that Wes was going to be a hit wherever he went.

During the 1961/62 season there was no international touring team and therefore no Test matches, as occasionally happened in that era. The focus of cricket attention would be almost entirely on the Sheffield Shield competition with each State having their Test players available for all matches. It was a great time to have a high-profile West Indian player in the team, as Queensland did with Wes Hall. After all, a part of my job was to do what I could to increase revenue by getting more people to come to the cricket at the Gabba.

In what was really the beginning of 'imports' to the Sheffield Shield, there was an influx of West Indian cricketers to Australia for the 1961/62, season with three States strengthening their line-ups by recruiting star players who took part in the tour of Australia by Frank Worrell and his team a year before. Apart from Wes Hall, Gary Sobers had been lured to South Australia and the dashing Rohan Kanhai was signed by Western Australia.

With Hall to spearhead the attack, Queensland looked to have a strong team. Test players Ken Mackay, Wally Grout and Peter Burge had returned from the 1961 Australian tour of England while Tom Veivers, Sam Trimble and Barry Fisher were on the fringe of Test selection. Then there were stalwarts like Jack McLaughlin, Des Bull and John Mackay, plus some promising young talent. All in all, there was good reason for cautious optimism that this just *might* be the season for Queensland to win its first Sheffield Shield since entering the competition in 1926/27.

Big Wes was sensational, taking 43 wickets in the eight matches, the highest ever to that time by a Queensland bowler. He played a huge part in Ken Mackay's team winning five of their eight matches, ending the season in second place with a total of 36 points. While this was a great improvement on the previous year's 24 points, it was nowhere near enough to topple the all-powerful New South Wales team, led by Richie Benaud, which amassed 64 points to win the Sheffield Shield for a record ninth successive time.

This was a phenomenal achievement by the NSW teams of that era, but not a surprising one when you recall the names of the star players they had at their disposal. For example, the team that took the field against Queensland at the Sydney Cricket Ground in January 1962 was Richie Benaud (captain), Bob Simpson, Ian Craig, Neil Harvey, Norm O'Neill, Brian Booth, Grahame Thomas, Alan Davidson, Johnny Martin, Frank Misson and Doug Ford. Ten members of that team had played Test cricket or would go on to do so, wicketkeeper Doug Ford being the exception. Included in that ten were five Australian captains, Benaud, Simpson, Craig, Harvey and Booth.

Following his productive first season Wes Hall was keen to come back to play for Queensland in 1962/63, particularly as the West Indies had no international commitments that clashed with the Australian season. We were able to sign Hall up again for another season thanks to the generous sponsorship of Esso, as Atlantic Union had now become.

In 1962/63 Wes was again the leading bowler, taking 33 wickets. Queensland once more finished second in the Sheffield Shield, this time a solitary win behind Victoria, which finally broke the decade of domination by New South Wales.

It was becoming obvious late in that second season that the constant round of cricket for 12 months of the year was taking its toll on Wes. In his final three matches he took just eight expensive wickets. The big fellow then headed off to take part in a full tour of England by the West Indies team in 1963 and, despite a lot of correspondence between us, my efforts to lure him back for a third season were unsuccessful. The main reason for this was that Hall knew his body wouldn't carry him through another demanding season of Sheffield Shield cricket and he didn't want to let anyone down.

During the two seasons he played for Queensland Wes just couldn't do enough whenever I asked him, although it wasn't always easy going. I quickly discovered that with Wes, punctuality was not a strong point. There were very few occasions when he didn't make it to wherever he was supposed to be at the appointed hour, but it often took planning and patience on my part.

Only once, I think, did I fail to ensure that Wes was at the right place at the right time. The occasion was a match between a Queensland team and a Combined Country Xl in Toowoomba, that great sporting town west of

Brisbane on the edge of the beautiful Darling Downs. Interest in the match was tremendous with Test players Ken Mackay, Wally Grout, Peter Burge and Wes Hall taking part. Predictably there was a large crowd in attendance.

As the team manager I was normally required to do little more than make sure that the players got on the bus each way and all the cricket gear was safely on board. During this game, however, there was to be more to the job than I had anticipated, with repercussions that were not really serious then, but would make headlines now.

Ken Mackay won the toss. The Queensland XI batted first and was going along nicely when Wes, an avid punter like many other cricketers past and present, asked me if he could dash down to the local race track as he had a 'sure thing' he wanted to bet on.

This was fine as far as I was concerned, but to play it safe I checked with the captain. 'Slasher' had no objection as Wes was listed to bat at number ten and, given the strength of the Queensland batting, it was unlikely that he would be required to pad up at all.

Mackay made just one stipulation though: 'Make sure that the big fella is back here to open the bowling.' He added that he would probably declare the innings closed at a given time. According to my calculations this allowed Wes well over an hour to make the short trip to the Toowoomba racecourse, get the bets on, watch the race and return to the cricket ground, hopefully with some extra money for himself, me and the others who had asked him to back his sure bet.

Having a personal financial interest in the outcome of the race, I was tempted to go to the track too but felt that I really should stay at the cricket. I arranged for one of the local officials to take Wes. Big mistake! 'Slasher' duly declared his team's innings closed, but earlier than anticipated. Ominously, there was no sign of Wes.

After the break between innings, our star fast bowler, whom most of the big crowd had come especially to see in action, was nowhere to be seen. There was no choice for the skipper other than to take to the field without Hall, while I dispatched a search party.

You can imagine the reaction of the locals, as well as the QCA officials who were present, when 'Slasher' opened the bowling with Barry Fisher, who was reasonably quick but not in Hall's category, and himself with gentle medium pacers. Besieged by questions about where he was, I assured everyone, my fingers firmly crossed, that he was not far away.

Eventually big Wes turned up looking a happy man, that beaming smile wider than ever. Oblivious to the panic stations, he rushed onto the ground and grabbed the ball straight away.

Understandably there were many officials and spectators who wanted to know what on earth was going on, me included – I was, after all, responsible for the management of the team. My problem was that I couldn't explain why Hall was late taking the field. There simply hadn't been any time for me to find out what had kept him.

It transpired that the race in which Wes's good thing was running had been delayed before the start. When they did get under way his horse flashed over the line first past the post, only to have a protest lodged against it. So there was this giant Barbadian clad in his cricket attire in the betting ring at the Toowoomba races, bookmaker's tickets in hand, awaiting the verdict of the stipendiary stewards.

According to the local official who took him to the races, there was no way Wes was going to leave the track until the result was known. The stewards took an age to hear the protest, which was eventually dismissed and correct weight was signalled. Wes collected his – and our – winnings and returned to the cricket match.

We had another horse-racing 'incident' in the same match. Peter Burge, who also liked to have a bet, decided to put his small transistor radio in his shirt pocket so that he could follow his fortunes, using the earpiece when required.

Burge was fielding in the gully, where a thick outside edge flew in his direction. Instinctively he flung his right hand out, succeeding in knocking the ball up in the air – followed by the radio, which flew out of his shirt pocket in the same general direction. In the space of a millisecond Peter needed to make a decision. The ball or the radio? The radio won and was neatly caught, while the ball went to ground amid cursing from bowler and captain.

The batsman was dismissed shortly afterwards, so no damage was done on the scoreboard, while the spectators had put it down to a dropped chance. But to my discomfort the matter was not allowed to rest there, as it became news far and wide that some fancy juggling had taken place out on the field.

At the next QCA executive meeting a couple of members demanded to know just what had happened during the match up at Toowoomba. In those times the Executive was made up of people who were appointed by the individual clubs and affiliated bodies, many of them being there simply because they had been around for a long time, not because they possessed any special administrative skills. Some of them made a habit of asking questions simply to be heard which – I suspect, was the case that night. I did my best to maintain a straight face while explaining 'the incident'. The committee insisted that its displeasure be conveyed to the individuals concerned, which I did in my own way, and that was the end of both matters.

It is interesting to reflect that Wes is now president of the West Indies Cricket Board and Peter, until his sudden death in October 2001, was an International Cricket Council match referee.

Had all this happened in these days of cricket gambling and match fixing, I wonder what the consequences might have been. Fortunately these two innocent incidents happened in a long-gone era when cricket was just a game.

The stories about Wes Hall and the impact he had on Queensland cricket are numerous. Some are funny, others very serious, like the one involving Wes and his great mate Wally Grout. In Hall's second year with Queensland, England was touring Australia – or, as it was in those days, the Marylebone Cricket Club was touring and England played in the Test matches.

As was the custom at the time, the first Test was to be played in Brisbane early in December, with a four-day match against Queensland leading up to the Test. Unlike the current practice in many countries where key players are rested for matches against touring teams, Queensland fielded a full-strength combination against the MCC, including Ken Mackay, Wally Grout and Peter Burge, all of who had been chosen for the first Test a week later. Big Wes, of course, was in the team.

In a high-scoring match the home team made 7/433 before declaring and the MCC replied with 5/581. During the long MCC innings and on the last day of the match, Wes was still off his long run as he let go a fast short-pitched delivery that went through to wicketkeeper Grout, bouncing for the second time just short of him on the half volley. Unfortunately for Wal the ball hit a rough piece of turf and slammed into his jaw with a sickening thud as he dived to stop it.

It was obvious straight away that the Queensland and Australian wicket-keeper was in big trouble. He had blood streaming from his mouth and, by the time he was assisted from the field, a lump the size of an orange on his jaw. We got him straight to hospital where X-rays revealed that his jaw was broken in two places, requiring immediate surgery, including the need to wire it together.

The first Test was only days away, and Wally had no chance of playing. The Australian selectors wasted no time in picking South Australia's Barry Jarman as the replacement keeper.

Wally was devastated by the injury. He valued his place in the Australian team with a passion that had been fired by having to wait in the wings until he was 30 before he got his chance. Grout's motto in life was 'never give a sucker an even break', and there was no way he was going to give anyone a chance of taking his spot if he could avoid it. But there was absolutely nothing the tough Queenslander could do about his plight, missing out on three Tests while recovering.

As for Wes Hall, he was distraught at the accidental damage he had inflicted on his teammate. Breaking Wally's jaw was not exactly the sort of impact he wanted to be remembered for. It took a while before Wal could open his mouth to talk coherently, but once he did big Wes was constantly reminded of the physical and financial damage he had caused his good friend. Unlike the current system of contracted players and minimum payments, in those days it was no play, no pay.

Wes was the trailblazer for a parade of overseas stars who played for Queensland in the relentless pursuit of its first Sheffield Shield. Tom Graveney, Majid Khan, Rusi Surti, Alvin Kallicharan, Viv Richards, Kepler Wessels, Ian Botham and Graeme Hick all came and went but it made no difference. Lord Sheffield's trophy still couldn't find its way up north.

I have nothing but fond memories of Wesley Winfield Hall, 'the fastest man on earth' as the West Indies team calypso proclaimed in 1960/61. The most vivid recollection I have of the big fellow is of him running in to bowl from the Vulture Street end at the Gabba, the end he invariably chose to operate from.

Wes didn't bother too much about measuring out his run-up. With the bowling marker in one hand and the ball in the other, he would wander off towards the players' dressing rooms, pause when he got near the boundary fence, look to the right where he had a spot marked out at the end of the old wooden grandstand, look to the left where the curator's shed stood, line the two points up, toss down the marker, scratch out a line in the turf about a metre long and he had his starting point.

He would amble back a bit further from there and begin to run in slowly, almost kicking off from the sight screen. Gradually he would gather momentum, with the golden crucifix he always wore around his neck bouncing off that massive chest. He would accelerate gracefully as he neared the crease, landing in his delivery stride with the left arm vertical before he let the ball go with awesome speed, finishing off this classic bowling action with the perfect follow-through. Poetry in motion.

Over the years since Wes played for Queensland he has been a regular visitor to Australia as a player, team manager, chairman of selectors, celebrity speaker and a member of the Barbados parliament. His contribution to West Indies cricket has been enormous, as is reflected by his appointment as President of the West Indies Cricket Board.

An articulate, intelligent and compassionate man who has now found his true calling in life as an ordained minister of religion, the Reverend Wesley Hall has all the credentials required to handle the delicate role of steering cricket in the Caribbean back in the right direction after the troubled times of recent years.

3

IAN MECKIFF: CHUCKER OR SACRIFICIAL OFFERING?

There have been many moments of high drama during the Test matches I have been involved in as an administrator over the years. Among them all, eight gut-wrenching minutes stand out in my mind like a beacon.

The day was 7 December 1963, the place the Brisbane Cricket Ground, the occasion the first Test of an Australia–South Africa series. At centre stage were Australian fast bowler Ian Meckiff, who had just been 'called' for throwing, and umpire Colin Egar, the man at square leg who was not absolutely satisfied with the fairness of four deliveries from Meckiff in his first over.

Egar's verdict on Meckiff's bowling action that day sent shock waves around the cricket world. It also ended Ian's cricket career there and then.

There was tremendous public and media interest in the Test match, largely as a result of Meckiff's inclusion in the Australian team after three years in the wilderness. The popular Victorian fast bowler's action had been subjected to examination of almost microscopic proportions because of doubts being raised whether some of his deliveries were thrown, not bowled, as required by the Laws of Cricket.

As secretary of the Queensland Cricket Association, I was the designated manager of the Australian team for that Test match, so I had a close view of what was going on. There was an air of expectancy around the Gabba as the teams prepared, unknowingly, for what would be Meckiff's last Test and Richie Benaud's final Test as captain of Australia.

Ten years later Eric Beecher, the founding editor of Australia's *Cricketer* magazine, asked me to write an article about the 'Meckiff Test' as part of a special edition. Under the headline 'Mateship against the odds', this is how I described things in 1974:

Even though a decade has passed since Ian Meckiff was so unceremoniously removed from the cricketing scene, I still have a vivid mental picture of his humiliation at Brisbane's Gabba which is as clear now as it was ten years ago.

In half a lifetime of involvement in sport, the no-balling of Meckiff by umpire Colin Egar that steamy day on December 7, 1963 is without a doubt the most dramatic and emotion charged single sporting moment I have ever witnessed.

And yet, with the benefit of hindsight, it really should have come as little surprise that the popular Victorian fast bowler was to become another chapter in the sensational history of the Gabba.

Looking back to the events building up to Meckiff's moment of cricketing judgement, there were several happenings that gave a clear indication something was about to give.

When the South African team arrived at Eagle Farm airport to commence the Queensland part of their 1963/64 tour, they hadn't heard that Meckiff had been included in Australia's team for the first Test. The announcement of the team came while they were airborne on the way to Brisbane and when the news was broken that Meckiff was to again play for Australia it was greeted with a mixture of stunned silence and incredulity by the Springbok party.

This left me in no doubt at all as to the South African view of Ian's bowling action despite the fact that they hadn't seen him in action for six years when he had toured South Africa with the Australian team in 1957/58.

It struck me then as quite strange that the Springboks should be prepared to pre-judge Meckiff as a 'chucker' when he bowled over 1000 balls in four Tests in South Africa and had passed the scrutiny of South African umpires who have not built up an unblemished record over the years for impartiality.

There was no Victoria v South Africa fixture in Melbourne on the South Africans' progress around Australia to Brisbane for the first Test, instead there was a match against an Australian XI in Melbourne – a match in which Meckiff took no part.

Before the Test, Brisbane was buzzing with rumours that Meckiff was going to be called, that he had been set up by officialdom as part of a purge to get rid of bowlers with suspect actions.

With this build-up the air was electric as the Australians took the field just after lunch on the second day of the match. Richie Benaud threw the ball to Graham McKenzie to open the Australian attack and then a strange event occurred. Big 'Garth' began marking out his run from the Stanley Street end which meant that he would have to run up a fairly steep incline to the wicket, something which opening bowlers just don't fancy in the hot sub-tropical Brisbane sun.

Strange, I thought to myself, as in two full seasons for Queensland I could only remember the great West Indian fast bowler Wes Hall sending down one solitary over from the Stanley Street end. He invariably chose to bowl down the slope from the Vulture Street end regardless of the wind direction.

Whether it was nerves or the fact that he wasn't used to running up hill, McKenzie bowled an untidy first over from which the South African openers Trevor Goddard and Eddie Barlow scored 13 runs.

This then left Meckiff bowling from the northern end, and of course, umpire Egar standing at square leg to him!

It was precisely 2.05 pm as Meckiff began his fateful over in an atmosphere which was unreal in its quietness.

I had been asked by the South African team manager, Ken Viljoen, if I could take him around to the scoreboard so that he could take some moving pictures from an elevated position. By the time Meckiff started his now famous over we just happened to be at a position square on to the wicket and we paused to watch Ian bowl, an event which Viljoen was busy recording with his camera!

The first ball, a normal Meckiff 'warm up' delivery, passed without any drama.

Meckiff then ran in to deliver his second ball, which was greeted by a shouted call of 'no-ball' by Egar from square leg.

A simmer of excitement began to erupt in company with looks of total disbelief on the faces of the Australian players. That call was to reverberate around the entire cricket world and in fact 10 years later it still hasn't died down.

Meckiff's third ball got the same treatment from Egar as the crowd began to realise what was taking place and they turned their attention to the South Australian umpire in no uncertain manner.

Two more no-balls were called by Egar amid uproar while Benaud and Meckiff conferred. The way things were shaping it looked as though Ian's over would never finish.

Mercifully for all concerned, Egar approved the last three deliveries and that was that.

There before our very eyes a bowler with 18 Tests under his belt had been summarily banished from the game he loved in a space of just eight minutes. A great sportsman had suffered the indignity of having his sporting qualities questioned and one of the most popular players to wear the Australian cap had temporarily at least had his spirit broken.

There were questions to be asked aplenty then about the chain of events leading up to the Meckiff affair, many of which are still unanswered.

The rest of that infamous day is now history. Ian became the hero of the Brisbane crowd and was carried from the field then accidentally dumped in the players' race.

I couldn't help but feel the irony of that situation. He had been dumped out in the centre of the field quite positively then just four hours later dumped again quite by accident.

The Australian dressing room after stumps that day was deathly quiet as players sat around not knowing what to say. Even the normally jovial Wally Grout was silent. Eventually Colin Egar came to the Australian dressing room door and after receiving the nod from Richie Benaud to allow him in, Egar entered to join the silence.

After what seemed an eternity he spoke to a few of the players and then to Meckiff. Just briefly mind you but enough to break the ice.

From that point on my estimation of Colin Egar as a man, which had always been high, rose even higher. His action in walking into the proverbial lion's den at that time, with a hostile crowd still milling about, took guts. This was something Egar proved he had plenty of on that day in more ways than one.

It was not until later that evening that Meckiff and Egar resumed what had until then been a close personal relationship.

Knowing that a few of the Australian team were going back to their hotel for a quiet drink to get away from it all, without telling them or Colin I brought him along as Ian was going to be there.

When he walked into the room you could have heard a pin drop. The two central characters in one of the biggest dramas in the history of cricket looked at each other, shook hands and then put their arms on each others shoulders.

The ice had thawed.

> The two of them sat quietly away from the rest of us as they discussed the events of the day and it was obvious that there were no hard feelings.
>
> Yes, December 7, 1963 will long live in my memory, not only as a day of sheer cricketing tragedy but it will also be just as long remembered as a day when real mateship prevailed against overwhelming odds.

Now, more than 25 years after I wrote that piece, my recollections of the events that took place are as firmly entrenched in my mind as ever. So are the many questions that the no-balling of Ian Meckiff raised at the time, questions such as:

- With the Australian Board of Control, of which Sir Donald Bradman was the *very* influential chairman, having issued clear instructions before the season began to State cricket associations to adopt a get-tough approach towards bowlers with suspect actions, why was Meckiff suddenly recalled to the Australian team after an absence of almost three years?
- Considering the fact that Meckiff had been 'called' by two umpires in Sheffield Shield matches during his absence from the Test match arena, was he used as a sacrificial offering in a campaign to eradicate bowlers with doubtful actions?
- Why did Graham McKenzie open the bowling for Australia from the Stanley Street end, not the Vulture Street end?
- Why didn't Richie Benaud put Meckiff on to bowl from the other end so that umpire Lou Rowan could have a chance to have a look at the legality of his deliveries?
- Would Lou Rowan have done the same as Colin Egar and no-balled Meckiff?
- How did the media generally, and some newspapers in particular, get to know in advance that Meckiff was going to be called?

- Why were the South Africans stunned by Ian's inclusion in the Australian team when they had looked very closely at him a few years earlier and apparently had no problems with his action?
- Was the whole episode some sort of conspiracy at the top level of Australian and indeed International cricket, and if so who was involved?
- Did the Australian selectors *all* believe that Meckiff's action was fair under the Laws of Cricket?
- Why did Australia go into that particular Test with only five specialist batsmen, *three* fast bowlers, two spinners and a wicketkeeper after South Africa had suffered a humiliating defeat at the hands of Queensland only days before on a pitch that turned, played low and started breaking up early on day three?

These and other questions were sweeping around Brisbane like wildfire after Ian Meckiff's day of reckoning. We now know the answers to some and others we can speculate on. For example:

- Graham McKenzie, being the tireless worker he was, *may* have preferred the challenge of starting off up-hill with the new ball, indeed, his captain may have asked him to do so.
- Richie Benaud had said on record early in 1963, that he would not continue to bowl anyone called for throwing by an umpire. This was a policy he had decided upon well before the Brisbane incident and it applied to any bowler in any team of which he was captain. By not asking Meckiff to bowl from the other end, Benaud was being true to his word.
- Lou Rowan, referring to the calling of Meckiff by umpire Egar, wrote in his book *The Umpire's Story*, that; 'There is nothing I can now say that will alter the opinions already expressed that his delivery was unfair.' From that it appears that Rowan would have passed judgement on Meckiff's action in the same manner as Col Egar did.

As for the other questions, I hold the view that they will largely remain unanswered, which adds to the mystery and intrigue of the whole sorry affair.

I have a number of lingering doubts in my own mind regarding the Meckiff incident, including one aspect I have already briefly touched on that, to my knowledge, has not had much of an airing in the subsequent debate. I still wonder about the composition of the Australian team for this Test. It was top heavy with bowlers. In batting order the team was Bill Lawry, Bob Simpson, Norm O'Neill, Peter Burge, Brian Booth, Richie Benaud, Graham McKenzie, Tom Veivers, Wally Grout, Ian Meckiff and Alan Connolly, with Barry Shepherd, a specialist batsman, as twelfth man.

To see this in perspective, understand that the South Africans were extremely concerned about the standard of the pitch prepared for the lead-up match against Queensland. Their manager, Ken Viljoen, had taken the unusual step of asking me to accompany him to look at the badly deteriorating strip at the end of the third day's play during that game.

The Springboks had reason to be anxious, as they had lost 11 wickets in the day, including 9/91 in the first innings before being asked to follow on. Eight of these batsmen had been dismissed by the Queensland spinners, Tom Veivers and rookie David Hale, on a pitch which was devoid of grass, played low and slow, and offered no encouragement at all to the fast bowlers.

With the Test match starting in four days time and a new curator having recently taken over at the Gabba, players and officials from both sides were understandably worried that the pitch would be a spinners' dream.

On that evidence, it would be reasonable to assume that Richie Benaud with his leg spin, which had already netted him well over 200 wickets, and Tom Veivers wheeling down his off-spinners, were going to do the bulk of the Australian bowling, with Bob Simpson providing spinning support. Why then would the Australian selectors play three fast bowlers at the expense of a sixth batsman?

Could the reason for playing only five batsmen and three fast bowlers have been that the selectors felt an extra paceman was needed as 'insurance' in the event that one of the trio was already destined to play little part in the match? In the end the pitch played truly and the Test fizzled out to a draw, but it is worth noting that in the South African first innings the Australian spinners bowled 92 of the 128 overs, taking eight wickets between them.

This sad Test match produced unusual scenes in Australian Test cricket: a hero destroyed, a captain and umpire booed. Indeed Egar was on the receiving end of death threats that the police took so seriously they provided official protection to the umpires for the remainder of the Test and for the following one in Melbourne. Meanwhile the game went on – but never quite the same.

This Test match left me with many memories, two of which stand out. The first is the indelible impression of a proud, loyal and extremely popular man being publicly humiliated and, in the process, displaying enormous courage. On that day, 7 December 1963, 22 years exactly after the bombing of Pearl Harbour, Ian Meckiff took the horrendous blow he had been dealt full on and handled it with great dignity. I will never forget the emotion.

My second memory is of an unexpected gesture by the Australian captain. At that time Test players were given an Australian cap, blazer and jumper at the start of each series, or on gaining subsequent selection. With the first Test being played in Brisbane, this gear was sent to the QCA and it was the job of the secretary, as Australian manager, to hand it out when the team assembled. As I gave Richie Benaud his new clothing to my surprise he tossed the jumper back, saying, 'Here you are Gibbo, you can keep this one.'

With that I became the proud possessor of the last Australian jumper Richie ever received. This exceedingly kind, but typical gesture assumed even more significance soon afterwards when Benaud, injured, vacated the Australian captaincy during the series.

Spectator interest was high following the tension of the first Test, with over 500,000 people attending the five matches, the highest ever for a South African tour in Australia.

Ian Meckiff returned to Melbourne and his family to begin life without cricket, a situation that had been suddenly thrust upon him. Ian was a sales representative and he threw his energies into his work. For sport he concentrated on golf, which he played extremely well. He went on to become captain of the prestigious Victoria Golf Club for a number of years.

These days Ian is a senior executive with Boyer Sports Media, in which capacity he has frequent dealings with administrators of the sports and venues throughout Australia, with a focus on cricket. He gets to visit the Test match grounds, including the Brisbane Cricket Ground, regularly. When he looks out at the new look Gabba, surely the memories come flooding back from that day in 1963.

Every year now for well over a decade Ian, Colin Egar and I have made a point of getting together for a few drinks and a chat about old times during the wonderful festival that occurs at Adelaide Oval over the five days of the Test match at this most picturesque of grounds.

Occasionally other people who figured prominently in the 'Meckiff Test' join us from interstate or overseas. Lou Rowan has been one, as has Peter van der Merwe, the vice-captain of South Africa in 1963/64 and now an International Cricket Council match referee; another was Bob Simpson when he was coaching the Australian team.

There were times in recent years when Meckiff, Egar, Rowan, Sir Donald Bradman and Benaud have all been at a Test match at Adelaide Oval on the one day, but never to my knowledge in the same place at the same time. It is interesting to contemplate how the discussion between these five key figures in that day of drama would have gone had the opportunity presented itself and, of course, had the group been inclined to discuss the affair.

As for those occasions when Ian, Colin and I have got together to enjoy each other's company and the mandatory cold drink, there has *never* been a mention of the events of December 1963 in Brisbane. Nor, I am sure, will there ever be.

The same situation applies between Colin and me. I have known Egar for over 40 years, enjoyed his company in many parts of Australia and overseas, socialised with him often since moving to Adelaide in 1988 and class him as a good mate. In all that time, while we have talked about some of the happenings which took place off the field, and even some events which occurred on the field during that fateful Test match, there has been absolutely no discussion at all between us about *that* over.

Ian Meckiff's life changed forever on 7 December 1963. He was banished from the game he loved, and in a very public and hurtful way.

After 18 Tests spread over a six-year period it was suddenly all over. Most men would have struggled to carry the cross Ian has had to bear all these years as a 'chucker'. Many would have taken the easy option and faded into obscurity, perhaps never to be heard of again. Not Meckiff – he walks tall, looks you in the eye and, I know, has a clear conscience. As someone who was there that day and saw it all happen, I have nothing but the utmost respect for Ian Meckiff the man, and admiration for his strength of character.

3

TOURING THE OUTBACK WITH DEAFY & CO.

The late Harry Bolton was a prominent Brisbane accountant, cricket lover and man with a vision to allow people in outback Queensland to see big name-cricketers in action without having to travel to the city. With the approval of the QCA, he fulfilled his dream by sponsoring a touring team for a number of years, starting in 1964.

The team was known as The Cobb & Co. XI, taking its name from the passenger bus and transport company of which Bolton was a director. It was an appropriate name as, like the old Cobb & Co. coach trips, these were pioneering journeys to far-flung places. Harry needed some assistance in pulling the idea together, he recruited me to help get things rolling, so to speak.

Bolton employed star players Peter Burge and Barry Fisher in the accounting practice he headed up, so he had a good foundation for the team. His idea was to pick a touring party comprising a former Test great as captain, add the nucleus of the current Queensland Sheffield Shield team, toss in one or two promising young players who looked as though they could go places in the game, maybe add a 'name' player from interstate, take a State selector along and fill the other spots with club players.

I was playing District cricket with the Toombul club and was fortunate enough to be selected as a member of the first three Cobb & Co. touring teams. The inaugural trip in 1964 took us out west to some far-away places including Roma, St George, Dirranbandi and Longreach. Our former Test player was the legendary Australian wicketkeeper, Don Tallon, whom we enticed out of retirement at the age of 48. Don went with us on the proviso that he didn't have to keep wickets, could bat way down the order and, if he felt like it, could bowl a few overs of his leg spinners.

With players such as Peter Allan, Barry Fisher, Sam Trimble, Des Bull, Grahame Thomas (from NSW), Ross Duncan, Jack Lihou and Tallon in the party, we had a team that boasted four Test players, two others who had toured overseas with Australian teams and a couple of very handy Sheffield Shield players. Bolton excused Peter Burge on this occasion as he had a better offer – touring England with the Australian team. But he did include a young solicitor, John McKnoulty, who is now the president of the QCA.

The grounds we played on varied from clay pans devoid of grass to verdant green ovals, while the pitches ranged from rolled ant bed with coir matting laid on top through to surprisingly well-prepared turf tracks.

Transport for the team was a mixture of Cobb & Co. buses, chartered light aircraft, scheduled regional airline services and private motor vehicles. Accommodation, too, provided enormous variety. In some centres we stayed on large grazing properties, their magnificent homesteads replete with private airstrips, tennis courts and swimming pools, while in the smaller townships we holed up at tiny outback pubs, complete with a route march down the hall to the bathroom and toilets.

Wherever we went the hospitality was remarkable, so much so that the trips became endurance tests the further we got into them. Two weeks on the road can take a toll on the body, particularly when you spend one or two nights in each place being filled with the milk – or other beverages – of human kindness. It was sometimes nice to draw breath on the bus, plane or car for a while – knowing that waiting at the next stop would be a fresh welcoming committee, raring to go.

On the first Cobb & Co. trip we played at a little spot called Kelly's Creek. It is not even on the map, just a cricket ground out in the vast cattle country in the western outback of Queensland, somewhere between Longreach and Corfield. But I won't forget Kelly's Creek in a hurry.

Des Bull, the accomplished Queensland left-handed opening batsman of the time, and I were staying on a nearby property that we had been driven to after flying into Longreach. The plan was for us to go by car to Kelly's Creek the next day for our match against a local team, but it didn't quite work out that way.

During the night it bucketed down with rain, rendering the unmade roads unusable. Even a four-wheel drive vehicle couldn't have travelled more than 100 metres before bogging in thick black mud. If we had to wait for the roads to dry out Des and I were either going to miss the match, or arrive very late indeed.

A telephone call by our host, who had an all-weather airstrip on his property, solved that problem. This is where I first met Sandy Whitehead, a local grazier, who soon arrived in his four-seater Cessna to fly us to Kelly's Creek. In we got and off we flew to our destination, only to discover that there was no airstrip and we were going to land on a bitumen road. After checking up and down the road for traffic, cattle, power lines and other hazards, Sandy calmly executed a perfect three-point landing on the road.

By this time Des Bull was white as a sheet. As soon as the aircraft came to a stop he dashed to the safety of terra firma, where he spontaneously bent down and kissed the ground. I was in better shape than Des, having experienced hairy moments in light aircraft over the years, but neither of us made much contribution to the team effort that day.

On the subject of dramatic arrivals, later in the day an official-looking car pulled up at the ground and out jumped Test umpire Lou Rowan, who just happened to be in the vicinity. Lou, a police officer, had recently been assigned to duties with the transport police that took him all over Queensland. In his deadpan manner, Lou explained that we needed an umpire to keep the peace.

Soon Rowan was standing in a cricket match far away from the Test match grounds of Brisbane, Melbourne, Sydney and Adelaide, where he and Colin Egar had officiated in all five Tests of the South African tour a few months earlier.

By the end of the day Kelly's Creek could boast that it had hosted a cricket match with a significant international flavour, not a bad achievement for a place that doesn't even appear on the map. Locals undoubtedly remember the Cobb & Co. visit and I'm sure that Des Bull has stayed true to his vow never to set foot inside a light aircraft again.

The next stop on the Cobb & Co. team's first marathon was Longreach, now the home of the superb Cattleman's Hall of Fame. By this time Don Tallon, who had not been called on to do much at all on the tour – not on the field, anyway – was warming to the idea of donning the wicket-keeping gloves one final time.

Don had taken a wicket with his leggies against a combined Central

West Xl and was happy not to bat while Sam Trimble and Grahame Thomas put on an opening partnership of nearly 200 in rapid time. We declared with an hour or so of playing time left, just long enough for Tallon to convince himself that it was time to put the gloves on.

It was as though the clock had been wound back more than a decade. This great keeper, many say the finest ever, gloved the ball in the same smooth fashion I can remember watching as a teenager from the old Southern stand at the Melbourne Cricket Ground looking down the pitch from above the sight screen.

It wasn't long before 'Deafy', as Tallon was called by his team-mates when he played for Queensland and Australia, made a brilliant leg-side stumping off Sam Trimble's medium-pacers. You would have missed it if you blinked.

With the game as good as over, I was invited to try my luck bowling gentle off spinners. Before trotting in to deliver the first ball I glanced down the pitch only to see this weather-beaten face crouching behind the stumps. Reality struck – I was about to bowl with the great Don Tallon keeping wicket to me.

Somehow I managed to land one in the right spot. The batsman played and missed, Tallon elegantly gloving the ball. For about ten overs he provided everyone at the ground that day with an unforgettable cameo, a reminder of the golden days of Sir Donald Bradman's team of 'Invincibles'.

From Longreach it was back to Brisbane for a rest. All the reports we had received along the way indicated that the trip had been a huge success, on and off the field. Harry Bolton was delighted, the players were happy and the people we visited in those far-flung communities had demonstrated by their enthusiastic response that the Cobb and Co. touring concept was a winner.

There was one unfortunate post-script. Don Tallon, who was a quiet, even shy, man with no pretensions to grandeur, had been working as a pump attendant at a petrol station in Vulture Street close to the Gabba when I first approached him on behalf of Harry Bolton about touring with us. I had explained that we would be away for about 12 days, which was fine with him.

It wasn't until I saw Don at the Queensland Cricketers' Club several weeks after we returned home that I learned something was amiss. It turned out that he 'forgot' to tell his boss that he was going away. When he finally did report for work – after being missing for more than a week – he found that he no longer had a job. He soon got another one with a little help from his friends, so there was no real damage done other than an unexpected hole in his pocket.

Harry Bolton felt that a change of scenery was appropriate for the next Cobb & Co. tour. It was decided that we should go north to visit some of the flourishing regional cities dotted along Queensland's coast.

The tour selection committee – Bolton, Peter Burge, Barry Fisher and Gibbs – persuaded Ray Lindwall, the former great Test fast bowler, to come on this trip as captain. This was a job in itself, as Ray had to convince his wife, Peg, that the booming florist business they ran in Brisbane could exist without him for a week or two. Lindwall had retired from first class cricket five years earlier after a distinguished career in which he took 228 Test wickets, making him Australia's highest wicket-taker at the time.

First stop for this Cobb & Co. XI was Rockhampton. Again we had a fairly useful team that included current Test players Peter Burge and Tom Veivers, both back from the 1964 England tour, some Queensland Sheffield Shield regulars and a sprinkling of capable young talent. Umpire Lou Rowan accompanied us, this time as an official member of the party. Sam Trimble and Peter Allan, both great tourists thanks to their cricketing talent and the ability to mix with people from all walks of life, couldn't make it as they were touring the Caribbean with Bob Simpson's 1965 Australian team.

On this trip I actually enjoyed some success on the field, especially during the second two-day match played in Mackay. After dismissing the home team for 180, Cobb & Co. belted up a massive score before inviting the Mackay team to bat again. The locals were cruising at 1/65, relieved at not having to contend with the pace and swing of Ray Lindwall and Barry Fisher as 'Lindy' had decided they both needed a rest after knocking up seventies.

Des Bull and Peter Burge took the new ball even though neither, in a total of over 130 Sheffield Shield matches, had taken a single wicket. The captain used six bowlers with very little success before, in a moment of desperation, he called on me.

In my first over of straight off breaks I dropped one short. The batsman pinned his ears back and thumped the ball high towards the mid-wicket boundary for what looked like a certain six. Out of nowhere one of our promising youngsters, David Hale, sprinted towards the disappearing ball, leapt high and pulled in a sensational catch. B Gibbs 1/0!

From there on it just got better. In my next over a couple of unwitting batsmen played for turn that didn't exist, paying the price and were caught behind. Flushed with that success it was time for the coup de grace when a most unlucky local lad by the name of Alan Morelande came to the crease. Alan played back to a ball pitched about middle and off; it went straight on and stayed low, hitting him on the pad just above ankle height. Up we all went for the lbw, which looked very adjacent, as they say.

Lou Rowan was standing at the bowler's end. As many a first-class bowler will attest, Lou was not renowned for answering lbw appeals in the affirmative unless they were *absolutely* plumb. I whirled around, but there was this endless pause before Rowan, with a look of mock pain, said to the batsman in that laconic voice of his: 'As much as it hurts me to tell you my friend, I am afraid you are out'. He slowly raised his right index finger.

Somehow I finished with 6/21 from six overs. The local paper generously reported my effort in these terms:

> Barry Gibbs almost bowled the Cobb & Co. side to victory late in the afternoon. In his first over Gibbs claimed a wicket and with the Mackay batsmen willing to take risks looking for runs, Gibbs' spinners kept the wickets falling, but the tail enders managed to hold him out for the final fifteen minutes of play.

The next year's trip again took us to the outback on an eleven-day excursion that turned out to be unforgettable in a number of ways. It was by far the most diverse of the Cobb & Co. tours I went on, covering places such as Cunnamulla and tiny Thurulgoonah way out west near the Queensland/New South Wales border. From there we travelled north-west through Charleville, Longreach, Aramac and Mt Isa.

Maintaining the standard of previous years, we had selected another strong team. We figured that Peter Burge, although he was still captain of Queensland, had done enough in his illustrious career already to qualify as the Test 'legend' for the tour. The party also included Sam Trimble and Peter Allan, back from the West Indies. The selectors rounded up the usual suspects from the State team and also took along a promising 17-year-old leg spinner, Bob Paulsen, who went on to represent both Queensland and Western Australia in Sheffield Shield cricket. Bob is now one of the WA directors on the Australian Cricket Board.

We were fortunate to have the services of two Test umpires this time. Colin Egar joined his friend and colleague Lou Rowan, by now a permanent fixture on Cobb & Co. tours. Between them Col and Lou had officiated in 55 Tests, 19 of these together, a record for Australian umpires.

In a hectic schedule we travelled nearly 3000 kilometres. Day five of the official tour itinerary provides an insight into just how busy it was:

> Tuesday, April 12: Travel Thurulgoonah to Cunnamulla by road, fly Cunnamulla to Charleville by Goss Air Transport chartered aircraft, fly Charleville to Longreach by TAA flight 536, arriving Longreach at 11.05 am, travel Longreach to Aramac by road – coaching of schoolboy and local cricketers at 3 pm followed by a civic reception in Aramac. Drive to stations where members of the party will be billeted.

During the day we journeyed more than 1000 kilometres by various modes of transport, starting near the New South Wales border and finishing up north of the Tropic of Capricorn in western Queensland. Meanwhile we somehow found time to carry out official duties before our hosts took us in different directions to their properties to enjoy old-fashioned country hospitality that lasted well into the night and a fair part of the next day.

Lou Rowan later described the rigours of touring Cobb & Co.-style in *The Umpire's Story*:

> There could be no rest days as trying as those during the Cobb & Co. tours to the north and west of Queensland. Only those people who have made these epic journeys understand the stamina needed to survive the hospitality. Some of the recipients of this overwhelming hospitality were known on one occasion to have spent hours walking through the cane fields at Mackay ... an unusual form of relaxation. And Colin Egar will not forget – or be allowed to forget – the rest day at Glenample Station, Aramac. There, thanks to the skilful driving of Peter Burge

who managed to pile up the jeep, we walked three miles home through heat and dust with nothing better than hot bore-water to drink.

Bear in mind that the team had played three successive days cricket at Cunnamulla and Thurulgoonah *and* enjoyed four nights of hospitality in that area before embarking on the cross-Queensland trek to Aramac. Fortunately for all concerned the next day was the only real rest day on tour, so we took the opportunity to charge our batteries for the run home.

In front of us was a one-day friendly at the tiny outpost of Rankin near Aramac, and then a more serious two-day game against an Invitation XI in Mt Isa. It all seemed straightforward at that stage, but there were some surprises in store, especially for me.

The match program produced by the Aramac District Cricket Association for the game at Rankin contained individual player profiles. I was described as 'a bowler of some class though his action is somewhat suspect'. Scandalous stuff, I thought when it was drawn to my attention but, alas, they turned out to be prophetic words.

When I came on to bowl Col Egar was standing at the bowler's end and Lou Rowan was out at square leg. With memories of what happened to Ian Meckiff still fresh in my mind, the thought occurred to me that it was lucky Col was standing at my end. Nothing untoward occurred in my first over, although I did notice Col and Lou in discussion at the end of it.

In my next over I was surprised to hear a shout of no ball from the bowlers end *and* another from square leg. Col pointed out that I had overstepped the crease and would need to come back a bit, but Lou's call from square leg was obviously made because he felt that it was not a fair delivery – in other words I threw the ball according to his interpretation of the Laws of Cricket.

Not at all happy at this turn of events, I went back to my bowling mark, mumbling to myself that this was supposed to be a friendly match and here are these guys treating it as though they were umpiring a Test match. In I trotted, making sure that I bowled from well behind the crease. The batsman edged the ball straight into the hands of the lone slip fielder who gleefully tossed the ball in the air.

Then I heard this very late call from umpire Egar: 'No Ball'.

'What on earth was that for Col', I demanded. His reply was brutal. 'If you are going to continue to throw them, there is no way you are going to get a wicket from my end.'

By now I was a most unhappy traveller telling everyone within earshot that I had come on this tour to enjoy my cricket and not to put up with this sort of treatment. I suggested to Peter Burge that there was no point in me completing the over the way these two so-and-so umpires were carrying on. Peter was most unsympathetic, growling at me to 'just get back there and bowl.'

I finished the over without further incident and for the remainder of the trip the umpires had no problem with my bowling action. Clearly Col and Lou had made their point and had decided to leave it at that. Well almost.

The final match of the tour was in the mining city of Mt Isa. At the end of the game umpires Egar and Rowan insisted on making a presentation to me that they felt would assist in the development of my bowling action – they produced a boomerang and handed it to me.

I didn't know until years later that I was the second recipient of the Egar and Rowan boomerang trophy, the first being given to genial England off spinner Freddie Titmus at the Melbourne Cricket Ground at the end of the 1965/66 Test series a couple of months earlier. Not that there was ever any real doubt at all about the legitimacy of Freddie's bowling action. He received his boomerang in a light-hearted gesture from these two umpires following the publication of a newspaper article by some misguided journalist that inferred Titmus should have been called for throwing.

My boomerang still sits on the sideboard at home as a reminder of delightful people, wonderful places, unforgettable experiences.

After the usual end-of-tour drinks it was back to Brisbane on what we all thought was going to be just another flight. It started out that way as we took off from Mt Isa at 7 am, stopping off at Longreach on the way.

On take-off from Longreach the plane shuddered and seemed to veer sideways before becoming airborne. Once we were in the air things appeared normal enough until the captain, Karl Muske, announced that the aircraft was experiencing problems with the hydraulic system that operated the landing gear, but we would still be proceeding on to Brisbane. What he didn't tell us was that Brisbane was considered a better option than

Longreach because of the availability of full-scale emergency services at Eagle Farm airport.

The mood grew tense when the captain advised us that we would be required to circle over Moreton Bay on arrival at Brisbane for 20 minutes or so to dump fuel before attempting a landing. Meanwhile the cabin crew gave us instructions on how we should brace ourselves for an emergency landing and explained how to use the escape hatches and over-wing exits.

The co-pilot began undoing a hatch in the floor at the rear of the cockpit, then climbed down below carrying a device that looked like an oversized metal syringe. It was, in fact, a manual pump and the idea was to use it to insert oil into the landing gear in an attempt to boost the hydraulic pressure. While this was going on, Karl Muske was flying the four-engine aircraft without a co-pilot.

The captain may have looked calm. His 27 passengers were anything but as we contemplated what might happen during the last minutes of the two-hour leg of our flight which by now was nearing Brisbane.

As Moreton Bay loomed up we began circling to get rid of as much fuel as possible as a safeguard against a crash-landing. We circled for what seemed an eternity, discovering later this was in part to use up time to allow the airport authorities to institute emergency procedures involving fire appliances, ambulances, the blood bank and police. Hospitals had been alerted, traffic was stopped on the major routes near Eagle Farm airport and finally the moment had arrived to commence our descent into Brisbane. You can imagine the tension on board. Then out of the blue one of our party, Peter Burge I suspect, said in a loud voice for all on board to hear: 'Right now the odds about Queensland winning the Sheffield Shield next season are about 5/1. There's a fair chance in the next few minutes those will blow out to 100/1.'

By now we had taken up our emergency landing positions, leaning forward towards the seat in front with arms folded in front of our faces. At first everything went according to the book as the two main wheels touched down while the aircraft maintained a 'nose-up' attitude, which Karl Muske skilfully held until the forces of gravity took over. The nose wheel then made heavy contact with the tarmac and the aircraft began to shudder, slewing along the runway before veering sharply to the right and, with warning sirens on board screaming, eventually coming to a halt well into the adjacent grassed area.

All of a sudden it became very quiet in the cabin. I looked up to discover that everyone appeared to be in one piece, then glanced out of the windows to see fire engines, ambulances and police cars all over the place. Fortunately none of them was required. But there was a smell of smoke in the aircraft, and we needed no prompting at all to evacuate through the emergency exits, urgently. Some passengers slid down the chutes to the ground and others, myself included, climbed out onto the wing and then jumped down.

Passengers and crew were transported by bus from the middle of Eagle Farm airport to the terminal building for a cup of tea, coffee or something stronger if you wished. I went for a very stiff brandy, despite the fact that the sun was nowhere near the yardarm.

That was the last Cobb & Co. tour I went on as I had resigned from my position as Secretary of the Queensland Cricket Association and was about to return to Melbourne to commence a new career in the finance industry. The trips continued on for a few more years, fulfilling Harry Bolton's vision.

5

REMINISCENCES FROM THE OLD GABBA

Wally Grout: A Tragic Sporting Hero

I only knew Wally Grout for eight years before his untimely death in 1968 at the age of 41 but in that short time a strong bond was forged between us. Wally, a genuine friend, lived life to the full and was prepared to share his highs, as well as his lows, with those around him. Above all what stood out about the man was his great courage in adversity.

When he died Wally held the record for the most dismissals by an Australian wicketkeeper with 187 to his credit in 51 Test matches, a remarkable achievement for a man who didn't play his first Test until he was 30 years of age. For someone who carried a potentially fatal heart condition, as he did for several years while establishing the record, this was an accomplishment that almost defies belief.

It was not widely known that Wal suffered a heart attack in the early 1960s and was privately advised by his doctors to give up cricket there and then if he wanted to continue living any sort of normal life. He chose to continue on despite knowing the risks involved in playing Test cricket and touring overseas with a time bomb ticking away inside him.

The alternative for Grout would have been to apply himself full time to his job as a representative with cigarette manufacturer, Rothmans, but he was not ready to hand over the role as his country's keeper, a spot he had coveted for so long.

I was right there on the spot when Grout collapsed on the oval at the Gabba after jogging a few laps at State training. He was just near the dressing rooms and was obviously in trouble. Fortunately we were able to get the team doctor there to attend to him quickly.

After a thorough checkout, Wally was sent off for some further tests that verified what the doctor had suspected; Australia's number one wicket-keeper had suffered a mild heart attack. Wally's condition was kept very quiet, so much so even some of his Queensland teammates didn't know what had occurred other than that he had suffered a 'turn'.

For the rest of his career Wally, and those of us who knew what had happened, kept his secret. He retired after the final Test of the 1965/66 Australia series against England, playing his last Test at the Melbourne Cricket Ground when he was nearly 39 years of age. Less than three years later he was dead.

Grout was a very proud man with an outgoing personality that made him universally popular. He was a genuine working-class hero who related wonderfully well to the man in the street and had a great affinity with the cricket fans at the Gabba.

He absolutely hated being called 'Grouty'. 'Grout is my name,' he would bark, 'call me that if you must use my surname.' To his teammates he was 'Griz', perhaps because he used to growl at them if returns from the field were sloppy. I have seen him stand there and allow a high throw to deliberately go over his head while he remonstrated with the fieldsman – though he always made sure someone was backing up the throw.

Wally was generous to a fault, frequently going out of his way to help a good cause. A classic example of how he gave freely of his time occurred early in 1968, months before his death. By this time I had left the QCA for greener pastures and was living in Townsville, working with a large finance company, Custom Credit Corporation.

I was part of a committee that had been formed to raise money for the Australian team to go to the 1968 Olympic games in Mexico City. As a fundraiser we were holding a gala sportsman's dinner on Magnetic Island just off the coast from Townsville. Each of us on this committee of 'prominent citizens' had the task of arranging for a well-known identity to attend the dinner and to say a few words. I put a telephone call in to Wal, who agreed to be there without hesitation, or a fee.

He flew the 1600 kilometres from Brisbane to Townsville on the day of the dinner courtesy of his employers, Rothmans, then made the boat trip to Magnetic Island, spoke at the function which finished about midnight, got back on a boat to the mainland, grabbed a few hours sleep then hopped into a car to drive to Mackay, 400 kilometres away, where he had a promotional job to do for Rothmans at 9 am.

When I left Wally at Townsville's Hotel Allan that night after a couple of night caps, which neither of us really needed, I had no way of knowing that I would never see him again.

As for his courage, this was never better exemplified than when he had his jaw broken by that errant delivery from Wes Hall days before the first Test of the 1962/63 series against England. A few people around the place suggested that this injury might signal the end of Wally's Test career. He was, after all, nearly 36 years old while his replacement, Barry Jarman, was nine years younger and had been standing in line for years. These pundits clearly didn't reckon on A.T.W. Grout's enormous pride in playing for Australia, nor his fierce determination.

Wal let it be known that he believed he would be fit to play in the second Test in Melbourne more than a month later. A Brisbane specialist confirmed this view in a report to the QCA ten days before the second Test, declaring Grout fully fit to take his place in the team for Melbourne. I rang Alan Barnes, the secretary of the Australian Board of Control, to advise him of the contents of the specialist's report as soon as I had received it and presume that this information was passed straight on to the Australian selectors.

The selectors decided however, that Jarman should be retained in an unchanged line-up, no doubt feeling Wally needed more time to recover from his injury and that Barry had done well enough for them to have another look at him. Grout was devastated at this turn of events; clearly he expected to resume the place in the Test team he took to be his right.

There was a Sheffield Shield match between Queensland and New South Wales in Sydney scheduled for the same time as the second Test and the Queensland selectors had no hesitation in picking Grout in their team.

Wally had a good match, holding four catches and experiencing no problems with his jaw. He was confident about his chances of getting back into the Australian team for the third Test in Sydney, but Jarman held his place and it was not until the fourth Test in Adelaide, late in January, that Grout finally got the nod again from the selectors. He went on to play 24 more Tests over the next three years.

Father time and the continuing battle with his health eventually caught up with Wally. As much as he would have loved to play on, he knew deep down that physically and mentally this was no longer an option. Reluctantly, as he neared his 39th birthday, the popular Australian keeper announced his retirement from cricket at the conclusion of the 1965/66 series against England.

People close to Wally had been concerned about his well-being as he continued to push himself during the last few years of his career. In the dressing-room after a hard day he would sit alone for long periods, ashen-faced and exhausted. We felt relief for the man when he told us of his decision to retire.

Cricket was Wally Grout's life. After waiting in the wings for what must have seemed an eternity while Don Tallon was the automatic choice as wicketkeeper for Queensland and Australia, Grout grabbed his chance with gusto when it was offered. No man has worn the baggy green cap with more pride.

Arthur Theodore Wallace Grout lived by the credo 'never give a sucker an even break'. Sadly, in the end he died by it.

The Duke of Norfolk Drops In

Brisbane, November 1962: The 28th Marylebone Cricket Club team to tour Australia has arrived in Brisbane to prepare for the first Test of the 1962/63 series. There is more than the usual interest in this touring party, as it is being managed by no lesser a personage that His Grace, The Duke of Norfolk, KG, PC, GCVO, who apart from being a member of the MCC committee, is the premier Earl and Duke of Great Britain.

Alec Bedser, the former England bowling great, is the assistant manager. Alec knows his way around the cricket grounds of Australia and is able to steer the Duke in the right direction, having toured here as a player on three previous occasions.

Not that His Grace, a man of tremendous influence, is any slouch at organisational matters. Among a myriad of other duties back home, he has responsibility for arranging the major ceremonial occasions involving the British Royal Family.

I must confess to being a little daunted at the prospect of dealing directly with such a high-ranking nobleman, particularly as this is to be the first Test match I have been directly involved in as an administrator. This is the first member of Britain's House of Lords I have ever met, let alone the premier Earl and Duke. I take little comfort from the knowledge that it will be the first Test the Duke has had anything to do with on a hands-on basis away from England.

The MCC has briefed us on the correct protocol when addressing the Duke. The first greeting each day, for example, is to be 'Good morning your Grace', and thereafter he is to be referred to as 'Sir'. The next day the same procedure is to apply and so on it goes.

The touring party is to be in Brisbane for more than two weeks and I have mentally convinced myself that I will be doing a normal job working with the MCC team manager – who just happens to be one of Great Britain's most influential people. I am also aware, without being unkind to the Duke, that most of my contact with our visitors will be with his assistant, Alec Bedser.

The tourists arrive and we have the mandatory official reception in the form of a dinner, at which the Governor of Queensland, Sir Henry Abel Smith, extends a hearty welcome to everyone. So far events are proceeding well – in fact it is quite a pleasant night.

I seem to be managing not to breach any etiquette. There is, however, one extremely close call. The telephone rings at home one evening and is answered by my wife, Peg. A man with a very cultured voice announces himself as the Duke of Norfolk and asks if 'Mr Gibbs' is at home.

I'm sceptical about the bona fides of the caller; after all what would the Duke of Norfolk be doing ringing me at home around 8 pm? We all have friends who love to play practical jokes like ringing up pretending to be someone else. Peter Trethewey, the former South Australian fast bowler, now living in Brisbane, seems the most likely suspect.

As I pick up the phone, I am on the verge of blasting Trethewey when it occurs to me that this just might be the Duke. 'Good evening your Grace,' I whisper, ready to blast my prankster mate if I recognise his voice.

It is in fact the Duke calling. He explains that Freddie Trueman has a back problem that needs urgent medical attention and, as Alec Bedser is out at a function, asks if I could arrange for a doctor. Happy to oblige I ring the QCA medical officer, Dr 'Lefty' Comino, who takes some convincing that the request is genuine before he agrees to go to the hotel to help Freddy out.

The first Test goes by without incident. The Duke relinquishes his managerial responsibilities for a few weeks so that he can return home to Arundel Castle for Christmas to attend to pressing matters. His role is taken over by the secretary of the MCC, Billy Griffiths. The Duke returns to Australia, Billy Griffiths goes back to Lord's, while the England captain, dubbed 'Lord' Ted Dexter by the media because of his regal bearing, continues trying to recapture the Ashes. All in all, a noble tour.

Ken 'Slasher' Mackay: The Complete Team Man

The late Ken Mackay was one of the real characters of Australian cricket. This statement may come as a surprise to a lot of people who only saw his dour side. Not blessed with natural flair, he did however possess a tremendous amount of dogged persistence and a fierce competitive instinct, as well as droll sense of humour, all attributes that made him an invaluable member of the Australian team during his Test career from 1956 to 1963.

One of the few Australian players to make 1500 runs and take 50 wickets in Test cricket, 'Slasher' will forever be remembered for his heroic part in Test cricket's most famous draw, played between Australia and the West Indies at the Adelaide Oval in January 1961. Mackay and Lindsay Kline batted for over 100 minutes in an unbroken last wicket stand of 66 to force the draw, and in the process they almost brought the nation to a halt as it tuned into the ABC radio broadcast.

I was in a little hotel in Brisbane's Queen Street, not far from the QCA office. Fortunately there was no such thing as six o'clock closing in the enlightened northern State so, as time ticked away, I was able to continue listening intently to the radio coverage in a packed bar, introducing myself to some of the locals and to the now extinct Bulimba beer.

Performing extraordinary deeds on the cricket field was not new to Mackay. He was a schoolboy superstar. As a 14-year-old playing for Virginia State School against Sherwood State School in 1939 he took all 10 wickets in Sherwood's innings and then proceeded to make 367 not out, a feat that put his name in *Wisden* at a very early age.

Mackay went on to rate many more mentions in the cricketer's bible, but I fancy the entry that would have pleased him most is listed among the slowest individual Test batting statistics, an innings he played in his very first Test match against England, at Lord's in 1956.

The record shows that Slasher made 31 in 266 minutes, but does not reveal that Ken came to the crease with Australia 3/69 and saw the score plummet to 6/112 before Richie Benaud joined him. Benaud hammered a rapid 97 in a partnership of 117 with Mackay, laying the foundation for Australia's only victory of the series.

As well as excelling at cricket, Ken was an accomplished tennis, golf and squash player. The Mackay traits of concentration and determination made him an opponent in all of these sports to be respected. My wife, Peg, and I played tennis regularly against Ken and his wife, Jean, at the home of Barry Fisher, the former Queensland fast bowler. These were no weekend social games. They were full on, with no quarter asked or given.

Slasher was the first exponent of the now fashionable two-handed backhand I ever encountered. His serve was a lot like his bowling, not really fast but invariably deadly accurate with lots of variety; as for ground-strokes, they were a combination of slice, top-spin and power, while his agility and court coverage were frustratingly persistent. He simply never gave up on a point.

Golf was much the same story. We used to play at the Virginia Golf Club, where Ken's younger brother, Sommy, was club champion on numerous occasions. Slasher would hit the ball a reasonable distance and, importantly, almost always straight as an arrow. He rarely missed a green and when he got there the uniqueness of Ken Mackay would be clearly evident. His putting stance was hardly out of the textbook; Slasher had his own distinctive method. Ken's putter was specially made, with the shaft at a 90-degree angle to the blade and joined at its centre. He would stand on the green, feet astride, facing the hole front on as he proceeded to use the putter like a croquet mallet. It looked dreadful, but was highly effective. There is every possibility that Ken had something to do with this type of putter subsequently being outlawed!

As for squash, all I can say is that it brought out every bit of the determination, innovation, cunning, competitiveness and sheer bloody mindedness that this wonderful character possessed. Again there were no easy points; every one was chased down in that dogged Mackay fashion. Anyone who played squash against Slasher was going to be very leg weary at the finish of the match.

When Ken retired from cricket he was 38, had played in exactly 100 Sheffield Shield matches and more than 200 first-class matches spread over 18 seasons. In that time he scored nearly 11,000 runs and took just on 250 wickets.

These impressive statistics give some indication of Mackay's contribution to Queensland and Australian cricket, but they don't tell how important he was to the team. It was *when* he got his runs, took his wickets, held his catches, occupied the crease while the going was tough or tied up an end with tight bowling that made him such a valued all-round cricketer.

Richie Benaud summed up Mackay's importance to the Australia team when he said that: 'Slasher was perhaps under-rated in some quarters but no one who played with him was ever in any doubt as to his value, particularly his captain. He was the complete team man.'

Ken Mackay died suddenly while on holiday at Queensland's Stradbroke Island in 1982 at the age of 56. I will always remember him as a generous man with a big heart. He had an unflappable temperament, was fiercely competitive, the master of 'leaving' the ball just fractionally outside off stump and possessed of an uncanny ability to hit a boundary with no apparent back lift.

Another great Australian captain, Steve Waugh, never had the chance to see Ken Mackay in action; had he done so I am sure he would have liked what he saw. In the areas of mental and physical toughness, it might have been like looking in a mirror for Steve.

The Slack Sec and Justa

Cricketers are renowned for coming up with clever nicknames for people involved in the game. Not only players find themselves with a moniker that sticks – administrators, umpires, ground staff, journalists and commentators also find themselves endowed with witty sobriquets.

A case in point is the name given to the late Alan Barnes, secretary of the New South Wales Cricket Association and, at the same time, of the Australian Board of Control for International Cricket as the national controlling body of the game was known in the 1960s. Alan suddenly became 'Justa' when he was managing the NSW team on a trip to Brisbane in 1962.

This name came about in a convoluted way. I had already been dubbed 'The Slack Sec', by the NSW team as I recall. The derivation, so I was told at the time, had nothing to do with any lack of competence on my part, but reflected the fact that I was young and laid back by comparison with most of my predecessors and contemporaries.

Frequently on tour the manager gets to be called by the shortened term of 'Ger' by the team. On this particular trip to the Gabba many of the NSW players would greet me with 'Good morning Slack Sec', while Alan was just plain old 'Ger'. It didn't take the boys long to come to the conclusion that their own highly respected secretary deserved a more deep and meaningful handle.

They seized on the fact that Barnes, understandably, had not taken on his managerial duties as assiduously as might the normal tour manager, who was frequently a zealous honorary administrator let loose away from home for possibly the first time with an elite cricket team. This inevitably led to comparisons with the performance of others in the past and the fairly predictable tongue-in-cheek judgment that Alan was 'only just a manager'.

From then on Barnes, the most senior full-time administrator in Australian cricket, was affectionately referred to by the New South Wales players as 'Justa Ger', later shortened to 'Justa'. I can assure you that these names, once they take a hold, survive the passage of time and, like information on player strengths and weaknesses, are quickly passed from State to State through cricket's version of the bush telegraph.

Even now, nearly four decades on, if Ian Chappell rings me he will start off with 'Slack Sec – it's Chappelli here.' Many other players from that era, such as Bob Simpson, Doug Walters, Norm O'Neill and Keith Stackpole, will greet me along the lines of 'How are you Slack Sec?'

Over the years, exchanges like this have produced some very quizzical looks on the faces of people within earshot. I don't even attempt to explain. It is just part of the camaraderie of the great game of cricket.

Never on a Sunday

Adelaide Oval is one of the loveliest cricket grounds in the world. The beauty of this serene place is never more evident than on a fine Sunday morning before play commences in a Test match, or any other match for that matter. With the bells of nearby St Peters Cathedral peeling in the background there is an ethereal atmosphere that creates a feeling of tranquillity, one of those wonderfully simple pleasures in life that we too often take for granted.

Sunday play was not always part of the Australian cricketing calendar. In fact it took a spirited campaign by the Queensland Cricket Association in the early 1960s before Sheffield Shield matches were finally scheduled on a Sunday by the Interstate Conference, the body that controlled the competition at the time. Even then the approval was limited to 'those States who were mutually agreeable to playing on Sundays'.

Only Queensland and Western Australia were in favour of this innovation. It was no coincidence, therefore, that the first Sheffield Shield match to include Sunday play was staged between those two States at the Brisbane Cricket Ground in November 1964, as was the second, at the WACA Ground in December 1964. I was fortunate enough to be present on both occasions as I managed the Queensland team on its trip to Perth.

The match in Brisbane attracted Australia-wide attention and more than 4000 spectators turned up at the Gabba on Sunday despite drizzly conditions. The local press was enthusiastic about 'the family picnic atmosphere' of the day and they accurately predicted a big future for Sunday cricket.

New South Wales and South Australia remained opposed to Sunday play, but Victoria put its toe in the water by agreeing to play in Brisbane late in the 1965/66 season. It took a few years but eventually Sunday play became the norm and a key factor in the marketing of the game in Australia as administrators realised the significance of being able to attract families to the cricket.

It intrigued me that South Australia would not initially agree to Sunday play in Sheffield Shield matches, while they were happy for their normal late December home match against Queensland to include Christmas Day. I remember being in Adelaide with the Queensland team in 1964 and for once there was no play on Christmas Day in the match against South Australia. The reason? Christmas Day fell on a Sunday!

As QCA secretary in those days I was at the forefront of the campaign to establish Sunday play on a regular basis. Little did I know when we were successful in our push that it would bring so much personal enjoyment in South Australia many years later.

Which leads me to urge anyone who has not been at Adelaide Oval on a Sunday morning before play starts to take in the aura and hear those cathedral bells ringing to take my tip and make the effort. You will not regret it.

Having a Beer with Duncan

Duncan Hall is a legendary figure of Queensland and Australian Rugby League. A big, tough and versatile forward, he became a bookmaker and a publican after he retired from football, both pursuits that ideally suited this wonderful character.

I got to know him quite well as he used to drop in at the Queensland Cricketers' Club for a cool Fourex on a hot day. As part of my three-pronged job I was secretary of that wonderful establishment situated on the boundary near fine-leg at the Vulture Street end of the Gabba.

The Queensland cricket team's pre-season program during my time there one year included a match against a North Queensland Xl in Bundaberg. It so happened that Duncan Hall ran a very successful hotel there.

Bundaberg is a town steeped in sporting tradition. It is the birthplace of numerous internationals in various sports, including the great Don Tallon.

I drove up there a few weeks before the match to finalise accommodation, transport and match conditions for the State team's visit, and naturally called on Duncan Hall at his pub. Over a beer I mentioned that I was returning to Brisbane the next morning, and Duncan asked me if I could give him a lift as he had business to do in the capital. I was delighted. His company would make the five-hour drive much more enjoyable.

As the driver I had been warned about Hall's penchant for stopping at 'watering holes' along the road from Bundaberg to Brisbane. Apparently he liked to keep up with what was going on in the hotel trade. As a precaution I suggested that we should concentrate on getting to Brisbane and, when we arrived, head straight to the Cricketers' Club to quench our thirsts.

Duncan was relaxed about this idea, but he put forward a proposition that we could stop at the towns along the way with names starting with the letter 'G', as it was going to be a hot day. A mental flick through the road map to Brisbane brought to mind just one town that qualified – Gympie, which was about half way down the track. That seemed reasonable, so I agreed.

Before I picked Duncan up the next morning I had a good look at my road map. Gympie was indeed the only town we would have to stop at if we went down the direct coastal route. Then I noticed an inland route, which would have taken us through towns such as Gin Gin, Grosvenor, Gayndah and Goomeri. But it was a longer route, along the Burnett Highway, so we agreed that the coastal road it would be.

Off we set and within an hour my travelling companion announced that we would have to stop at the next town. 'What town is that?' I asked. 'It's G-childers', Duncan replied with a wink as we approached the nice little town of Childers.

From there on I knew I was in trouble. Another stop was called for at 'Gmaryborough' and we were only a quarter of the way to Brisbane. By the time we got to 'Gnambour', just before the Sunshine Coast, I was drinking soda water but Duncan was still enjoying a glass or two of Fourex.

We eventually made it to Brisbane but, as far as I was concerned, the Cricketers' Club was out – I had waved the white flag long ago, so I dropped my travelling-mate off in the city and went straight home.

The moral of the story is two-fold. First, always make sure that you know what the real touring rules are when you offer a thirsty publican a lift; and second, never try and argue with a 20-stone former international Rugby league forward.

6

AN UNLIKELY SPORTS WRITER

Brisbane in the 1960s had two daily newspapers, the broadsheet *Courier Mail*, published in the morning, and the tabloid *Telegraph* which hit the streets in the afternoon. Both papers employed excellent cricket writers – including Jack Reardon and Max Hawkins – so the sport generally received good coverage.

There were also two Sunday papers, the *Sunday Mail* and the *Sunday Truth*. Coming as I had from Melbourne, where no Sunday paper existed until the 1970s, this was a pleasant change. Both publications boasted extensive circulation but were different in style. The *Sunday Mail* was conservative while the *Sunday Truth* was much more sensational in its content.

The *Telegraph* transferred Max Hawkins to Canberra as bureau chief in 1963, and with his departure came a marked decline in the paper's cricket coverage, particularly at club level. By then I had been in the job as QCA secretary for nearly three years and had worked hard at building close relationships with the media, the general view among their representatives apparently being that it was a nice change to have someone in the job who was accessible and actively promoting Queensland cricket.

I raised the matter of the falling off of cricket coverage in discussions with John Wakefield, editor of the *Telegraph,* and he explained that following Hawkins' move to Canberra they had the space to devote to cricket, but didn't always have the manpower to write it. He suggested that if the QCA had someone who could contribute regular material on cricket, the paper would be happy to publish it. As no one else wanted the job, with the blessing of my executive committee I decided to give it a go. So began my cricket-writing career, which has continued on now in some form or other for nearly 40 years.

The arrangement was that I would do a weekly column, which was given the somewhat unimaginative title *'Barry Gibbs' Cricket Score'*. The column appeared in the *Telegraph* each Wednesday throughout the cricket season for two years, commencing in 1964. It didn't reach any great literary heights, but it did provide a forum for the publication of all manner of cricket news, particularly from the club level, that otherwise may never have seen the light of day.

My cricket-writing was put on hold for a while after I left the QCA in 1966 to begin a career in the finance industry with Custom Credit Corporation. This took the family from Melbourne to Sydney to Townsville and then, in 1968, back to Melbourne.

During this period I occasionally managed to branch into other sports-reporting pursuits. I covered a VFL match between Essendon and Hawthorn at the Sydney Cricket Ground in 1966 for the Melbourne *Sporting Globe* and hosted a weekly Monday night sports television show on TNQ7 Townsville.

While I was secretary of the QCA I got to know a number sporting journalists from various parts of Australia, including Ian McDonald, the chief cricket, football *and* tennis writer of the *Sporting Globe*, colloquially referred to as 'The pink paper with the punch'. Macca had a distinguished career in journalism, going on to become the first sports editor of the Melbourne *Sunday Press,* the first media manager of the Victorian Football League and then the first media manager of the Australian Cricket Board.

By now I was back living in Melbourne, and this prompted Ian, who was aware that I had written a cricket column in Brisbane, to put the proposition to his editor, the legendary Geoff Hawksley, that it would be a good idea for the *Globe* to have a similar type column in its mid-week edition.

'Hawkeye', as Geoff was known in the trade, readily agreed, dubbing the column 'The Score' and in the process unwittingly giving me yet another nickname to go with Gibbsy, Gibbo, Bazza, Slack Sec and BG , among others. Even now there are people in the media who refer to me as 'the Score'.

So began a Sunday morning ritual, observed from October through to March for a number of years, when I would turn up at the *Sporting Globe* offices at the rear of the fourth floor of the old Herald and Weekly Times Limited building in Flinders Street. The offices doubled as the telephone copy-takers' room, where stories were phoned through on Saturday afternoons from reporters all over Melbourne and many other parts of Australia.

After my first year as a cricket columnist with the *Globe* I found out that there would be no such thing as a formal invitation to come back next season. It was simply a matter of turning up straight after the VFL grand final, sitting down at one of the old typewriters and picking up where you left off six months earlier. 'Hawkeye' would acknowledge my presence with a jovial welcome. 'It must be cricket season again, "The Score" is back. I thought I could hear the twang of leather against the willow.'

Like millions of people over the years, I grew up with the *Sporting Globe.* For those who are not familiar with this unique newspaper, it is difficult to explain the extent of the influence that it had upon the lives of sports lovers. Sufficient to say that the *Globe* was an institution, particularly in Melbourne, where it was published twice weekly, on Saturday evening and Tuesday morning.

The staff of the *Sporting Globe,* from Geoff Hawksley through to the newest cadet, could easily have jumped straight out of the pages of a Damon Runyon novel. 'Hawkeye' was from the old Sydney school of journalists, some of whom lived by the ethos that you should never let the facts get in the way of a good story. He was a remarkable character. Dress sense was not one of his strong points, and he would often turn up at the office on Sunday in shorts, an old shirt, thongs and minus his dentures.

McDonald was a hard-nosed former police rounds reporter who learnt his trade at the Melbourne *Argus.* He broke more than his share of major sports stories, many of them through his amazing number of contacts, who included senior politicians, business leaders, a virtual who's who of sporting greats and then ranging through society to some of the toughest criminals in town.

The other senior football writer was John Rice, nicknamed 'Hoppit' as Hawksley continually asked him to hoppit here and there during his cadet days. 'Hoppit' would occasionally use the office as a crèche for his children. One of them, Dean Rice, developed into a talented, uncompromising AFL footballer who played with distinction in the superb Carlton premiership side of 1995.

Chief racing writer was Rollo Roylance, known as the 'Cheery Chestnut', a stand out character in an industry that was full of characters.

Trotting was covered by Peter Bye, 'the biggest man in trotting', a phrase coined as much as a reflection of his massive frame, which would have tipped the scales at well over 20 stone, as his peerless knowledge of harness racing.

Boxing was the domain of the one and only Merv Williams, a former Australian champion himself and a legend in the world of fisticuffs. Merv was a gentleman in every sense of the word. Quietly spoken and mild-mannered, had it not been for the battered nose he could have passed as a retired preacher.

Williams also wrote on wrestling as the need arose. I have a vivid recollection of Merv bringing a former world heavyweight wrestling champion, Navajo Indian 'Big Chief Little Wolf', into the *Globe* office one Sunday morning where he interviewed the American wrestler in his colourful feathered tribal regalia.

The *Sporting Globe* prided itself on featuring just about every sport there was, though VFL football and horse-racing accounted for a large part of the paper. The reporting of each Saturday's six VFL games was done by McDonald and Rice, together with a panel of former stars such as St Kilda Brownlow medallist Neil Roberts, North Melbourne great and future VFL president Allen Aylett, and champion Essendon full forward, now chairman of the AFL Commission, Ron Evans.

An assortment of other permanent and casual staff carried out all manner of duties, not the least important of which was making sure there was an ample supply of liquid refreshment conveyed from Lou Richards' nearby Phoenix Hotel back in the days when the pubs were shut on Sundays.

After a year or so of churning out a cricket column for the *Globe*, I became 'phone man' for Allen Aylett in the football season, assisting him with statistics, goal kickers and best players, as well as filing match details on the VFL reserves curtain-raiser. This meant being at the ground around 11 am and leaving about 6 pm, after the injuries and reports for the main game had been obtained from both teams and the umpires.

If the game we were covering was at Geelong, Footscray or Essendon, all of which were miles the other side of Melbourne from where I lived, it could mean heading off at around 9 am and arriving home roughly 12 hours later. This allowed little time for a well-earned drink at the ground after the match – or networking, as it would be called these days.

The financial rewards from writing were meagre, but it was part of a great learning experience that took me to many memorable games of football. High on this list was the late Ted Whitten's 321st and last match, played on a wet, miserable and very emotional day at Footscray's Western Oval, which now carries his name. I also got to see about 15 VFL grand finals from the press box, including some of the great Carlton premierships of the 1970s and early 1980s.

It wasn't long before a vacancy came along as one of the *Globe's* main game writers and I got the nod, having covered a few games here and there when someone was away. Never did I dream when I was a young man growing up in Melbourne in the 1950s, when we would congregate outside the local newsagent on Saturday evening waiting for the last edition *Sporting Globe* to arrive hot off the press, that I would one day be writing football for the revered pink paper.

The Saturday edition of the *Globe* ceased publication in the early 1970s, the paper then coming out on Tuesdays only. Shortly afterwards the *Sunday Press* arrived on the scene. This was a joint venture newspaper between The Herald and Weekly Times Limited (publishers of the Melbourne *Herald, Sun News Pictorial and Sporting Globe*) and David Syme & Company Limited, which publishes *The Age*.

Both the Herald and Weekly Times and David Syme & Company had left the Sunday newspaper market in Melbourne alone, which was quite surprising considering the circulation figures for Sunday papers in Sydney, Brisbane and Adelaide ran into well over a million copies each week.

When Ian McDonald was appointed as sporting editor of the *Sunday Press,* he recruited a number of former Saturday *Sporting Globe* writers, myself included, to cover VFL football matches and, in my case, cricket. Gone was the pressure of the very tight early Saturday evening deadline and the need to phone copy through as matches progressed. Now there was the luxury of a little time in which to take a more critical view of proceedings and to write an overall summary of matches *after* they had finished, replacing the kick-by-kick type of match description that had been the *Sporting Globe* style for decades.

Over the years I filed copy for both the *Sporting Globe* and the *Sunday Press* from many parts of Australia and overseas, often when I was away from Melbourne on business or on holiday. Occasionally I got lucky and managed to rate a front-page story, such as the time in 1982 when Australian fast medium bowler Terry Alderman suffered a career-threatening injury to his shoulder during a Test match against England in Perth.

Alderman had chased after a spectator who had clipped him behind the ears after running onto the WACA Ground during play. When he reached the intruder, Terry brought him to the ground with a perfectly executed rugby-style tackle, only to dislocate his shoulder in the process. The aftermath of this incident was an all-in brawl between Australian and England supporters, one of the ugliest episodes I have seen anywhere in sport.

The Falkland Islands war was in full swing at the time and this prompted Jeff Hook to draw a clever cartoon to accompany my article. It portrayed British prime minister Margaret Thatcher holding a newspaper with headlines reading 'Battle For The Ashes. Crowd Invade Pitch! 2 Injured.' She was issuing orders to two high-ranking naval officers to 'Have a task force headed by HMS *Invincible* sail for West Australia immediately!'

In 1974 I was on a business trip to London when the chairman of England selectors, Alec Bedser, called a press conference to announce the team to tour Australia in the 1974/75 season. I headed off to Lord's to renew acquaintances with my good friend Alec and hear what he had to say about the omission of star fast bowler, John Snow, from the touring party. In the *Sunday Press* a few days later I boldly predicted that Australia would regain the Ashes. The headline, which read 'No Snow No Show', turned out to be accurate. Australia won the series by four Tests to one.

During a trip to Hong Kong in 1980 another friend, the former champion Australian jockey Geoff Lane, took me to a Wednesday night race meeting at the magnificent Shatin racecourse. Geoff had recently retired from riding and was on the staff of the Royal Hong Kong Jockey Club.

The Shatin complex had recently been developed by the RHKJC in the new territories of mainland Hong Kong at a cost of A$85 million. This was a massive capital outlay two decades ago, illustrating the popularity of thoroughbred racing in that part of the world. It also gives an insight into the financial strength of the Club.

That night the races were held on a sand track with 40,000 people in attendance. It was a great spectacle, which started me wondering why night time thoroughbred racing had not been tried in Australia.

In discussion with Hong Kong Jockey Club officials, my curiosity was further aroused when I learned that work was just about completed on the installation of a new multi-million dollar lighting system and grass track for night racing at the headquarters of the Club, Happy Valley, on Hong Kong island. They had already held a successful full-scale dress rehearsal and had scheduled the first official night meeting on a grass track for 23 December 1980, in what was being promoted as a world first.

When I returned home I wrote an article in the *Sporting Globe* extolling the virtues of night racing as I had seen it in Hong Kong and suggesting that it would be marvellous in Melbourne during the summer. The suggestion was not embraced by the racing fraternity, with various reasons being put forward as to why it couldn't work.

I didn't give the matter much thought from then on until I read more than a decade later that the Victorian Amateur Turf Club was seriously considering upgrading the grass track at its magnificent Moonee Valley facility, as well as incorporating provision for future lighting. This was to be in addition to the magnificent flood-lit harness-racing track that runs inside the racecourse proper.

Shortly afterward the grass track upgrade got the go-ahead with work starting in 1995. It is now history that the first night race meeting on grass in Australia was staged by the VATC at Moonee Valley on 26 January 1998 with a massive crowd in attendance. The Sport of Kings had finally joined just about every other major sport in Australia chasing a slice of the lucrative evening entertainment market.

In addition to sports reporting I began to write articles on the financial markets, drawing on the experience I had gained in that industry, which was then my full-time occupation. I have Des Keegan, the finance editor of the *Sun News-Pictorial* in Melbourne, to thank for getting me started in that direction. Des and I knew each other through having a beer together at the journo's watering hole, Lou Richards' Phoenix Hotel, where we discussed what was going on in the world of finance as well as footy, cricket and the races.

Over lunch one day Des mentioned that he wanted to extend the *Sun's* small financial section to include items about the rapidly evolving capital markets. He asked if I would be interested in writing an occasional piece, and I was more than happy to accept the brief. The arrangement was that I would submit material that I thought might be of interest from time to time and, conversely, I could be called upon to write an article on a specific subject when there was a need.

There was one problem involved in extending my journalistic endeavours to include financial matters. I was reluctant, due to professional etiquette, to have my name appear on articles I had written. As any journalist will attest, the reverse normally applies, with a by-line being of paramount importance.

We overcame that little matter when a character by the name of Brian McGee started to write in the finance pages. McGee happened to be my mother's maiden name and the initials, BMG, were identical to mine. Brian McGee didn't have a long career on the *Sun,* though he did feature fairly regularly in 1971 and 1972, fading from the picture about the same time as the finance editor headed off interstate to greener pastures!

As time went by I found myself being invited to write features on various aspects of the financial markets for national newspapers such as the *Financial Review* and the *Australian,* especially in their banking and money-market supplements. This increasing involvement in newspapers and other publications brought with it another concern to me; no matter how hard I tried I just could not become a member of the Australian Journalists' Association.

For some years whenever I enquired about becoming an AJA member, I was invariably told by the then secretary of the Victorian branch, Graham Walsh, that I was not eligible to join the Association under its rules as the bulk of my income was not derived from journalism. Obviously this was a matter over which I had no control, but I felt uncomfortable about it, particularly as I was paid for my contributions at what were referred to as 'AJA rates'.

The impasse was eventually overcome when I took time off in between jobs to cover a season of cricket full time in 1975/76. I finally joined the

AJA in October 1975, retaining my card for some years after returning to merchant banking.

The opportunity to write – whether on cricket, football, finance or other topics – has been a creative diversion for me, one that has enabled me to get away from the different sorts of pressures of my full-time occupations. Writing has given me a tremendous amount of pleasure, opened many doors, taken me to new places and enabled me to meet wonderfully interesting people.

7

SUDDENLY I AM A TELEVISION HOST

I can't be certain, but there are compelling reasons for me to suspect that I have Wally Grout to thank for becoming a TV sports show host in Townsville, north Queensland, in 1967. I was living there at that time, working for Custom Credit Corporation.

Wally had retired from Test cricket in 1966, but continued to work as a promotional representative with Rothmans, which took him regularly to far north Queensland. During one of these trips he was working on the pilot launch of a new cigarette brand in Townsville, a city that Rothmans had identified as being suitable to measure the national market potential.

Part of Wally's role in the lead-up to the launch was to locate a suitable person locally who could do a short introductory television commercial for the new brand on TNQ7 in Townsville. Wally put my name forward as someone who fitted the bill, so I duly had an audition of sorts – with the result that I didn't get the gig.

Not long after this I had an unexpected telephone call from Keith Christensen, the general manager of TNQ7, asking if I could meet him. My curiosity was aroused, so we got together a few days later. Keith outlined plans he had for a new weekly sports TV show. Would I be interested in hosting it?

To say that I was surprised by this offer would be an understatement. My television experience at that point had been limited to occasional behind-the-scenes outside broadcast commentaries on local Australian rules matches for ABC TV in Brisbane, plus a few short guest appearances on sporting and current-affairs programs during the time I was secretary of the Queensland Cricket Association.

Despite the fact that I was in north Queensland to work in the finance industry, not television, I warmed to the prospect of having my own locally produced TV sports show. After discussing the situation with Peg and my employers, I decided to give it a go. So began *Barry Gibbs' Sporting Scene* on TNQ7.

These were pioneering times in television, particularly in the far north. The medium had only been operating in Australia for about a decade and for a considerable lesser time in remote areas such as Townsville, which is 1600 kilometres from Brisbane. You couldn't just flick a switch or push a button to link distant cities together, video cameras were still in the future, satellite transmission was years away and Neil Armstrong had yet to walk on the moon.

Doing a weekly TV show placed demands on my 'free' time as I juggled my full-time job around sporting events and the availability of personalities passing through the region. The offices and studios of TNQ7 lay high up on Mt Stuart in rugged mountain ranges just west of Townsville. This was a great location for transmitting a signal over a widespread area, but a nightmare if you were in a hurry to get there.

Doing *Sporting Scene* was a real buzz. It provided me with a crash course in the workings of a television station. Not only was I the host of the show, I produced it and even got involved in the technical side, helping to splice film amid the chaos before we went to air.

As host I would open and close the show, introduce segments and make comments live to air. Most of the interviews were done at the studios at Mt Stuart and pre-recorded for the Monday evening show. Occasionally we would do an interview on the night, which meant driving guests in pitch dark up the steep, windy and narrow road to reach the station.

Once I was driving to the studio in torrential rain to interview former Test umpire Col Hoy, who was in the car with me. Halfway up the mountain we suffered a flat tyre. There we were in the downpour, me jacking the car up on a wet, sloping road while Hoy, sheltering under an umbrella, shone a torch on the offending wheel. We got it changed eventually and arrived at the studio looking like two drowned rats. But the show went on!

We travelled north, south, east and west of Townsville filming segments for the program. Wherever there was a sporting event of interest within about 100 kilometres, off we would go to get some footage for *Sporting Scene* – 'taking our cameras', as I was wont to say on air with great regularity, much to the amusement of my wife and friends.

For Peg, me and our three daughters, *Sporting Scene* made the time we spent living in Townsville one of the most enjoyable periods in all of our lives. One of the highlights was a trip to beautiful Magnetic Island, located only a few kilometres offshore. I was a member of Townsville's Mexico Olympic Appeal Committee, which organised a fund-raising dinner on the island in 1968. Among the celebrities who attended this highly successful function was champion athlete Ron Clarke.

Clarke was a totally dedicated athlete who was not about to waste any spare time during his visit to Townsville as he was in serious training for the Olympics. He came out to our home for a visit with his wife Helen and their small baby – and promptly left the family with us before setting off on his own to put in a few hours of running.

Ron wanted to achieve two goals during this run, firstly to cover a lot of kilometres and secondly to do some work in altitude, bearing in mind that Mexico City is over 7000 feet above sea level. I suggested that he could combine his two objectives by running out to Mt Stuart, up the mountain, turn around and descend it and finish off with straight stretch of eight kilometres back to his hotel in the city. Ron, who was the current holder of every world record from two miles to ten miles, thought this was just the ticket, so off he went. We estimated how long it would take him to complete the journey and, when the time was right, drove the rest of the Clarke family to the hotel so that they could be there to greet him after another day at the office.

Townsville in those days was the second-biggest city in Queensland and, like most provincial areas in that decentralised State, had a proud sporting tradition. There was plenty of material to fill a half hour sports show each week, particularly with towns like Ayr to the south, where we would cover the Burdekin Delta Turf Club Races from time to time, Ingham in the north where the 1968 Queensland hard-court tennis championships were held, and the old gold-mining town of Charters Towers out west, which hosted a big annual regional cricket carnival. In recent times Ayr has become famous as the home of Karrie Webb, the world's leading woman golfer, while Ingham is where cricketer Joe Scuderi was born.

A parade of prominent sporting personalities passed through Townsville, providing me with a stream of interview opportunities. Occasionally there were superstars in town like tennis greats Roy Emerson and Margaret

Court or world snooker champion, Horace Lindrum. These great sportspersons added a stamp of class to a local sporting show that prided itself in covering everything from rugby to racing, cricket to canoeing, tennis to trots and sailing to swimming.

All too soon came the news that I had been transferred back to Melbourne after less than two years in tropical Townsville. My career in the finance sector was about to take off, but my short and thoroughly enjoyable time in TV was over.

As fate would have it Wally Grout, the man who unwittingly played a part in my becoming a television show host, appeared on the last edition of *Sporting Scene*. He was one of the celebrity guests at the Olympic Games dinner on Magnetic Island in April 1968, which we filmed for the program. Wally left Townsville the next day before the show went to air; sadly I never got to see him again.

8

CODES OF BEHAVIOUR

Not long before the start of the 1984/85 cricket season I received a telephone call from David Richards, chief executive of the Australian Cricket Board, enquiring if I was available to come in and talk to him about a cricketing matter. At the time I was working with a Melbourne-based merchant bank, Capel Court Corporation, and was more than happy to have a chat with David who I had known from the time when he was secretary of the Victorian Cricket Association.

I went down to the ACB's offices in Jolimont near the Melbourne Cricket Ground a few days later. David told me that Bob Merriman, a prominent VCA official who had for a number of years been the Board's cricket committee coordinator and arbiter on player code of behaviour matters, had accepted the job as full-time manager of the Australian cricket team for the next two years. Merriman was to retain his cricket committee role, but this left vacant a newly created position as ACB Code of Behaviour Coordinator.

My name had been mentioned as a likely candidate for this honorary position, which was effectively a one-man independent tribunal set up to hear charges laid against first-class cricketers throughout Australia under the players' Code of Behaviour. In the main these had to do with breaches of a player's contract or invitation to represent his State, as provided for in the code.

On-field charges of breaching the code would continue to be dealt with by a small peer group comprising the player's captain, vice-captain and cricket committee representative, as had been the case since the introduction of the code in 1980. In a change of direction, any appeals against the decisions of this group were now to be referred to the Code of Behaviour Coordinator for hearing and his decision would be final.

This was never going to be an easy position to fill. Merriman was a professional arbitration commissioner and therefore quite at ease in hearing charges of this nature. For my part, however, I had little experience in this field, other than the few appearances I had made before the Arbitration Commission during the time I was secretary of the Australian Air Pilots Association 25 years earlier.

After thinking it over for a short while and being assured that a legal background was not essential to the job – but that a knowledge of the first-class game together with an ability to apply common sense were – I decided to give it a go for a year. My appointment was officially announced by the Board in October 1984 and from then on it was just a case of being available if, when and where required.

I must admit that I had reservations about how I would handle the situation when I did get around to hearing a charge against a player. Over the years, I believe, I had enjoyed good relations with first-class cricketers across the board, both as an administrator and as a writer. Clearly there now was the potential for this to change, particularly as the job might well involve taking disciplinary action against players by imposing monetary fines or suspension, or both. I knew full well that this responsibility went with the territory and had to face the fact that the onus was on me alone to manage it.

Taking Strike Against 'Thommo'

I didn't have to wait long to hear my first charge as Code of Behaviour Coordinator. Fast-bowling great Jeff Thomson was writing a regular column in the Brisbane *Telegraph* in conjunction with journalist Wayne Smith. In an article published early in January 1985, Jeff expressed surprise that South Australian Rodney Hogg had regained his place in the Australian team for the forthcoming one-day internationals, saying that Queensland's Carl Rackemann would have been far better value. He also wrote he was not convinced that leg-spinner Bob Holland should be a definite starter for the tour of England later in the year, despite taking 10 wickets in a recent Test match against the West Indies at the SCG.

Jeff was approaching the veteran stage by this time but he still had an

ACB contract and accordingly was bound by the player/writer clause, which stipulated that players must not comment on team selection. David Richards took a dim view of what Thomson had written and advised him formally that he had referred the matter to me under the breach-of-contract provisions of the Code of Behaviour.

Queensland were to play a Sheffield Shield match against Victoria in Melbourne a few days after the offending column appeared, so it was decided to hear the complaint during that match. Queensland was batting first so there were no problems with Jeff in arranging a time for the hearing, both of us agreeing that we might as well get it out of the way on the first day.

There I was, less than three months into my new job in cricket, and first up I am confronted with the prospect of hearing a charge against one of the legends of the game, a charge laid by the most senior full-time administrator in Australian cricket. As if to get the adrenalin flowing even more quickly, the venue I had chosen, for the sake of convenience, was the players' dining area down in the bowels of the western grandstand at the MCG. Talk about Daniel entering the lion's den!

By this stage I had memorised the entire Code of Behaviour rules and rehearsed in my mind the way I wanted the hearing to be conducted. I was as ready as I was ever going to be, so Ron Steiner from the ACB office, who was assisting me, set off to bring 'Thommo' into the hearing. This gave me a moment to question what on earth I had got myself into.

The hearing itself turned out to be an anti-climax after the build-up I had given it in my own mind. There were four people in the room: Jeff Thomson, the Queensland wicketkeeper Ray Phillips, who had accompanied Thommo, Ron Steiner and me. I read the charge out, explained the alleged breach of the code and asked Jeff what he had to say about the matter.

Thomson conceded the words in the column were his but said that the reference to Rodney Hogg was intended as a statement on the Australian team's fitness-testing process (Hogg didn't have a test after coming back from injury), and not as a direct comment on team selection. In other words, he said, there was a 'double meaning'.

After I had pointed out to Jeff the responsibilities of contracted players and satisfying myself that there was nothing further anyone wished to raise, I adjourned the hearing for a short time to consider what action I should take. Crunch time.

It didn't take long to reach the conclusion, virtually on Jeff's own admission, that he had breached his playing contract and in particular the player/writer rule. This in turn meant that he had contravened the players' Code of Behaviour. Having decided that, it was then a matter of determining an appropriate penalty, which I set at a $300 fine.

Jeff was called back into the hearing where I advised him of my decision and the penalty I had imposed. He accepted both with good grace and then quietly left the room. For all that has been said and written about the fiery and aggressive Jeff Thomson on the cricket field, in my dealings with him off the field he has always been courteous, friendly and straight to the point. There are no frills – what you see is what you get: an eminently likeable person.

Apart from tidying up some paperwork for the Australian Cricket Board, that was the end of my first hearing as Code of Behaviour Coordinator. Although it was a fairly painless experience all round, except perhaps for Thommo who was $300 lighter in the pocket, I was pleased that the matter was behind me and I now felt reasonably comfortable about my decision to accept the Board's invitation to take on the position.

'Flipper' Fronts Up

For some little time the Australian Cricket Board had been concerned about how effectively the Code of Behaviour system was working, with cricketers sitting in judgment of their team mates in the event of charges being laid for on-field misconduct. In general it appeared that the umpires had lost confidence in the process.

There were a number of flash points throughout the 1984/85 season, mostly involving Australian and West Indies players during the six-Test series in Australia. West Indies manager Wes Hall had severely criticised the domestic disciplinary system. He strongly felt that some members of the

Australian team should have been charged with on-field breaches of the Code of Behaviour. There were also quite a few ACB directors, as well as some senior players, who felt that after five years of 'peer discipline' the procedures needed overhauling.

After discussion on the matter the Board changed the Code of Behaviour rules in October 1985, taking away from players the authority to hear initial charges of breaches and giving that task to independent commissioners to be appointed by each State.

My initial appointment was extended for a further year and the name of the position changed to Australian Cricket Board Code of Behaviour Commissioner. In this new and slightly upgraded role I was to be responsible for the hearing of any appeals lodged against decisions made by the various State commissioners throughout Australia and would continue to hear complaints laid against players for contractual breaches and the like.

The new arrangements clearly had a greater level of acceptance by umpires and officials, with six individual charges against players for on-field breaches of the Code in 1985/86 being heard by commissioners in four States. This was double the number for the previous season. Four players were found guilty and either fined or reprimanded, while the other two had their charges dismissed. In each case there was no appeal made by a player against the State commissioners' rulings, which meant that my services were not called upon for the whole of the season.

It was beginning to appear that the words of David Richards in his letter of appointment to me in 1984 – 'we sincerely trust that you will have little to do in this role' – would be spot on.

But in May 1986 South Australian batsman and keeper Wayne Phillips took it into his head to describe the national selectors as 'idiots' in an interview with Melbourne *Age* journalist Garry Linnell after Phillips had been overlooked for the Australian team to tour India. All of a sudden I had a dicey issue to deal with.

The chairman of the Australian Cricket Board, Fred Bennett, took a very dim view of the comments by Phillips, deciding that they constituted a breach of the players Code of Behaviour, with his criticism of the Australian selectors being seen as detrimental to the best interests of the game. David Richards concurred with Bennett's opinion, formally lodging a report form with me together with a request for an early hearing of the matter.

The ACB supplied me with a copy of the offending article in which Phillips, when questioned about his immediate future after being dropped, was quoted as saying: 'I'm going to live … I'm going to do what I want to do and not be at the beck and call of these idiots who pick the side.' These were strong words from a contracted player who had been a member of the Australian team for nearly three years.

We arranged for Wayne to come from Adelaide to Melbourne for the charges to be heard at the Board's offices on 6 May 1986. I had a fair idea that this would be no low-key affair, which was confirmed when I arrived for the hearing to be greeted by a large media contingent in Jolimont Street.

Wayne Phillips is one of the most likeable cricketers I have ever met, immensely popular with his peers and devoid of malice. Not that this view had anything to do with my deliberations – but it did add an intriguing personal twist to my first major hearing as Code of Behaviour Commissioner.

Having got the formalities out of the way, I asked Wayne if he had anything he wished to say in relation to the charges and his reported comments. He admitted to making the statement about the selectors to Linnell who, Phillips said, had rung at a 'terrible time when I had had a gut full'.

He agreed that the comments, which he had made off the cuff and not expecting them to be printed, could be viewed as being detrimental to the game. He deeply regretted having made them. Wayne indicated that, having made the comments, he was prepared to cop it sweet and went on to say that he wished to apologise to the selectors. He then left the room while I considered what action should be taken.

From what he had said, Phillips was clearly in breach of the code, as well as his contract with the ACB. But it was far more difficult to determine what penalty should apply. This was not your run-of-the mill on-field sledging matter in which I could be guided by ample precedents. In fact, I doubt that any player before had publicly referred to the selectors as 'idiots', although some had no doubt harboured such thoughts privately over the years.

After a lengthy and lonely period of careful consideration, I asked Phillips to return to the hearing and informed him that I had found him guilty of breaching the Code of Behaviour by making comments detrimental to the game and in commenting on team selection. I also reminded him that I was empowered to suspend him from playing in matches under the control of the Board or impose a fine, or both.

I made it clear that I viewed this as a most serious breach of the code. I said that I accepted he would have been disappointed at not being selected for the tour of India and acknowledged his contrition over his 'off-the-cuff' comments. But as a contracted player, I pointed out, he must have been aware of the possible consequences of his statements.

Summing up, I said that I had given serious thought to suspending Phillips for a period to begin from the commencement of the 1986/87 season but had finally decided a fine was more appropriate under the circumstances. With that I imposed a fine of $2000, adding that I genuinely hoped the penalty would ensure he did not breach the code again.

Before closing the hearing I asked Wayne if there was anything further he wanted to add. His only request was for it to be recorded that he felt the charges against him had been very fairly heard, which says a lot about the character of the man.

As he left the room to head back to Adelaide, Phillips must have had an inkling that his 27 Test-match career was very much in the balance. Despite some excellent form for South Australia in 1986/87, when he scored 882 runs at an average of better than 55 including three centuries, the elegant 28-year-old left-hander never played for Australia again.

The $2000 fine caused a kerfuffle in the media and in cricket circles generally. At the time it was the highest monetary penalty imposed since the introduction of the players' Code of Behaviour six years earlier, although I don't think there were too many people, including Wayne Phillips, who considered the amount to be excessive in the context of what was said.

In his autobiography Allan Border wrote at length about the shortcomings of the Code of Behaviour in the early days. As the former Australian captain put it: 'How silly it was to have teammates sitting in judgment on you. There was no way your own colleagues were going to crucify you, but some attempt at realism should have been made.'

He went on to comment about the changes the Board had made to the procedures in 1985, saying:

> Thankfully the Code of Behaviour set up has been tightened considerably and justice is now seen to be done. No longer are teammates obliged to pass judgments and sentences. It was a function they neither sought nor desired. The position of 'Code of Behaviour Commissioner' has been created by the ACB and it seems to have filled a need. The position is currently occupied by Barry Gibbs, and if you think he doesn't mean business, you should seek the opinion of Wayne Phillips. Barry fined Wayne $2000 for his 'idiots' outburst against the selectors who left him out of the 1986 party to tour India. I don't think Wayne will want to cross swords with the commissioner again.

Two years later, in May 1988, I was appointed to the full-time position as Executive Manager of the South Australian Cricket Association, so Peg and I were on the move interstate again.

Phillips was still a prominent member of the South Australian team and naturally we saw a lot of each other. Of course it didn't take long for the subject of *that* fine to be raised. With a straight face Wayne suggested to me, jokingly I think, that as I had cost him $2000 a couple of years earlier, it was only fair, now that we were living in the same town and as both of us enjoyed a cold beer on a hot day, that I should shout whenever we got together until the ledger was square.

For over thirteen years now this repartee has been going on with one of us invariably coming up with an estimate of the amount still owing, often to the bemusement of people in our company who don't have a clue what on earth we are talking about.

Tim Zoehrer Appeals – Unsuccessfully

In February 1987 I was transferred in my employment from Melbourne to Brisbane. The ACB was happy for me to continue on as Code of Behaviour Commissioner while living in Queensland, although I was hoping that my services would not be required for some time while I settled into Brisbane after an absence of 21 years. Unfortunately it didn't work out that way.

I had been back in the Sunshine State for a month when I received a telephone call from Ron Steiner at the ACB office to let me know that Tim Zoehrer, the Western Australian wicketkeeper, had been charged by umpires Peter McConnell and Terry Prue with two breaches of the Code of Behaviour. The report alleged that Tim had used crude and abusive language, and also engaged in conduct detrimental to the game, in a match against Tasmania in Perth. WA State Commissioner Vic Fisher heard the charges, finding Zoehrer guilty and applying a fine of $260, the equivalent of a full match payment.

Tim lodged an appeal against Fisher's guilty decision, as he was entitled to do under the code. For the first time, I was required to hear an appeal by a player and to do so with as little delay as possible. Under normal circumstances this would not have posed a problem, but my life wasn't normal. I was in Brisbane trying to get a newly licensed bank up and running at the same time I was house-hunting, while Zoehrer, McConnell and Prue were all in Perth, about 4000 kilometres away.

After briefly discussing with ACB general manager Graham Halbish the possibility of hearing the appeal in Brisbane due to the pressing demands of my new job, we agreed that logistically and financially it would be preferable for me to fly to Perth where there was a Sheffield Shield match between Western Australia and Queensland scheduled at the WACA Ground in a few days time.

At short notice I was on a plane for Perth where, to fit in with playing hours, the hearing was held at the WACA offices before play started on the first day of the game. Zoehrer and WA captain Graeme Wood were present, along with umpires McConnell and Prue and WACA cricket manager Ian Brayshaw. The proceedings were short and sharp, with virtually no evidence being tendered to influence me to overturn Commissioner Fisher's guilty finding.

By now I was pretty unhappy about the whole matter. I had flown diagonally across Australia from Brisbane to Perth the night before only to find that Zoehrer's appeal was apparently founded on the mere fact that he could appeal, not on any substance.

After a short adjournment, during which I seriously considered increasing the original penalty, I dismissed the appeal and in doing so reprimanded Zoehrer for his behaviour leading up to the charges being laid, and for the bad example he had set as a Test player. I went on to warn him that if he had to appear before me on a similar charge in the future he could expect far more serious consequences if found guilty.

Two positives came out of that hearing. The first was that the ACB decided to amend the Code of Behaviour to make it possible, if appeals could be proven to be of a frivolous nature, for the person lodging the appeal to be held responsible for the costs involved. In the case of the Zoehrer appeal, the Board would have been out of pocket by more than $2000 for my airfares and accommodation expenses, while I lost nearly two days at work during a very busy time while carrying out my honorary role.

The second positive was that, in the opinion of some senior WACA officials I subsequently spoke to, Tim Zoehrer had listened to what I had to say. He was finally beginning to mature as a cricketer and was showing signs of being prepared to accept the responsibilities expected of a senior player. With that change of attitude came a return to international cricket for the talented Western Australian. Tim was chosen for the 1989 and 1993 Australian tours to England, where he was understudy to Ian Healy but could not add to his tally of 10 Tests.

'Fat Cat' Faces the Music

I have been amazed over the years how experienced cricketers – including ones who have signed an Australian Cricket Board contract that precludes them from commenting on team selection – can let their guard down when being interviewed by journalists.

A case in point was the enormously talented and likeable Queenslander, Greg Ritchie. 'Fat Cat', as Greg became known due to his propensity to put on weight more easily than most, decided for some reason to tell Melbourne journalist Ken Piesse that he was still smarting at being left out of Australia's 1987 World Cup team. No doubt he was very unhappy about his omission when the squad was chosen several months earlier, but what on earth possessed him to go public in November 1987, *after* Australia had just won the World Cup for the first time, I simply do not know.

ACB general manager Graham Halbish was unimpressed with Greg's comments in the *Sun-Herald* and promptly reported him for a breach of the Code of Behaviour. Halbish believed that Ritchie had breached his playing contract by making comments in relation to his non-selection that were detrimental to the game and in breach of the player/writer rule.

Being a charge of a contractual nature, this one was referred directly to me for hearing. As Greg and I were both in Brisbane, the matter was heard the next day so that it did not interfere with a vital Sheffield Shield match between Queensland and Victoria at the Gabba one day later. Greg conceded that he made the comments, although he said that they had been taken slightly out of context. In finding him guilty I imposed a $400 fine, which was promptly paid.

Facing D.K. Lillee Off the Long Run

In October 1987 the great Dennis Lillee was coaxed out of retirement at 38 years of age to play for Tasmania after a three-year absence from the game. I didn't know it at the time but I was to have a fair bit to do with D.K Lillee late in the season, even though he was based temporarily in Hobart and I was living in Brisbane.

The 1987/88 season turned out to be a busy one for State Code of Behaviour Commissioners as well as for me, with ten charges being laid, the highest number since the introduction of the code. In each instance the player was found guilty, with two appeals being lodged, both of them by Lillee.

The first of these appeals was against a fine of $300 imposed by South Australian Commissioner Justice John Gun, who found proven a charge by umpires Tony Crafter and Daryl Harper against Dennis for the use of crude language in a Sheffield Shield match at Adelaide Oval. Lillee appealed on the grounds that more than one similar instance had occurred in the same game and that he was the only player singled out.

It was not possible to get all the parties together at short notice for an early hearing and the appeal date was eventually arranged for three weeks later on 12 March 1988, when South Australia were to play Tasmania in a McDonald's Cup semi-final in Adelaide. I flew to Adelaide from Brisbane that day and heard the matter after the match had finished.

After listening to what Lillee had to say, as well as to umpires Crafter and Harper, I dismissed the appeal and ruled that the fine imposed by Justice Gun would stand. In doing so I pointed out that even if there were other similar breaches, which the umpires said they did not detect, I was of the opinion that these would not have over-ridden the fact that Dennis had breached the Code of Behaviour in the manner reported and should meet the consequences of his actions.

The great fast bowler was not at all happy. Tasmania had lost the semi-final, he had not taken a wicket and now his appeal had been rejected. He left the hearing abruptly!

I had to stay overnight in Adelaide and went to my hotel to wait for friends who were coming for a drink. What I didn't know was that the Tasmanian team was staying at the same hotel – when I walked into the bar most of them were there. I recall getting that famous Lillee glare, the one normally reserved for a batsman who had snicked him for four. I immediately thought to myself that there had to be more congenial spots in Adelaide to have a beer.

My trepidation was eased when that wonderful cricketing character, Brian Davison, formerly of Rhodesia (Zimbabwe), Leicestershire and Gloucestershire, who was captain of Tasmania at the time, came over and insisted that I have a drink with him and some of his team. I accepted, staying for a short while – but the glare was still there!

The next morning I flew back to Brisbane. On the way the thought ran through my mind that while this had been a different way to spend a weekend, it was not one that I would recommend. But that was in the past and by now it was nearly the middle of March, with the first-class cricket season due to conclude in two weeks. Surely I would have no more official duties to carry out in relation to the Code of Behaviour, at least not until the 1988/89 season got under way.

I didn't know then that another incident had already taken place, one that would upset my thoughts of a quiet end to a busy year. This matter, which involved Dennis Lillee, Ian Botham and some damage to the Queensland team's dressing-room, took place after play had ended in a McDonald's Cup match between Tasmania and Queensland at Launceston on 28 February 1988. Botham was playing for Queensland at the time.

For reasons best known to officials of the various cricketing organisations that then controlled the game in Tasmania communications between them on the affair had been slow. The Northern Tasmanian Cricket Association, which was responsible for the administration of cricket in the Launceston region, did not notify the Tasmanian Cricket Council, the peak body for the sport in the State, that there had been a problem until nine days later. The TCC in turn did not advise the Queensland Cricket Association for a further five days. By now it was 14 March and I had already returned to Brisbane after hearing Dennis Lillee's appeal on the Adelaide matter.

The wheels ground on slowly with Peter Hadlow, Executive Director of the TCC, formally charging both Lillee and Botham on 19 March with breaches of the Code of Behaviour, alleging that they engaged in conduct detrimental to the game by causing damage to a dressing-room at the NTCA Ground in Launceston. By this time Dennis had finished his season with Tasmania and was back home in Perth. Ian was also in Perth as part of the Queensland team playing in the Sheffield Shield final against Western Australia and was scheduled to be back in Brisbane on 24 March for a brief period before returning to England.

Due to the somewhat unusual geographical location of the parties involved, the Australian Cricket Board agreed with a proposal that the Tasmanian Commissioner, Ted Stokes, should hear the charge against Lillee in Hobart and the charge against Botham should be dealt with by Queensland Commissioner Ron Archer in Brisbane. The Botham hearing was held on 25 March and the Lillee hearing, which he decided not to attend but to send a written deposition instead, took place on 28 March. Both players were found guilty and fined $1800 each.

Ian Botham did not appeal against Ron Archer's finding, but on 29 March Dennis rang Richard Watson, the Administration Manager of the Tasmanian Cricket Council at that time, to advise that he wished to appeal against Ted Stokes' decision. Lillee followed that up with a letter to the TCC on 31 March. He failed to specify the grounds for his appeal in either the telephone call or the letter.

After a telephone discussion with me, ACB General Manager Graham Halbish wrote to Dennis on 31 March informing him that, subject to receipt of the required form containing the reasons for the appeal, I had agreed to hear the matter in Brisbane on 16 April. This was just before he was due to play in a Centenary Test 'replay' match in Brisbane, one of three being held in aid of charities around Australia.

By 13 April there was still no sign of Lillee's appeal form so the ACB sent him off a letter by fax asking that he contact me directly. Dennis rang me two days later when he got to Brisbane and between us we made sure that the form was completed and in order.

The appeal was held in the QCA offices at the Gabba and it turned out to be almost a carbon copy of the hearing in Adelaide five weeks earlier. After listening to what Lillee had to say and showing him various photographs and documents tendered as evidence, including statements Ian Botham had made to Ron Archer in relation to the same charges, I had no hesitation in dismissing the appeal. Not surprisingly Dennis was not at all pleased with my decision, again leaving abruptly.

In what had been an agonisingly slow process, taking seven weeks from the original incident to the appeal, that was to be the last Code of Behaviour charge I heard. A week later I was appointed Executive Manager of the South Australian Cricket Association, starting duties in Adelaide on 1 June 1988. I relinquished the Commissioner's position after four years.

Despite some drama here and there, I am glad that I decided to accept the role when David Richards offered it to me. It enabled me to experience at close quarters a rare aspect of cricket administration. I have no doubt that serving as Code of Behaviour Commissioner stood me in good stead during the nine hectic years I spent with the SACA before retiring from that job in 1997.

The only regret I had was a souring of relations between Dennis Lillee and me, which took quite some time to sort out. We were not ever close friends, but I had known Dennis for over a decade from my days as a freelance writer on the game and admired him greatly as a cricketer. It saddened me that he seemed to have taken personally my decisions as the independent arbiter on Code of Behaviour matters. In more than 25 years of close involvement with cricketers at the first-class level up until then, I could not recall any other instance where I had felt at all uncomfortable in my dealings with a player.

Three years later Dennis and I shook hands and put the past behind us. This came about in a most unlikely manner, with Rod Marsh, the staging of the Adelaide Formula 1 Grand Prix and Elle MacPherson all playing a part.

Rod, in a universally popular appointment, had recently taken on the job as head coach of the Adelaide-based Commonwealth Bank Cricket Academy. As the South Australian Cricket Association CEO, I had a lot to do with the Academy staff and scholarship holders as they used the practice facilities at Adelaide Oval. Rod and I saw a lot of each other on and off the field.

Dennis and Elle MacPherson were both competing in the celebrity drivers' event at the 1991 Grand Prix, while I was an invited guest at one of the corporate hospitality marquees dotted around the picturesque Adelaide street circuit. I was able to obtain a pass that admitted me to most areas, including the compound where the celebrity drivers cars were garaged.

I had secured this pass in the hope that I could win a bet with my great mate Les Burdett, the incomparable SACA Oval Manager, that I could secure an autograph from the beautiful Elle. With this in mind, as soon as the final practice session for the celebrity event had started I headed off to the vehicle compound to await the return of the contestants.

The cars returned to base and, after a quick debriefing, most of the drivers gathered briefly together. I couldn't spot Elle, which in itself is remarkable, but did see Dennis Lillee talking to his long-time buddy Rod Marsh.

This was clearly too good an opportunity to let pass so I wandered up to where the two of them were standing and was greeted by Rod in his usual jovial fashion. I said hello to Dennis and shook his hand. The three of us then chatted away about what a buzz it was to go for a burn on a Grand Prix circuit. From that point on, I am happy to say, Dennis and I have shared a drink and enjoyed each other's company whenever our paths have crossed.

Getting back to the Grand Prix, I hadn't overlooked my original mission. I left the two great cricketers briefly, located the charming Elle, got the signature – personalised at that – *and* won the bet. All told it had been a good day.

9

IAN BOTHAM CREATES A STORM

In the long history of Queensland cricket there have been seasons that will never be forgotten and others that slip easily from the memory of even the most passionate follower of the game. The summer of 1987/88 was a curious mix, starting out as one of the most memorable and finishing in a way that many players, officials and cricket fans would prefer to forget.

This was the season when Ian Botham and his cricketing caravan arrived in Brisbane with a bang, moved though every State like a juggernaut, was dramatically halted in Perth and finally saw the man they call 'Beefy' leave Australia on a very sour note.

The great England all-rounder had agreed to play for Queensland for three years from 1987/88. The contract had been negotiated by the Queensland Cricket Association with his Worcestershire sponsors, The Carphone Group, by Botham's manager, Tom Byron. Tom ran Byron Sports International, a company based in Worcestershire.

I had been transferred in my banking job from Melbourne to Brisbane earlier in the year and had accepted an offer from the QCA to take on a part-time media liaison position for the season. The job had been created in an effort to lift the profile of the Queensland team and cricket in general.

It was an exciting time for cricket in the Sunshine State, with expectations running high about finally winning the Sheffield Shield after 60 years. Not only was Ian Botham's presence going to boost the strength of the Maroons, there was the added bonus of Carl Rackemann, John Maguire and Trevor Hohns being available after they had spent the previous two seasons with an Australian 'rebel' team in South Africa. On top of this, Allan Border and Craig McDermott were due home for the start of the season after playing key roles in Australia's 1987 World Cup triumph in India.

Not everyone at the QCA was over the moon about Botham's pending arrival in Queensland. There was a view that if a parade of star imports over 25 years hadn't been able to deliver the Shield, then Ian Botham, with his best years behind him, was unlikely to make the difference.

Former Australian captain Greg Chappell, who was then living in Brisbane, was one of those opposed to the signing of Botham. Greg had a number of concerns about the star recruit, among them that the former England all rounder was not renowned for putting in the hard yards at practice. Chappell maintained that this would set a poor example to younger players.

Despite these reservations, Botham arrived in Brisbane on 10 November 1987 to a hero's welcome. The sporting public were ready to embrace him with a degree of enthusiasm that may have surprised even the gregarious Englishman.

At the official season's launch at the Cricketers' Club the next day, The Carphone Group announced a $500,000, three-year sponsorship of the Queensland team. So already, it seemed, Botham's presence was working wonders.

That morning Border and McDermott had flown in from India complete with the World Cup trophy, which I managed to borrow from the Australian captain so that it could go on display at the launch. For a few hours this symbol of international supremacy in the one-day game reposed on the kitchen bench of the Gibbs home in suburban Brisbane.

There was optimism around the Gabba leading up to the first match of the season against Victoria, which was just a few days away. The feeling was enhanced when Queensland won outright in front of a large crowd. More that 11,500 people turned up on the Sunday, many being attracted by the prospect of seeing the great Ian Botham in action. The big all-rounder didn't let the fans down, making runs, capturing wickets and clinging onto catches as he took centre stage in a promising start to his first season in the Sunshine State.

Brisbane was buzzing, cricket was front-page news – making my media liaison role almost a full-time one for a while as I happily dealt with the huge number of media requests for access to Botham and Border in particular, and the team generally. The Sheffield Shield seemed within reach.

The only cloud on the horizon was the loss of giant fast bowler Carl Rackemann with a stress fracture in the right ankle that would keep him out of first-class cricket until January. But Queensland was rich in fast-bowling talent, with McDermott, Maguire, Dirk Tazelaar and Botham providing fire power. They took 15 wickets between them in the win against Victoria.

Game two was against South Australia in Adelaide, where the home team, surprisingly, took first-innings points. But Botham made an entertaining half-century and snared three more wickets. The crowd of more than 18,000 for the match was the biggest at a Sheffield Shield match at Adelaide Oval for many years, thanks largely to the Botham factor.

Next stop was Newcastle for the away clash against New South Wales. The Maroons won in a canter, making it two outright wins from three matches. Beefy, who was only called on to bowl in the first innings, claimed another three wickets.

Back in Brisbane for game four against the current Sheffield Shield holders, Western Australia, Allan Border's men again won outright in three days, moving to the top of the table. Again it was the quicks who did the damage, with Botham adding yet another three to his tally. He also belted another half-century, his third for the season to date.

By this time the Queensland team, and Ian Botham in particular, had captured the imagination of the northern State's sporting public. The star import looked a man on a mission, ready to really cut loose with bat and ball.

Off the field a number of the marketing initiatives I had been involved in – including 'dollar days', barbecues on the hill, days sponsored and promoted by the media, and live rock bands during breaks – were working well. My role as media liaison officer had been made easier by the on-field success Queensland were enjoying, but it was personally satisfying to see large crowds at Sheffield Shield games and to have all sections of the media getting behind the team.

The next match, against New South Wales at the Gabba, marked the half-way point of the season. It was crunch time – for the first time in the season, Queensland did not have the services of internationals Border and McDermott. The visitors were also missing stars, but still fielded a team that included eight former or future Test players.

The Maroons welcomed back Carl Rackemann from injury and Trevor Hohns finally reclaimed his spot in the team. Both players were making their first appearance since returning from the rebel tours of South Africa.

Brisbane's cricket fans sniffed the sense of occasion, particularly on the Sunday when 12,500 people turned up in what was the largest single day's crowd at a Sheffield Shield match at the Gabba since Don Bradman was in his prime half-a-century before.

Queensland won an epic battle, giving the Maroons four outright victories from five matches. Fast bowlers Rackemann and Tazelaar were the heroes, along with batsman Greg Ritchie. Botham failed with the bat, but he grabbed four wickets at crucial times to take his tally for the season to a respectable 16.

A week later, still without Border and McDermott, the rampaging Queenslanders played bottom-placed Tasmania in another home game. This looked like a mismatch from the start, particularly with David Boon absent from the Tasmanian team. The Maroons won by an innings before tea on the third day. Tazelaar and Rackemann wrecked the Tasmanian batting twice. Botham chipped in with yet another three wickets but, ominously, he still hadn't really fired with the bat.

With six games completed Queensland had amassed 30 points for the season and were set for all the advantages that finishing on top of the table brings – a home final playing in familiar conditions, the support of a partisan crowd and knowing that a draw would be good enough to win the Shield.

In a season that was condensed due to the absence of the Australian team in India and Pakistan for the World Cup until the second week in November, the Queenslanders found themselves in Perth just three days after polishing off Tasmania, preparing for an extremely important clash against Western Australia. This was a vital game: victory would almost guarantee that Gabba final. But in a sign of misery to come, WA won a hard-fought encounter by three wickets.

I had been back in Brisbane while the team was away, busily dealing with the continuing appetite of the media for news on anything to do with cricket, especially Ian Botham. There was also a lot of planning to do for the anticipated climax to the season.

The Queenslander's came home for a break of about three weeks after a hectic month zigzagging the continent. Time for the team to recharge the batteries and await the return of Allan Border and Craig McDermott for the crucial last three games against bottom-ranked sides, South Australia, Tasmania and Victoria. It looked a relatively easy run home.

David Hookes and his South Australian team gave the Maroons a fright at the Gabba before the game ended in a draw, Queensland sneaking in the first-innings points.

Tasmania in Launceston was next and six points beckoned, or so it seemed. David Boon, however, was back and he had other ideas, scoring a century in each innings to lead his team to a memorable win, Tasmania's first in 45 first-class matches. The island State's cause was helped by Border's declaration when the Maroons were 118 runs behind with five wickets in hand in a desperate bid for the crucial six points. This was a calculated gamble by 'AB' as the hard-hitting Glenn Trimble was in full flight on 138 not out and first innings points seemed in the bag. Eventually Queensland were set a target of 409 to win which they failed to reach, crashing from 1/221 to be all out for 314.

The late-season wobbles – so often the despair of Queensland fans – had set in; two points from three matches was not the form of a side that aspired to winning the Sheffield Shield. Moreover, there had been a noticeable dropping off in the contribution of Ian Botham, and there were reports filtering through from within the team about friction in the camp. These centred largely around the star import and his conduct – on and off the field. They had been swirling below the surface for some time but were now becoming harder to keep a lid on. The early season promise had started to dissipate into gloom.

Allan Border's team still only needed a win in the last match of the season, against Victoria at the MCG, to finish on top of the Sheffield Shield table. But it was not to be. The home team took outright points easily. To make matters worse Botham suffered a back injury that forced him out of the attack in Victoria's second innings and severely restricted his movement when batting. During the match he also managed to collect a $500 Code of Behaviour fine for abusing spectators.

While this latest debacle for Queensland was going on, Western Australia thrashed South Australia by seven wickets in Perth, putting WA far enough ahead of second-placed Queensland to ensure that the Sheffield Shield final would be in Perth, not Brisbane. WA had collected 18 points from their last four matches while Queensland could manage just two.

There was a fortnight's break before the final, giving Botham time to have his injured back treated in an attempt to get him somewhere near fit to play. It also provided the team as a whole the opportunity to regroup and focus on the objective of winning just one more match.

The odds were clearly stacked in favour of Western Australia. They were playing at home on the WACA Ground and only had to draw the final to retain the Shield.

On 15 March 1988 the Queensland team flew out of Brisbane on Ansett flight 55, bound for Perth via Melbourne. They were given an enthusiastic send-off by a large crowd at the airport, accompanied by the biggest media contingent I have ever seen gathered to cover the departure of a Sheffield Shield team. Optimism was in the air again as the group boarded the aircraft. Surely the two-week break had rekindled the spark that had deserted Allan Border's men?

Pre-match planning had the team arriving in Perth earlier than normal so that the players could have more than two clear days to shake off the effects of the long plane trip from Brisbane, become adjusted to the time difference and get used to the extra bounce off the WACA pitch. Nothing, it seemed, had been left to chance, even to the extent of allowing for an extra player to be taken as insurance against any last-minute injury.

All this turned out to have been a waste of time and effort. Before the Queensland team even arrived in Perth, Botham became involved in a heated discussion with a patron in the bar at Tullamarine during the team's Melbourne stopover. By the time authorities arrived on the scene to investigate, the players had boarded the flight again and the aircraft was heading west.

It just got worse. Botham embroiled himself in an in-flight altercation with a passenger seated in front of him. The passenger had complained about the bad language being used by some of the players and the noise coming from the team 'ghetto blaster'. This prompted the captain of the aircraft to radio ahead to Perth, requesting assistance when the flight arrived.

The initial upshot of the in-flight disturbance was that Ansett airport officials interviewed Botham and the upset passenger when they got off the plane. The passenger declined to ask Federal police to investigate the matter, which could have led to charges being laid, preferring to leave the whole affair on the basis that he would write a strong letter of complaint to the airline's management. It appeared at this stage that the matter would go no further, especially as none of the flight attendants had seen fit to lodge a formal complaint.

While this drama was unfolding I was home in Brisbane initially oblivious to what was going on over in Perth. My role as media officer had, I thought, just about finished when the team got on the aircraft in Brisbane. The Queensland coach and team Manager, Ray Reynolds, had to deal with the fall-out and he kept us informed as well as he could with developments.

But Reynolds and other Queensland officials travelling with the team, were unaware that the Federal police in Melbourne had followed up the Tullamarine bar incident and had relayed details to their colleagues in Perth. The next day Federal police interviewed Botham, in company with his captain Allan Border and Ray Reynolds, at their hotel.

After taking statements, police escorted Botham to the East Perth watch-house, where he was charged with two counts of assault and one of disorderly conduct. He was released later that night on $5000 bail and ordered to appear in the East Perth Magistrate's Court the next morning. The matter was adjourned following that hearing and Botham was remanded on reduced bail of $3000 until 23 March 1988, the day after the Sheffield Shield final.

The saga had a devastating effect on the Queensland team's morale. They played poorly, and lost the final by five wickets. With court proceedings hanging over his head, Botham somehow managed to score a defiant 54 in the second innings after coming to the crease when it looked as though the match could be all over early on day four.

The next day Botham pleaded guilty in the Perth Magistrates Court to one charge of assaulting a passenger on the Melbourne to Perth flight and to one of offensive behaviour. He was fined $800 by the magistrate, who had harsh words to say in delivering his sentence.

The day after he returned to Brisbane Ian had an appointment with Ron Archer, Queensland's Code of Behaviour Commissioner, concerning two separate charges that had been made against him under the Australian Cricket Board's player Code of Behaviour. These related to the incident on the flight to Perth on 15 March 1988 and to his alleged part in damaging the Queensland dressing-room after a McDonald's Cup match against Tasmania at Launceston the previous month.

Ron Archer is a level-headed, no-nonsense sort of fellow who became a successful businessman after having his promising Test career cut short by a knee injury at the age of 22 while he was playing in Australia's first-ever Test match in Pakistan on the way home from the 1956 tour of England. Ron knew about the highs and lows of Test cricket, playing in 19 of them and being regarded as a potential Australian captain before injury struck.

In handing down his findings that Botham had contravened the ACB's Code of Behaviour on two counts, Archer imposed fines totalling $5000 and resisted the temptation to impose a suspension, mainly because the season had finished. The following statement, which was issued by Ron at the time, contained a stern and timely warning to Botham and to cricketers generally:

> If a similar breach of the Code comes before me during the next season then Ian Botham will have a long holiday from the cricket fields of Australia.
>
> I am cognisant of the fact that Ian Botham is a 'larger than life' personality and as such attracts attention from the media and public, some of which may be unfair. I am however convinced on this occasion his actions, while possibly exaggerated in the media, were extremely detrimental to the game of cricket and cannot be tolerated.
>
> As one of the great cricketers of the world his talents and actions both on and off the field are understandably studied and are undoubtedly emulated by many thousands of cricketers with lesser talents. I trust that this action is one that the budding young cricketers of Australia delete from their repertoire.

These were well-chosen words at an appropriate time from a man who has always had the best interests of the game at heart.

As the Australian Cricket Board's Code of Behaviour Commissioner I was more than a little interested in the outcome and particularly in whether Botham would appeal against Ron Archer's findings. If he did, the matter would under normal circumstances have been referred to me. But as I was would under normal circumstances have been referred to me. But as I was still working part-time with the QCA when both the charges against Ian were laid and, even though the season was now over and my job at the Gabba completed, there was clearly the potential for a conflict of interest to arise.

I had raised the possibility of such a conflict when I was first approached about taking on the role as Queensland Cricket's media liaison officer. Both the ACB and QCA had no problem with me remaining on as commissioner, although we did talk in general terms about the need to relinquish one of the positions under certain circumstances. I also took the opportunity to seek Allan Border's views on the matter shortly after he had returned to Brisbane with the World Cup. He too was quite relaxed about it.

As it turned out, Botham had no thoughts of appealing against Ron Archer's findings. He paid the fines imposed and flew out of Australia the next day to prepare for his re-enactment of Hannibal's epic trek over the French Alps to raise money for the Leukemia Research Program. Before leaving he told reporters he 'couldn't give a stuff' about his conviction on an assault charge and, as for the $5000 fine Ron Archer imposed, he said he could not care less, adding that '$5000 is about 50 quid at the present rate of sterling, so I'm not really too bothered'.

With two years of his contract still left, Botham indicated to the media that he had every intention of returning to Queensland to play 'unless things happen outside my control'. It didn't take long at all for the QCA Executive Committee, chaired by Norm McMahon, to make 'things' happen. At a meeting held on 29 March 1988, the day after Ron Archer's findings were made public, the Committee decided to terminate Botham's contract forthwith.

The newspapers were generally scathing in their comments about the way Botham had conducted himself, the *Australian* headlining an editorial 'Good riddance'. Andrew Slack, the much-respected Australian Rugby captain of the time and a keen student of cricket, was more moderate in his regular column in the Brisbane *Courier Mail,* coming to the conclusion that: 'If the silly actions of recent times result in some positive and thoughtful reaction, Ian Botham may have helped Queensland cricket more than he will ever know'.

It took a while before the words of the Wallaby captain to hit home, but they did, and he was right. There are no short cuts to achieving consistent success in cricket; quick fixes such as plugging gaps with itinerant superstars is not the long term answer to building a winning team.

The lessons from the 'Botham season' were taken on board, perhaps unwittingly at first. Queensland cricket had begun to learn from the mistakes of the past and to chart its own destiny by encouraging and developing home-grown talent, culminating in that unforgettable triumph at the Gabba in March 1995 when the Queensland Bulls, as the team was now known, finally won the Sheffield Shield after nearly 70 years of frustration.

Having finally got that monkey off their back, the Bulls have gone from strength to strength, firmly establishing themselves as the pacesetters in Australian domestic cricket.

10

THE LURE OF ADELAIDE OVAL PROVES IRRESISTIBLE

Looking back now on the events leading up to my appointment as Executive Manager of the South Australian Cricket Association in April 1988, it seems that I was destined to return to full-time cricket administration, even if it was 22 years after my time as QCA secretary.

I say that despite the fact that only twelve months earlier the possibility of me once again becoming a professional sporting administrator was far from my mind. I was happily pursuing a career in the financial markets that had already spanned more than two decades.

I had been transferred from Melbourne to Brisbane in February 1987 by my employers, the newly formed National Mutual Royal Bank, as General Manager, Queensland. This followed a hectic period during which I was a member of a task force that worked on the successful application for a banking licence for a joint venture between National Mutual Life and the Royal Bank of Canada in 1986

At that time I was 54 years of age and saw myself ending my working days in Queensland, then quietly retiring and enjoying some precious leisure time. But what I didn't know when I moved to Brisbane – two months after accepting the transfer – was that the bank's business plan of establishing retail branches in each State had been radically altered.

This policy change came about when an opportunity arose for National Mutual Royal Bank to merge with the large New South Wales-based United Permanent Building Society, thereby creating a vast number of ready-made retail banking outlets in NSW, where previously there were virtually none. The merger meant that the bank had grown in size to such an extent that it was now much bigger than even the most optimistic forward projections for years ahead.

As a consequence of the corporate indigestion that followed, there was no requirement to establish more than the one token Brisbane office, nor was there a need for a General Manager, Queensland. Put bluntly, the job I had been asked to do in 1986 had evaporated by the time I got to Brisbane early in 1987.

This necessitated a sudden change of direction for me, but not another move – not yet anyway. I joined another National Mutual Company, the burgeoning investment advisers Godfrey Weston Limited, in July 1987, and surprised myself by knuckling down to study for, and passing, the exams to qualify as a Certified Investment Planner.

As it transpired the timing of my move was absolutely appalling. The global share market collapsed in October 1987, decimating the investment advisory industry in Australia. My career in that area was over before it began.

Fortunately I had some consultancy work to fall back on and, importantly as it turned out, I was appointed to the part-time media liaison officer's job with the Queensland Cricket Association, a role that kept me in touch with what was going on in the cricket world.

Early in 1988 I learned on the cricketing grapevine that the South Australian Cricket Association might be looking for an experienced senior full-time administrator following the resignation of its general manager, Kevin Griffiths. The thought occurred to me that I might have something to offer the SACA so I made a couple of telephone calls to Adelaide to pass this thought on.

A short while later the South Australian team was in Brisbane for a Sheffield Shield match, giving me the chance to have a chat to its captain, David Hookes, who was kind enough to give me a run-down on the strengths and weaknesses of the SACA as he had observed them as a player. David said enough during our talk to encourage me to make further enquiries of a couple of longstanding friends in Adelaide.

By this time I was starting to think that the SACA job, if it became available, could well be the late career change I needed. My interest in cricket administration had been rekindled both through my appointment as the ACB Code of Behaviour Commissioner in 1984 and the QCA media position.

By coincidence I was required to go to Adelaide in March 1988 to hear a player code of behaviour matter. While there I had informal discussions with senior SACA committee members and learned that the new position of Executive Manager would soon be advertised nationally. I returned home to Brisbane and talked it over with Peg, who agreed that it was worth considering.

I sent off an application and about a month later I was offered, and accepted, the position of SACA Executive Manager on an initial five-year contract, to start work from 1 June 1988. The unexpected transition from banking executive to born-again cricket administrator had been completed.

The prospect of working at the beautiful Adelaide Oval, which I had visited many times as a spectator, administrator and writer, was genuinely exciting. There was much going on at the famous old oval, including the start-up of the fledgling Commonwealth Bank Cricket Academy and some serious talk of a major grandstand development. On the playing side, the great South African batsman Barry Richards had agreed to move from his home in Durban to take on the job as full-time coach of the South Australian Sheffield Shield team.

There was an added bonus for me in that I would be working with a committee that included some very capable administrators, including men I had known for decades such as Phil Ridings, Colin Egar, Des Rundle, Lance Duldig and Mel McInnes. The committee also included former South Australian Test and first-class cricketers Ian McLachlan, Neil Dansie, Gil Langley, Rex Sellers and Murray Sargent, all of whom I knew from my first stint in Queensland nearly 30 years earlier.

On a personal note our 19-year-old son, Peter, was working as a jackeroo on a property near Naracoorte in SA's south-east in preparation for going to agricultural college. We would now have the chance to see a lot more of him than had we remained in Brisbane.

I was also looking forward to renewing acquaintances with some long-standing Adelaide-based cricketing friends, including Alan Shiell, the former South Australian batsman and chief cricket writer for the *Advertiser,* and former Test players Barry Jarman, Neil Hawke and Terry Jenner.

So, one more time, Peg and I prepared for an interstate relocation, the twelfth in 27 years since we moved from our home town of Melbourne to

Brisbane in 1961. Moving thousands of kilometres away to begin a new life is always traumatic, but our move to SA proved to be one of the most straightforward we had made, thanks largely to many of the people I have mentioned previously and some we didn't even know.

The welcome mat was laid out in Adelaide for Peg and me. The president of the Adelaide Oval Bowling Club, John Jenkinson, and his wife, Dot, whom we had never met, even made their home in suburban Urrbrae available to us for a couple of months, furniture and all, while they wintered at Noosa Heads. All we had to do was move in.

It is difficult to express the feelings you experience when arriving for work each day at a national icon, as the National Heritage Trust has officially recognised the Adelaide Oval. Universally known for its beauty, charm and tranquillity, it is also one of those rare sporting venues where you can feel the sense of history the moment you walk through the entrance gates, even if there is no match in progress.

Think of the exquisite batting of Mark Waugh. His style and elegance at the crease sets him apart, and so it is with the Adelaide Oval when compared to any other cricket ground in the world. I don't believe for a moment it was a coincidence that Mark made a stunning century on his Test debut at Adelaide.

11

IT'S DON BRADMAN HERE!

Not long after settling into my new job at the SACA I received an unexpected, but most welcome telephone call. A distinctive, high-pitched voice was at the other end. 'It's Don Bradman here, Barry. I would have rung you earlier to welcome you to Adelaide but I thought it best to leave you in peace for a little while as you have no doubt been kept very busy since you arrived. If you have some time to spare I would like to come down to the oval some time to have a chat with you.'

Would I have the time to talk with the great Sir Donald Bradman? Naturally I jumped at the chance and we got together in my office a short while later. I had met Sir Donald a number of times when I was secretary of the Queensland Cricket Association in his dual roles as chairman of the Australian Cricket Board and of the Australian selection panel, but had not had the pleasure of enjoying a private discussion at length with him. In a meeting that lasted about an hour I soaked up the sage advice of a man who was not only the greatest cricketer of all time but, in the view of just about everyone I knew that had been closely involved in cricket for any length of time, was the game's finest administrator. I had been told numerous times by various chairmen of the Australian Cricket Board that Bradman dominated cricket as an administrator as much as he did when he was playing the game.

Digressing for a moment, one of those chairmen was my good friend Colin Egar, who held the post from 1989 to 1992. Egar's first match as a Test umpire was the tied Test between Australia and the West Indies at the Gabba in 1960. Col recalls a discussion he and fellow umpire Col Hoy had with Sir Donald before play began on the first morning of that Test. After years of dreary Test matches Sir Donald had obviously had enough and knew the game was about to change for the better. He said to Egar and Hoy, 'In my view this will probably be the greatest Test series ever played.' A big statement but, as usual, Sir Donald was right.

After the match had finished, Egar walked past where Bradman was standing and Sir Donald called out: 'You never umpired a football grand final as exciting as that, did you Col?', referring to the two South Australian National Football League grand finals that Egar had umpired in the late 1950s.

As the great Sir Donald gave me an insight into his intimate knowledge of the SACA and its workings I recall thinking to myself, 'Is this really happening?' There I was sitting across the desk from this hero of millions of cricket followers throughout the world, the man I had watched with reverence as a schoolboy over 40 years earlier batting at the Melbourne Cricket Ground in his last Test series in Australia. The same Don Bradman who had kept me awake at night while I listened to his feats on my home-made crystal set during that triumphant final tour of England in 1948.

Naturally we talked at some length about the Adelaide Oval, a place dear to Sir Donald's heart and one that he had been so heavily involved with as a player and administrator for more than half a century. Having been SACA president for eight years, vice-president for 15 years, a member of the Ground and Finance Committee for 43 years, a trustee of the Association for 30 years, a member of the cricket committee for 27 years, a State selector for 34 years, a SA delegate to the Board of Control for 35 years, chairman of the Board of Control for a total of six years and an Australian selector for 34 years, he was able to give me a marvellous insight into the past, and then a look at what he saw as the future, both of the SACA and Australian cricket. Even though the great man no longer held any official office he clearly still had his finger firmly on the pulse of the game, not just in South Australia but throughout Australia and internationally.

We chatted about the changing face of cricket and the need for administrators to adjust their attitudes to accommodate that change. He had a keen interest in the establishment of the Commonwealth Bank Cricket Academy and was aware of the need for improvements to be made to some of the facilities at Adelaide Oval, but he was not really in favour of digging too deeply into SACA's financial reserves to achieve this end. Bradman's up-to-date knowledge of what was going on in cricket circles was remarkable, especially as he had cut his last official ties with the Association on 30 June 1986 – two years earlier.

Too soon it was time for Sir Donald to leave. Before he did he told me that I should not hesitate to contact him if I had any matter or problem that he might be able to help with. In the years ahead there were several occasions when I took up his offer and invariably came away from those discussions with a fresh perspective.

During my first few months at the SACA Sir Donald turned 80 years of age. In typical fashion he wanted no fuss made of the fact that it was his birthday, but he did accept an invitation from the president, Jim Grose, and committee of the Association to be the guest of honour at a small dinner to mark the occasion. Appropriately the function was held in the Bradman Room at Adelaide Oval, an evening that I had the pleasure of arranging and attending.

In the knowledge that there was a toast to be proposed to, and a response made by, Sir Donald, with his concurrence arrangements were made for the proceedings to be recorded. He remarked at the time that as this definitely would be the last speech he intended to make, it might as well be recorded for the archives. As insurance against the possibility of a technical malfunction we made sure we captured the moment by connecting two tape recorders to the microphone and, for additional back-up, had a battery-operated micro-cassette recorder running!

Sir Donald's speech that night was brilliant. With little or no reference to notes he regaled us for 30 minutes, providing an insight into the good and bad times of his extraordinary life. It was a speech I will never forget, not only for the content, which encapsulated brilliantly so much his 80 years, but also for the eloquence with which it was delivered and the wonderful sense of humour he displayed.

Among the topics Sir Donald talked on that night was his premature obituary written for the British Press Association 54 years earlier when he was lying desperately ill in a London hospital. He had only recently been able to lay his hands on a copy and was carrying it in his pocket on his 80th birthday. Bradman went on to refer to the penalty imposed on Lady Bradman, himself and their family by the massive publicity and lack of privacy they had all suffered. He told us that the last thing he ever wanted in life was a knighthood and how he was still having difficulty in coming to terms with old and valued friends calling him 'Sir' rather than 'Don.' He recalled how he was persuaded by the Australian Broadcasting Commission to record a series of interviews for radio broadcast only by the thought that it would be wonderful if we could hear today the views of Dr W.G. Grace or Victor Trumper, which are gone forever.

Sir Donald then reduced his audience to tears of laughter when he recounted part of a letter he had received from a young lad who must have thought that Bradman had already departed this life. 'I have enjoyed reading some of your books, is it hot or cold up there?' the boy asked. Sir Donald was delighted that he said *up*, not down!

On the subject of money in sport, Sir Donald said:

> I believe in sports people being properly rewarded for their services, but in many instances I fear there is a great danger in the dollar being such a dominant factor that it erodes the underlying integrity and purpose of sport – I still think that it is important for people to be dedicated, and to love what they are doing, as distinct from the rewards – to give of their best the players have to have an inner commitment.

These were relevant words then and still are over a decade later, particularly in the light of the match-fixing allegations that have so badly damaged the game in recent years.

One of the guests at this memorable function was former South African batting star Barry Richards, recently arrived in Adelaide to coach the South Australian cricket team. Richards received the ultimate accolade from Sir Donald Bradman that night when he said:

> How honoured I am to see Barry Richards here tonight and to give him a welcome to his new home. In my view no player in the world is better equipped, technically and practically, to impart cricket knowledge.
>
> Only politics prevented his Test match figures matching those of all the great figures of history. I feel sure his presence in South Australia will give a great shot in the arm to our cricketers, who will do well to absorb his advice.
>
> I feel very keenly this terrible cricketing problem with South Africa, not least because I was chairman of the Australian Cricket Board when, regretfully, I had to announce the cancellation of Tests between Australia

and South Africa. The board had no option but to take the stance it did, but it was one of the saddest days of my cricketing life – to take a decision which effectively terminated Barry's Test career.

Unfortunately South Australia only had the benefit of Barry Richards' extraordinary talents and wealth of experience as the State coach for one season before he received an offer he thought too good to refuse from the Queensland Cricket Association to become its Chief Executive. With the reluctant approval of SACA, Barry headed north after he had guided SA from second last the previous season into the 1988/89 Sheffield Shield final against Western Australia in Perth.

Despite Sir Donald's intense desire for privacy, particularly after he had officially retired from public life, it was inevitable that the unique position he occupied in the hearts and minds of cricket people would make this wish impossible to achieve. There was always some event that he felt obliged to attend.

One such occasion was the official opening of the Clarrie Grimmett Gates at the northern entrance to Adelaide Oval in December 1988. That function remains in my memory for a number of reasons, one of them being the search we conducted to find an appropriate way to mount the bronze plaques that had been cast to perpetuate the deeds of Grimmett, one of the greatest leg-spin bowlers of all time.

The many thousands of people who have wandered through the northern entrance to Adelaide Oval over the last thirteen years or so will not have missed the plaques, which are mounted on a rock near the turnstiles. These plaques detail Clarrie's first-class and Test career, and there is a sculpture of the little fellow weaving his magic with his unique, almost round-arm bowling action.

Les Burdett, the SACA Oval Manager, came up with the idea of mounting the three very solid plaques on a rock. That was the easy part of the exercise; the difficulty lay in finding something big enough, and of the right shape, to appropriately display them. Enter Bernie Leverington, who at the time was chairman of a company that operated a number of large quarries around Adelaide. Bernie assured us that with his guidance we would be able to find a rock of the right dimensions to do the job.

We were told that our best chance of staking claim to a suitable boulder was to wait for a time when routine blasting was taking place. The day arrived, so Bernie, Les and I headed off to a quarry in the Adelaide suburb of Marino, and then drove down into the pit.

The temperature was nearly 40 degrees and a howling wind was blowing. It was like a Mallee dust storm. To top it off, the blasting was not finished when we arrived, which meant that we had to wait at a safe distance until the all-clear was given.

Wait we did, with the car ignition and air conditioning turned off, doors closed and windows up. It was stifling in that car, and then we had to contend with explosions that made the ground shake around us.

At last we were able to drive around until Les spotted a rock about the size he had in mind. It weighed a few tonnes and stood about four metres high, but was able to be conveyed later to the Oval on a massive low-loader and lifted into position over the northern gates by two giant cranes.

This monolith, now surrounded by roses and immaculate lawn, looks very much at home inside the northern gates to Adelaide Oval. If you get the chance to admire 'Clarrie's Rock', spare a thought for the three would-be geologists who nearly suffered heat-stroke locating it.

The opening ceremony was performed by the then Lord Mayor of Adelaide, Steve Condous. Among the guests of honour was another great Australian leg spinner, Bill O'Reilly, who despite ailing health flew from Sydney to take part. I had telephoned Bill in Sydney several months earlier to ask whether he could come to say a few words. He jumped at the opportunity, telling me that he would be honoured to pay tribute to his old friend, fellow leg spinner and team mate.

It is no secret that, from time to time, relations between Sir Donald Bradman and Bill O'Reilly had been strained for various reasons. O'Reilly was a man of forthright opinions that he expressed with vigour and eloquence during a long, distinguished career as a cricket correspondent after he retired from Test cricket. There was always going to be the possibility that he would make known his viewpoint on some controversial topic or other during the proceedings at the unveiling of Clarrie's Rock. A few people in the audience had their fingers crossed, me included.

O'Reilly opened his remarks by saying: 'Nothing could have possibly stopped me from being present here this morning – I was prepared to walk the 900 miles if necessary had not Barry Gibbs and the SACA so kindly arranged for Ansett to do the job for me.' Bill was 83 at the time and had thrombosis so badly in his legs that one of them had to be amputated a short while later. You can see the tremendous esteem in which he held Grimmett, and appreciate why O'Reilly was called 'Tiger'.

He went on to pay a moving tribute to Clarrie, telling the gathering that this was a debt he was very glad to repay. 'I am here to do honour to the man I reckon was the greatest bowler that ever walked onto a cricket field right round the world', O'Reilly said, adding, 'and I was lucky enough to have him as my work mate.' Coming from O'Reilly, the man Bradman called the best bowler he ever faced or saw, this was praise indeed.

After his heartfelt opening remarks, O'Reilly began to warm to his task, venturing into more controversial territory.

> The last time I played cricket with Clarrie Grimmett here at the Adelaide Oval was in that famous bodyline Test in 1933 when the cricket world almost fell apart. We are still, I think, paying the penalty for what happened at that time because lots of people, in various parts of the world, would not face up to the situation that was put before us then. A lot of people were too timid to take the steps which should have been taken.

By this time 'Tiger' O'Reilly was at his pugnacious and eloquent best. He announced that he was going to take us all on a quick trip up to Valhalla. 'Be careful when you come with me,' he said,

> dodge all those satellites, brush them aside and we will look for old Clarrie upstairs. He will be easy to find because he will be wearing his green cap, which he never took off, and he will be sitting beside the biggest peephole the place can supply – and it will be right over the top of this place. He will have a few mates with him. There will be Victor Richardson, who he helped carry this State on his back for twenty years or more, there will be Tim Wall, Charlie Walker, Bill Woodfull, Stan McCabe, 'Dainty' Ironmonger, Don Blackie – just think of them all.
>
> Imagine now, when I say to old Clarrie when we sit down up there: 'Why in the name of God didn't you come to England with us in 1938 – you made it terribly tough you know for us.' He said to us 'I was

too old' and Don Blackie replied, 'What, too old – you were only 46, you were a boy, old "Dainty" here and I made our cricket Test debuts at 46 years of age, the first time ever that we played for Australia.' And old 'Dainty' said to me: 'Do you remember that Test match in Brisbane where at 51 years of age I bowled all day long in the heat?' So I've never agreed with the fact that Clarrie Grimmett was too old – Clarrie could have done anything!'

Most people in the sizeable crowd were highly amused by Bill's mythical trip to Valhalla. What they either didn't know, or hadn't fully appreciated, was that Bill wasn't being humorous – he was deadly serious in his blunt criticism of the Australian selectors, one of whom was Bradman, for leaving Grimmett out of the 1938 tour of England.

Sir Donald, who was standing quietly only a few metres away, handled the situation with dignity, showing no reaction to what had been said. Later he happily posed for media photographers together with O'Reilly and Len Darling, another Test veteran of the bodyline series. If anyone was aware that the cricketing equivalent of a diplomatic incident had just taken place, they were certainly not letting on.

In his speech that day Bill O'Reilly was emotional, humorous, tenacious and controversial. He also ventured into the future. When talking about one of his favourite topics, the art of leg-spin bowling, he referred to the recently established Commonwealth Bank Cricket Academy in Adelaide. Addressing his remarks to all the young cricketers within earshot, he exhorted them to forget about trying to bowl fast and to consider becoming a 'leggie'. His words are well worth recalling:

> We haven't seen a leg spinner like old Clarrie Grimmett since the day he disappeared from the game. So boys I am telling you this, don't be satisfied to go back into the distance, drop your cap and then rush up because it's a long way to run and everyone says 'Gee, isn't he fast' – they are generally worn out by the time they get to the stumps. But remember this, a leather ball with a raised seam on it gives a boy with talent and imagination so many chances of introducing guile, and it goes whether you are quick, slow or indifferent, that any boy who decides to become a quickie instead of a slowie nowadays, is a ratbag!
>
> I say it straight out – are you listening carefully boys – because if ever

> I have known a time when there is an open door entrance to the Australian team, this is it – 1988. So pack your swags, hop into it, even if the Commonwealth Bank Cricket Academy doesn't want you yet, you make very sure that South Australia wants you in the very near future.

These were prophetic words. Less than two years later a young blond leg spinner from Melbourne by the name of Shane Warne was awarded a scholarship to the Academy, and the next season he made his Test debut for Australia. Now the same Shane Warne has taken 400 Test wickets.

Bill O'Reilly died in 1992, but he was just able to see Shane make his Test debut. It is a fair bet that Bill quickly found that great big peep hole 'up there' and sits with Clarrie Grimmett observing Warne, Stuart MacGill and the other leg spinners who now grace the game.

At the time the Grimmett Gates were opened, SACA had decided to demolish the ageing, dilapidated Creswell grandstand at the southern end of Adelaide Oval. In its place a modern structure was to be built containing corporate entertaining facilities and a state-of-the-art media centre. The challenge was to design a building that would be aesthetically appealing. The architects, Hassell Pty Ltd, succeeded brilliantly.

There was considerable debate, both around the SACA committee table and in the public arena, concerning the naming of the new building. The name was kept secret until the formal opening ceremony, which took place on Adelaide Oval before play started on the second day of the Pakistan Test match in January 1990. I say 'secret', but there was little surprise when Premier John Bannon declared the building opened and named it the Sir Donald Bradman Stand.

Sir Donald had been waiting patiently on the oval with the rest of the official party during the formalities. In this time he quietly said to me: 'I suppose you would like me to say a few words.' Naturally I replied that we would be delighted to hear from him. When Sir Donald walked up to the microphone you could have heard a pin drop. This is what he said:

> Mr Premier, my Lord Mayor, Mr President and ladies and gentlemen. It was nearly 63 years ago that I first walked out the players gate onto this oval to play my first first-class match. That was an accident, the selectors picked me to be twelfth man but on the morning of the game our star

batsman, Archie Jackson, developed a boil on his knee and couldn't play, so I was sent out to take his place. That was the start of what I hope was a long and honourable career in first-class cricket.

But little did I dream in those days that I would be standing here today with a stand which is in future to bear my name, and that is a compliment I greatly appreciate. The committee of the South Australian Cricket Association must have had a difficult job deciding what to call it. There were several names they could have used which would have added great lustre, I think, to the stand – a player like Vic Richardson, who was probably the greatest all-round sportsman South Australia has ever produced; or Clarrie Grimmett who was the best bowler who ever bowled for South Australia; even my late friend Les Favell, who gave so much enjoyment to people on the Adelaide Oval.

Perhaps the most difficult decision was to turn down a huge sum of money to sell the naming rights to some corporate body. Well anyway, eventually they apparently decided upon my name, which I appreciate very much, and as I have never been one to dispute the umpire's decision, I accept that with pleasure.

I don't think there is anything else that I can say, except to congratulate the architects and the designers on having produced a stand which, I think, if anything, enhances the beauty of this ground. It is, in my opinion, the loveliest cricket ground in the world and I am sure that the spectators seated up there will have a view of cricket that is unsurpassed anywhere in the world.

All I can hope, ladies and gentlemen, is that cricketers of future generations who play on this ground may be inspired by the stand to give us cricket worthy of the setting. Thank you very much.

So, to standing acclaim, Sir Donald Bradman had spoken publicly for what turned out to be the last time. To me it has always been appropriate that he should have done so on the oval he had graced for so long while performing remarkable cricketing feats.

Sir Donald remained on the oval while dozens of newspaper and television cameras captured the moment. Then I escorted him to the sanctuary of the committee room.

I really do mean 'sanctuary'. The police inspector in charge of the area had informed me before the official guests assembled that the Premier had recently received a death threat and, as a consequence, there would be a much greater police presence than normal. It was agreed that we should not unduly alarm anyone about the situation, so only a small number of people, including the Premier, the police and myself, were aware of the threat while the opening ceremony was being carried out. I have to confess to having tingling nerves while we were out on the oval, especially when I was talking to the Premier or standing near him!

Sir Donald's words struck a chord in me when he talked about the difficulty we faced in turning down a potentially huge sum of money for the corporate naming rights to the grandstand. I am an unashamed cricket traditionalist, but I also appreciate as much as anybody how necessary it is for any sport to attract sponsorships. While there was no formal monetary offer made to SACA for the naming rights we knew that there were companies keen to explore the possibility. In this instance, thankfully, tradition took precedence over corporate dollars.

Despite his decision to sever any official ties he had with cricket in 1986 and retire from public life, Sir Donald still attended some functions of special significance. One of these was the annual dinner to announce the winner of the Bradman Medal, which is awarded to the South Australian district cricketer of the season. For many years Sir Donald attended the Bradman Medal Dinner at Adelaide Oval and he would personally present the medal. It was often difficult to detect whether the recipient got the most excitement from winning the prestigious medal or being presented with it by the man himself.

In his later years ill health made it impossible for Sir Donald to attend this night, but the award will, I am sure, continue to carry his name in perpetuity – commercial free.

To my knowledge the last occasion Sir Donald appeared at a public function, was in November 1992 at the State Library of South Australia, where an exhibition had been mounted featuring a number of the items from his personal collection of memorabilia that he had donated to the Library some years earlier.

The 1992 exhibition ran for about four months, achieving the intended objective of raising awareness about the existence of this unique collection. Some five years later it was decided to give the Bradman Collection a permanent home and I was appointed deputy chair of the fund-raising committee.

With a lot of help from the corporate sector and the State Government, this committee chaired by Adelaide businessman and real-estate dynamo Michael Brock raised nearly $1.5 million, enabling the 142 items to be put on display in the beautiful old Institute Building situated in Adelaide's North Terrace, next door to the State Library.

The name Bradman fascinates people of all ages, not just throughout the cricketing world but far beyond it. Over the years I saw mountains of material flood in for Sir Donald to sign from every corner of the globe.

At the SACA office we used to have a room set aside to store these items that kept arriving for his signature. When they built up to a certain point, which never seemed to take long, a telephone call would be made to Sir Donald and he would make a time to come down to Adelaide Oval for yet another signing session.

He would park his car outside the SACA administration building, get out, pick up the little old brown leather case in which he carried the implements needed to sign that famous name on all manner of memorabilia, walk briskly inside past people in the reception area and make his way to the 'signing office', often without being recognised. Perhaps those people who didn't know that the greatest cricketer of all time had just walked past them had in their minds an image of the younger Don Bradman of his playing days.

Sir Donald stopped signing autographs about the time he turned 90. The task became so enormous that he had no choice but to call it a day. Apart from his advancing years, the onset of what was initially thought to be arthritis in his right hand but turned out to be gout had made signing almost impossibly difficult.

I doubt that any one person has ever signed his name more often than Sir Donald. His signature over the years on many thousands of articles has, conservatively, raised millions of dollars in aid of charities and other good causes, for which he personally never sought, nor expected, a cent. And he brought untold pleasure to countless cricket lovers all over the world, simply by writing those two magic words: *Don Bradman*.

Unfortunately, the 'Bradman Industry', a term I used even before the explosion of 'Bradmanphilia' since his death, attracted a number of people who worked hard on collecting his signature purely to sell it for personal gain. There was no realistic way of sorting the genuine cricket follower or dedicated charity fund-raiser from opportunists who sought to take selfish advantage of Bradman's generosity.

Even after Sir Donald did stop signing his autograph, the profiteering continued. In fact, the problem got worse. A number of times in recent years items of memorabilia said by their sellers to have been signed by him have turned out to bear forged signatures. Quite a few of these were the subject of police inquiries, some being successfully prosecuted in court. This illegal activity caused Sir Donald unnecessary stress in his later years, at a time when he was struggling against illness.

My strong advice to anyone contemplating the purchase of Bradman memorabilia is to insist on a certificate of authenticity before parting with your money. In fact I would go further than that and recommend that the bona fides of the certificate be validated by a reliable source.

In the twilight of his life there were a number of his favourite activities that Sir Donald could no longer enjoy. One of these was his regular round of golf. He was a gifted golfer, winning the Mount Osmond Golf Club championship in 1935 and again in 1949. He was also a pennant player for Kooyonga Golf Club, at one stage playing off scratch.

Sir Donald continued to play at Kooyonga until he was in his late eighties and hit the ball sweetly until well after he became an octogenarian. Even then you'd find the name D. BRADMAN featuring high up in the Kooyonga results published in the *Sunday Mail* and occasionally read that he had won the Saturday competition in his grade. Sometimes he would even complete a round of the demanding Kooyonga course in a score of less than his age, 'off the stick' as they say in golfing parlance. That always made him quietly chuffed.

Remember that Sir Donald was also South Australian squash champion in 1939 and an outstanding billiards player and you start to get some idea of the extraordinary physical and mental qualities he possessed. They made him the greatest batsman cricket has ever known.

Among Test batsmen Don Bradman sits right up there at the top with 6996 runs at the amazing average of 99.94. Next comes South Africa's

Graeme Pollock with 2256 runs at 60.97. If a Test average of 50 is considered exceptional, then D.G. Bradman – with just on double that – was a genius.

Bradman and the Media

When Sir Donald Bradman stepped down as a Trustee and member of the Ground and Finance Committee of the South Australian Cricket Association in 1986 he ended his involvement in the first-class game after 60 years. After such a lengthy and demanding period in the public spotlight, he justifiably felt that the time had come for him to be allowed to lead the private life he had so long coveted. This meant that he would no longer be available to the media.

Mission impossible. He was the most famous person in Australia, as well as the greatest cricketer the world has ever seen, and there would be no escape from the limelight.

From the time I took up the position as SACA chief executive in 1988, I was contacted almost daily by newspaper, radio and television reporters wanting to know whether Sir Donald would be prepared to make a statement on any manner of topic. Mostly these fell into a category where, with Bradman's consent, I was able to use my discretion and advise that he no longer commented on such matters.

In the following years I became recognised by the media as the un-official media spokesperson for Sir Donald. There seemed always to be a journalist, or an editor, who was keen to embellish a cricket story with a few words from the great man – not that I can blame them, having spent so many years in the sporting media myself.

Although I retired from the SACA job in 1997, still barely a week went by without someone in the local, interstate or overseas media contacting me about a Bradman-related topic. Whenever I had any doubt whether he might wish to depart from his no-comment policy I took the view that it was not for me to presume what Sir Donald might or might not want to do. I would discuss the matter with him before responding to the query.

Mostly these were about some player breaking a record, or reaching an important milestone; often it was the news of some well-known cricketing identity's death. If he felt it was appropriate, Sir Donald would agree to issue a statement that he would prepare himself and then read out to me over the telephone. After checking it back with him, I would arrange for distribution through the various media outlets on his behalf.

Over the years I lost count of the times I was contacted by reporters trying to confirm that Sir Donald was either on his deathbed, or had passed away.

On most occasions it was easy to dispel the suggestion of the great man's unexpected demise simply by checking around. One time, however, six or seven years ago, I was bombarded by telephone calls from all sections of the media about a persistent report 'from a very reliable source' that Sir Donald had died of a heart attack. As the calls became ever more persistent and from various parts of the world, I began to feel that something might indeed be amiss.

I wasn't able to contact any of Sir Donald's family, nor any of his old friends. I hadn't had any recent personal contact with him and just couldn't locate anyone who had. Meanwhile my phone just kept ringing; I was at my wit's end. I was reluctant to ring the Bradman home. Lady Bradman was ill, and I didn't want to disturb or alarm her if she happened to answer the phone.

At last I decided to take the plunge and call the Bradman's silent number. A familiar voice answered the telephone; to my immense relief it was Sir Donald. He was sitting quietly at home, oblivious to the fact that the world's media had their Bradman obituaries ready to run.

I apologised for the interruption and explained what had been going on. After assuring me that he was in relatively good health, Sir Donald said: 'There is absolutely no need to apologise Barry, I will always be very pleased to take your call on that particular topic.'

I told the media that Sir Donald was alive and well. Several of their number asked how I could positively confirm that fact, to which I simply replied that that I had got the information from the best possible source.

When the phone started ringing at my home on 25 February 2001 and continued through the next day with enquiries about Sir Donald's rumoured death, I initially thought it was the same situation again. This time, of course, the reports were true. Sir Donald had passed away at 92 years of age.

I am privileged in the extreme to have been in the right time and place to get to know well a humble and private man, the late Sir Donald Bradman AC.

12

THE RODNEY MARSH FINISHING SCHOOL

The Australian Cricket Board backed a winner in 1986 when it decided to apply to the Australian Institute of Sport for cricket to be admitted as one of the Institute's sports. I have no doubt at all that the decision to do so has been a key factor in Australia becoming the number one cricketing nation in the world.

In those early days there were a few sceptics around the place, but the Board, and in particular its general manager Graham Halbish, persisted with their vision until the Academy was up and running in 1988. This joint venture between the Australian Cricket Board, the Australian Institute of Sport and the Commonwealth Bank, has unquestionably succeeded beyond the most optimistic expectations.

When the AIS accepted the ACB's application in 1987, the Board's annual report for that year contained this mission statement:

> The Commonwealth Bank Cricket Academy will set a standard for the development of young players for many years to come, and the aim of the coaches will be to stress aggressive captaincy and positive play. It will be uniquely Australian, with the objective of restoring Australia as a cricket power.

Now, 13 years after the Academy program commenced in 1988, that mission has been accomplished, due largely to the tremendous work carried out by Rod Marsh, the head coach for most of that time, and his highly committed staff.

Over the years I have developed a close attachment to the Commonwealth Bank Cricket Academy and everything it has strived to do. The Academy is based in Adelaide and my appointment as Chief Executive of the South Australian Cricket Association in 1988 coincided with the first year of the program.

When I took on the job I was acutely aware that, to help the far-sighted program get off to a flying start, there needed to be good working relationship between Jack Potter, the first head coach of the Academy, his assistant Peter Spence and management of SACA. This was a high priority in those early days, when everyone was feeling their way.

One of the main reasons for mutual cooperation was that from the outset almost all of the Academy's activities were conducted in and around Adelaide Oval, which is leased by SACA from the Adelaide City Council. The indoor cricket centre at the oval had been extensively upgraded, making it the best of its type in the world at the time. The internationally renowned outdoor practice facilities at Adelaide Oval were at the disposal of the Academy scholarship holders and coaching staff. A comfortable, air-conditioned meeting and lecture room, complete with all manner of audio-visual aids, was created out of a century-old rotunda that had for many years served as a tea room.

Living quarters were originally located at St Mark's College, which is adjacent to majestic St Peter's Cathedral at the northern end of the oval. The Academy scholarship holders provided an interesting contrast to the usual occupants of St Mark's, which is a university residential college. There were times when some of the young men from the Academy had difficulty in adjusting to the cloistered culture of St Mark's, but overall there were no major problems thanks to the understanding of the then house master, the Reverend Peter Thompson.

The nearby University of Adelaide made its extensive gymnasium facilities available, as well as the services of legendary fitness guru Rob Crouch. Many of the scholarship holders from those early years will shudder even now at the mention of Rob's name. He devised a program of torture that enabled most of them to reach levels of fitness previously unheard of in cricket.

Adelaide Oval was almost a second home for the early 'scholars' as, for the best part of 12 months, they trained, lived, did their fitness work and played a lot of cricket there or nearby. The scholarship holders became part of everyday life at the oval, with many lasting friendships being forged between the pioneers of the Commonwealth Bank Cricket Academy and staff at the SACA.

Members of the Academy from outside Adelaide were each allocated to one of the district cricket clubs and, controversially as it transpired, became eligible to play Sheffield Shield cricket for South Australia. The playing conditions at the time allowed the selectors to choose interstate Academy members unless they were required by their home State. The selectors took up the offer with alacrity.

During the first two seasons of the Academy, Joe Scuderi (Queensland), Brett Williams (New South Wales), Darren Berry (Victoria), Phil Alley (New South Wales) and Michael Bevan (New South Wales) all began their first-class careers with South Australia. Scuderi never went back to live in Queensland, becoming a regular member of the SA team.

Michael Bevan, an incredibly gifted cricketer, announced his teenaged arrival on the first-class scene by scoring a nonchalant century in his first match for South Australia at the WACA ground in Perth in 1990.

'Bevo' was born and raised in Canberra and, like all players from the ACT, was deemed to be a New South Welshman as far as Sheffield Shield cricket was concerned. After his successful debut season with South Australia, he was faced with the prospect of trying to break into the strong New South Wales side after he returned to Canberra. This was not going to be an easy task. NSW had won the Sheffield Shield in 1989/90 and had plenty of talented batsmen, including Mark Taylor, Steve and Mark Waugh, Steve Small and Greg Matthews.

Not long after Bevan had graduated from the Academy and gone home, I received a telephone call from his father in Canberra who wanted to talk to me about Michael's cricket future. At the time it was no secret that the South Australian selectors were keen for young Bevan to continue to play in Adelaide – but would the New South Wales Cricket Association clear him? The situation had the potential to become very messy for all concerned.

After a few telephone discussions with Bevan senior, I found myself in a predicament. There was growing resentment building up in other States about SA supposedly trying to keep Academy players in Adelaide to strengthen its Sheffield Shield team. At the ACB level this trend was also a cause for concern. In addition some of the SACA district clubs were worried about interstate scholarship holders taking places in the State team that could otherwise be filled by local talent – they felt that it would be bad for player morale and detrimental to the game in the long run. I must say that I had sympathy for all of these arguments.

Michael's father wanted to make sure that his son did whatever was in the best interests of his cricketing future, and knew that he would be an automatic selection in the South Australian team. In the end I suggested that it would be in the best interests of all concerned if Michael stayed where he was and used his enormous talent to force his way into the New South Wales team. England was due to tour Australia in 1990/91, which meant that Mark Taylor and Steve Waugh for certain, and probably Mark Waugh, would be missing from the New South Wales batting order for a large part of the season. Obviously Bevan would be in the running for a spot in the NSW team when Sheffield Shield matches clashed with international duties.

Michael did decide to stay and the rest, as they say, is history. By season's end a new star had arrived. Bevan, who was still only 20 years of age, had accumulated 766 Sheffield Shield runs in eight matches at an average of nearly 70.

By this time the other States had strongly made their point to the Australian Cricket Board about South Australia picking their talented youngsters to bolster the SA team. For the 1991/92 season the Sheffield Shield playing conditions were changed, making scholarship holders eligible to play for their home State only; in addition they were required to return home for a minimum period of 12 months at the conclusion of their scholarship. I had been part of the discussion process leading up to the ACB making this decision and fully supported the change, believing it to be in the best long-term interests of SA cricket.

In 1990 a number of unexpected events impacted on the Academy program. Firstly both Jack Potter and Peter Spence resigned from their coaching positions, Potter to go into a business in Adelaide and Spence to take up a coaching position in Victoria. Two former South Australian Sheffield Shield players, Andrew Sincock and Barry Causby, replaced them for the remainder of the year.

In addition, St Mark's College was no longer available as a residence for the scholarship holders, which meant that alternative accommodation had to be found. A few were billeted with families in Adelaide and others stayed at the Alberton Hotel in Port Adelaide. The Alberton didn't exactly fit the regimented accommodation specifications of the Canberra-based Australian Institute of Sport, but it had a lot going for it, being run by the genial Peter Brien, who comes from a family with a strong sporting background and a great love of cricket.

Looking back now on the names of the young players chosen for the 1990 intake, it was clearly a vintage year for the Academy despite the changes. The 14 scholarship holders included future Australian Test players Shane Warne, Greg Blewett, Justin Langer and Damien Martyn, as well as a young New South Welshman, Jason Gallian, who went on to play Test cricket for England.

We had the pleasure of Warne's company as a casual employee in the SACA office for a few months as a part of the policy of the Academy to encourage scholarship holders to seek employment when they were not training. This was seen as part of the development of the all-round individual and the refinement of their life-skills.

It was no easy matter to find employers willing to offer work to young men who already had as their first priority morning and afternoon training commitments each day. To help out in this regard, I arranged for one or two scholarship holders to work at the SACA, either in the administration office or on the ground staff under the guidance of Les Burdett.

Shane was a breath of fresh air around the office. Nothing was too much trouble for him, however menial the task. In fact I credit him with creating some semblance of order out of the mountain of paperwork I had accumulated. I suspect that if we went looking into the SACA files even now, there would still be evidence of his handiwork. He was followed in later years by some other interesting characters, including Shane Lee and Paul 'Blocker' Wilson, both Australian Test representatives, and Murray Goodwin, who went on to become a regular member of Zimbabwe's Test team, where he was born, before returning to Western Australia.

The class of 1990 was loaded with talent, but it was also surrounded by drama. Much of it involved Warne, who at times felt that the strict Australian Institute of Sport style discipline at the Commonwealth Bank Cricket Academy was over the top. He was a free-spirited young man who enjoyed life to the full and, like others before and after him, occasionally got up to pranks that didn't endear him to the Academy's management.

After a couple of warnings Shane was placed on three months' probation by the Australian Institute of Sport in September 1990, a situation that was due to be reviewed just before Christmas. Unfortunately for all concerned, that review did not eventuate until early in January 1991 and the manner in which it was handled was, to put it politely, a classic piece of bureaucratic bungling.

Warne was initially told by AIS officials that the institute had decided to withdraw his scholarship, which meant that he would not be going with the Academy squad on its tour of Sri Lanka starting on 19 January 1991. He was further advised that it would be in order for him stay with the Academy until 31 January 1991 so that he could attend training and play with the Glenelg District Cricket Club, to which he had been allocated for the season. Officials stressed that he would not be able to train as a scholarship holder and that the AIS would cease paying for his accommodation and meals at the end of January. The unlikely bottom line of all this was that, from 19 January until 31 January, Warne was going to be the only member of the 1990 intake who was still in residence, even though he had been told his scholarship had been withdrawn.

Needless to say there was confusion all round, especially as far as Shane was concerned. Not surprisingly he felt that the situation had become ridiculous, and told Glenelg officials that he would be going back to Melbourne to live on 22 January and not returning to Adelaide. The Glenelg Club was most unhappy about the way the matter had been handled, prompting their president, Barry Walton, to write to the AIS letting it know about how upset the club was. He also said that Warne was a high calibre and very popular cricketer whose behaviour at the club had been excellent.

The saga went from bad to worse. Robert de Castella, then the director of the Australian Institute of Sport in Canberra, wrote to Shane in mid-January 1991, responding to an earlier enquiry from the young leg spinner in which he had asked for clarification about his position with the Academy. It seemed that the AIS had softened its attitude a little as de Castella's letter notified Warne that he was suspended from the program until 15 February, the date the squad was to return from its tour of Sri Lanka. At that time Shane's position was to be reviewed in the light of the way he conducted himself in the intervening period.

As a condition of his 'reprieve' Warne was not permitted to represent the AIS in any competitions. Well, he was the only Cricket Academy scholar in residence at the time, so there was no Academy cricket team to play for – and even then he was an unlikely candidate for selection in any AIS athletics meet. Other obligations placed on him included a requirement to train at the Academy three times a week, to fulfil his responsibilities with the Glenelg Cricket Club and to assist in the Academy/AIS office.

There was one problem with all this. By the time Rob de Castella's letter reached Adelaide, Shane had decided enough was enough and had left the program to return home to Melbourne. Within a month he was chosen to play Sheffield Shield cricket for Victoria, so that was one review that 'Deek' didn't have to worry about.

To top off his rise from suspension to stardom, on 31 December 1991 Shane was selected in the Australian Test team for the New Year Test against India at the Sydney Cricket Ground. I sent him a congratulatory fax message, concluding with the remark, 'What a difference a year makes!' It was indeed an unusual year for the young leg spinner – but for Shane Warne every year since then has been different, for all sorts of reasons.

In the middle of this drama a delegation from the Marylebone Cricket Club in London – including former England captain Sir Colin Cowdrey and the president of the MCC, Lord Griffiths – arrived in Adelaide for the day on 11 January 1991.

The purpose of their trip was to inspect the workings of the Cricket Academy and, in particular, the indoor facilities – the MCC was planning an indoor centre at Lord's. Colin Cowdrey was an old friend whom I first met in 1962/63 when he toured Australia as vice-captain of Ted Dexter's England team. He was particularly fond of Adelaide Oval, having scored 307 there against South Australia during that tour.

I collected our visitors from the MCC at their hotel and showed them around the oval, pointing out earlier improvements that had been made by SACA to accommodate the Academy, including the extensive upgrading of

The Gibbs family arrives in Brisbane in January 1961 to begin their cricket journey.
Peg, Susie, Lyn, Barry and Jenny.

Susie and Jenny in a Tiger Moth at Moorabbin Airport, 1960.

Keeping my eye on the ball as Bob Parker hears the death rattle at Bundaberg in 1963.

Farewelling Wes Hall at the Queensland Cricketers' Club in April 1963 after two outstanding seasons with Queensland.

Australian Test Team, First Test v South Africa, Brisbane, 1963.

Back row: Allan Connolly, Graham McKenzie, Barry Gibbs (Manager), Bill Lawry

Middle row: Brian Booth, Norm O'Neill, Tom Veivers, Ian Meckiff

Front row: Barry Shepherd, Bob Simpson (Vice Captain), Richie Benaud (Captain), Wally Grout, Peter Burge

Left: Ian Meckiff giving me instructions on how to keep my arm straight. The boomerang was presented to me by Col Egar and Lou Rowan to 'help me practice my bowling action'.

Right: Gary Sobers seeks my advice in Brisbane about an offer to play another season with South Australia.

With Sir Henry Abel Smith, Governor of Queensland who is being introduced to Barry Shepherd at the Gabba, 1965. Looking on: Peter Allan, John Mackay, Ken Mackay, Norm O'Neill, Richie Bena

Queensland Sheffield Shield Team, 1964–65

Back row: Ross Duncan, John Mackay, Peter Allan, Graham Egan, Jack Lihou, Graham Bizzell
Front row: Des Bull, Tom Veivers, Peter Burge (Captain), Barry Gibbs (Manager), Wally Grout (Vice Captain), John Brown, Sam Trimble.

Wally Grout, Barry Shepherd and Norm O'Neill – all Rothman's employees – at a charity match at the Gabba in 1965.

Greeting Wally Grout at Brisbane airport after he had played his last Test match. The pewter mug was presented to him by the Melbourne Cricket Club.

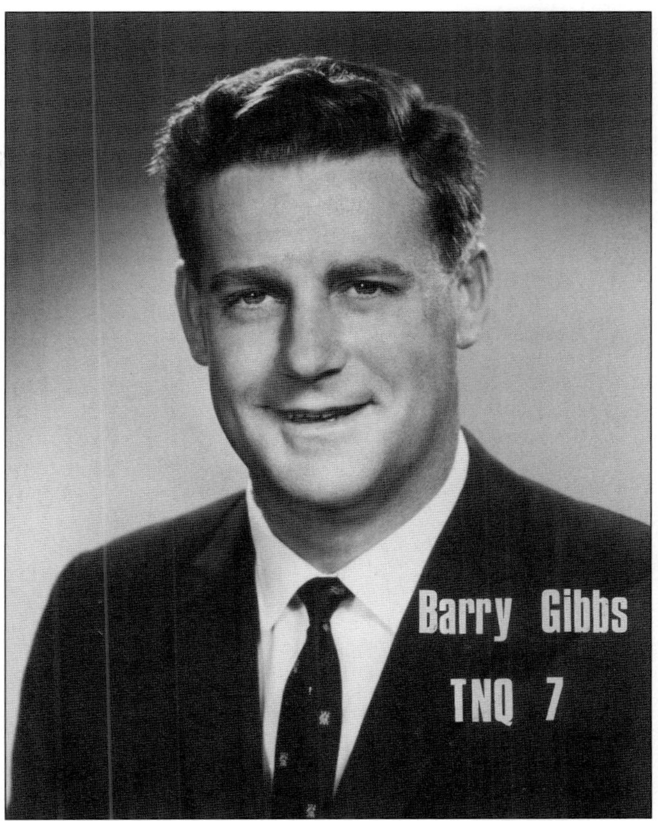

TV sports show host, Townsville, 1968

With world snooker champion Horace Lindrum at TNQ7 studios, Townsville.

Sir Donald Bradman giving me some friendly advice at the official opening of the grandstand named after him. Adelaide Oval, January 1990.

Left to right: Mel McInnes, Peter Jackson, Sir Donald, me and a worried premier John Bannon.

Sir Donald Bradman relaxing at Yalumba winery with Wes Hall and some West Indian visitors, 1975.

Dinner at the MCG, June 1986, in honour of Chris Chataway.
Barry Gibbs, Brian Watson, Chris Chataway, John Hasker, Herb Elliott, Derek Clayton, Peter Bartels.

The 1987 World Cup returns to Australia – and spends a few hours at our Brisbane home.

A young Darren Lehmann with SA coach Les Stillman in 1990. The next season 'Boof' was was playing for Victoria, and Les was still his coach.

Peter Sleep hits the winning run in South Australia's famous 506 run chase against Queensland in 1992. (*Advertiser* and Nicholas Wilson)

Sir Donald Bradman makes one of his very rare visits to the dressing rooms at Adelaide Oval. With South Africa's coach Mike Procter (left) and manager Robbie Muzzell (right), 1994.

State CEOs and ACB management relax at a farewell dinner for new ICC boss David Richards. Adelaide, 1993.

Back row: Graham Halbish (ACB), Bob Radford (NSWCA), Chris Smith (WACA), Barry Gibbs (SACA), Richard Watson (TCA), Ken Jacobs (VCA).
Front row: Ron Steiner (ACB), Ray Sneddon (ACB), Tony Mann (WACA), David Richards (ACB) and Barry Richards (QCA).

Winning the Shield – March 1996

A 'steadying hand' for the Shield.

Jamie and Deetha Siddons embrace after the win. (Bryan Charlton)

Jamie Siddons holds the Sheffield Shield aloft in front of ACB Chairman Denis Rogers, the South Australian team and me.

In the beginning … Excavations behind the south-east mound for light tower 2.

The smashed lighting frame lies next to the damaged cherry picker.
(*Advertiser* and Mike Burton)

My final Test match as SACA CEO, January 1997.

Left: 'Thanks, mate.' A quiet moment with kindred spirit, Les Burdett, after the Test. (Bryan Charlton)

Below: The Australian Test team makes sure I don't forget my last Test. (Bryan Charlton)

'Carrying my bat.' My last day before retiring as SACA Chief Executive.
(*Advertiser* and Ray Titus)

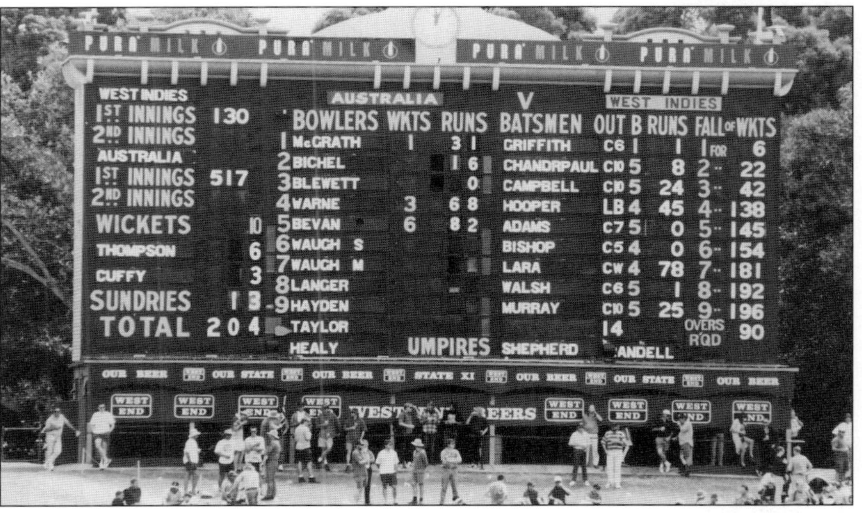

Adelaide Oval scoreboard at the end of my final Test match as CEO, January 1997.

Neil Hawke with his wife, Bev. At home, 13 December 2000.
(*Advertiser* and Ray Titus)

Courtney Walsh, Phil Simmons and Keith Arthurton celebrate the West Indies one-run victory against Australia. Adelaide Oval, January 1993.
(*Advertiser* and Peter Barnes)

the indoor centre as well as the meeting and lecture room. We made our way towards the fabulous outdoor practice facilities hoping that the Academy scholars would be going through their paces there at the time. Unfortunately they were engaged in activities elsewhere, but there was a Sheffield Shield match in progress and a couple of players were practising in the nets.

As we got closer I could see that the two players were Shane Warne and South Australian fast bowler Shane George. I took Sir Colin and Lord Griffiths inside the practice area so that they could have a good look at the set up, and introduced them to the two Shanes.

It wasn't until we got around to the committee viewing area that the irony of the situation struck me. Sir Colin Cowdrey and Lord Griffiths *had* in fact just met two scholarship holders – one who had been on probation and the other, Shane George, who dropped out of the first year of the program because it all got too hard for him!

When Warne went back home to Melbourne in 1991 it was not the end of his association with the Academy. In late 1992 he finally got to go to Sri Lanka, this time with the Australian team. Shane had by now played two Tests, both against India, that had yielded him just a solitary wicket; on his own admission this lack of success was partly due to the fact that he was overweight and lacking fitness. He knew he had a lot of work to do before he could make an impression at Test level.

Rod Marsh had by now been appointed as Head Coach of the Cricket Academy and he made sure the welcome mat was out for Warne again. The blond leg spinner headed back to Adelaide to prepare himself for the Sri Lankan tour – there was also the little matter of finishing off what he started as a scholarship holder in 1990. He put in many long hours in the nets at Adelaide Oval with Marsh and former Test leg spinner Terry Jenner, and the three of them also spent a lot of time talking about the game. By the time he had finished his second stint at the Academy, Shane was 15 kilograms lighter and genuinely felt ready for Test cricket.

It didn't take long for Warne to show just how ready he was. In the first Test against Sri Lanka at Colombo, he bowled Australia to an amazing 16-run win by collecting 3/0 in eleven balls to finish off the match. His foot was now on the ladder leading to success at the International level, thanks to his determination to succeed and, in no small way, to Marsh, Jenner and the Commonwealth Bank Cricket Academy.

Following the resignations of coaches Jack Potter and Peter Spence in 1990 their jobs were advertised nationally. Rodney Marsh, a veteran of 96 Test matches in which he broke the world wicketkeeping record, was the successful candidate. He was the perfect man for the job, and had as his senior coach an excellent deputy in Richard Done, a former New South Wales pace bowler. Together they set about a process of change to the Academy program.

The previous coaches, Potter and Spence, and 'caretakers' Andrew Sincock and Barry Causby, had all made significant contributions to the Academy's progress in the early years, but when Marsh accepted the job an air of expectation could be felt around the place. Marsh had been there and done it all at Test match level; he was a fierce competitor, a man who knew about winning, hated losing and was a tremendous communicator. In addition he was excited about having the opportunity to pass on some of his cricket knowledge to Australia's elite young cricketers.

One of Rod's first moves was to change the length of the Academy program from twelve to eight months, with the scholarship period finishing in December. This meant that interstate players were no longer required to play grade cricket in Adelaide. Instead the Academy took part in as many games as possible against quality opposition in Adelaide, interstate and, budget permitting, overseas.

The Academy, and the Australian Institute of Sport in South Australia, received a major boost in 1992 when the Australian Sports Commission purchased Del Monte, a grand old private hotel on the waterfront at Henley Beach. This delightful building is about 15 minutes drive from Adelaide Oval. At last the cricketers had a real home.

By 1996 the full-time coaching staff was increased to three by the appointment of the talented and popular South Australian and Australian batsman and wicketkeeper Wayne Phillips, who had recently retired from first-class cricket.

Rod Marsh and his staff made the Academy such a successful operation by continuing to look for new ways to expand their sphere of influence. They have used the 'old-boy' network extensively, bringing in as coaches former players of the calibre of Dennis Lillee, Ian Chappell, Terry Jenner, Kerry O'Keeffe and Doug Walters, to mention a few. These experienced, Test-hardened cricketers were able to pass on their intimate knowledge of cricket at its highest level and in their fields of expertise.

Cricket Academy teams have travelled to countries like England, South Africa, Sri Lanka, New Zealand, Pakistan, India and Zimbabwe as part of Marsh's plans for them to gain first-hand experience in what is required of players at international level. In turn, many of those countries have sent teams to Australia for matches against the Academy and State teams. Continuing this overseas theme, the Academy encourages young cricketers from countries around the globe to spend time in Adelaide participating in its world-renowned program.

The impact of the Cricket Academy is obvious when you look at the strength and depth in Australian cricket. Australia could select Test and one-day international teams comprised entirely of graduates from the Academy that would win a lot more games than they lose. Try this for a Test team: Michael Slater, Justin Langer, Ricky Ponting, Damien Martyn, Greg Blewett, Simon Katich, Adam Gilchrist, Shane Warne, Brett Lee, Jason Gillespie and Glenn McGrath. Actually that combination could do the job in the one-day matches as well, and if you add Michael Bevan, Ian Harvey and Andrew Symonds it takes on the look of a very formidable 14-man squad.

It is a comforting thought for Australian cricket that the national selectors haven't yet been required to tap into the 1998, 1999, 2000 and 2001 Academy graduates. The bad news for other cricketing nations is that there are more than 50 talented young cricketers who went through the Academy during those four years, along with others from earlier groups, waiting for opportunity to knock.

The turn-around in the fortunes of Australian cricket from the grim days of the 1980s didn't happen overnight, nor did the Academy do it single-handedly. The coaching and development programs implemented by the States under the auspices of the Australian Cricket Board, together with the remarkably effective system of talent identification that we have in this country, has had a tremendous amount to do with the results that have been achieved in recent years. But the main aim of the Cricket Academy is:

'To bridge the gap between youth cricket programs within Australia and first class cricket and to develop players who will be successful at the international level.' There is no question that the goal has been reached.

Now there are new challenges to be faced. Rod Marsh has moved on to his new role as the first director of the England and Wales Cricket Board's National Academy, while several other Test-playing nations have established cricket academies, or are in the process of doing so. Within Australia most of the States have developed their own institutes of sport, some with a focus on cricket.

All this adds up to stiff competition for the Commonwealth Bank Cricket Academy, but it is well placed to maintain the position it currently enjoys as the centre of excellence for cricket in the world, thanks largely to Rodney Marsh and the wonderful finishing school he and his staff developed during his eleven-year period as head coach.

13

HIJACKING DARREN LEHMANN

I had just arrived home from a solid day in the office in August 1990 when the telephone rang. It was Alan Shiell, a much respected cricket writer at the Adelaide *Advertiser.* 'Sheff' was calling to break the news to me that young South Australian batting sensation Darren Lehmann had been offered a lucrative contract to play cricket in Victoria.

Shiell had got the information from David Hookes, the South Australian captain, who had dropped the bombshell on his commercial radio program earlier in the evening.

Reports indicated that the Carlton Cricket Club had flown Lehmann to Melbourne a few days earlier and offered him a three-year deal, said to be worth over $100,000 a year.

'Sheff' needed a comment from me for the next morning's paper. After recovering from the shock I let forth with a quote about this 'unwanted invasion', giving full vent to my feelings of displeasure and frustration. Shiell's article was on the front page next day and was the lead story on the back pages. The poaching of Darren Lehmann, universally known as 'Boof', remained a news story in Adelaide for the next fortnight.

To put it mildly, I wasn't happy that a Victorian club had thumbed its nose at the Sheffield Shield player transfer rules, and in particular an addition to them that had been unanimously approved by the Australian Cricket Board just the week before. A rule had been widened to read: 'A State, and clubs within that State, shall not approach or discuss a transfer with a player from another State without the permission of that State or the club within that State.'

Clearly no such communication had occurred between Carlton or the Victorian Cricket Association and the SACA. If it had, I was the one person who would have known. Darren said in a radio interview: 'It's a good offer to secure my future. I've certainly got to look at it very closely.

Carlton is a prestige club and I will seriously think about it and come to a decision in the next couple of weeks.'

I managed to track 'Boof' down and he confirmed that Carlton had approached him with an offer that he was 'mulling over'. I told him that the SACA wanted to talk to him urgently with a view to keeping him in South Australia. A meeting of the SACA committee was hurriedly arranged for the next day, at which we planned to put together a package tempting enough to retain Lehmann's services.

That meeting never took place. Very early the next morning I was tipped off by Rod Nicholson, a Melbourne journalist friend, that Darren would fly to Melbourne that day to sign the Carlton contract. This news came out of the blue; all the indications had been that 'Boof' would not be hurried into signing anything. It was still only about seven in the morning, so I rang his home and managed to talk to him – just as he was about to leave for the airport.

Darren hurriedly explained to me that officials of the Carlton Cricket and Football Social Club had contacted him again overnight and had upped the ante significantly. He said that the offer now was simply too good to knock back and that he was about to accept it. I asked him to defer his decision to give us time to put together a counter-proposal, but his mind was already made up. Obviously the young fellow had been put under a lot of pressure by the heavies at Carlton to sign the contract that day.

The Carlton Cricket and Football Social Club is no ordinary sporting body. It controls Princes Park (Optus Oval) and is made up of representatives of the powerful Carlton Football Club and the Carlton Cricket Club, among them high-profile businessman John Elliott and Carlton's chief executive at the time, Ian Collins. Elliott is still calling the shots at Carlton while Collins, a hard-nosed negotiator, moved on to take up the job as football operations manager at the Australian Football League and is now chief executive of Melbourne's Colonial Stadium.

So, despite the fact that the Australian Cricket Board had just changed the player transfer rules especially to prevent players being poached from other States by cashed-up clubs, Darren was bound for Carlton in the blink an eye.

I rang Ken Jacobs, the chief executive of the Victorian Cricket Association, to let him know that I was livid about the unauthorised approach made to Lehmann. He told me that as far as he knew the VCA had nothing to do with the deal. Ken was quoted in the press the next day as saying that neither the VCA nor Carlton had breached any ACB regulations in relation to Lehmann's transfer. He added that no official advice had been received from ACB management about a change in regulations. I thought this was strange, as the SACA had definitely been notified.

The matter wasn't finished just yet. Despite the fact that Darren had now been contracted to play for Carlton, if he was going to play for Victoria both he and the VCA would have to satisfy another of the Sheffield Shield rules and playing conditions. This rule stipulated that 'a player who has represented his State and who transfers to another State may play for that other State in the Sheffield Shield competition only with the approval of a majority of the competing States.'

With six States taking part in the Sheffield Shield competition, if Lehmann was to become eligible to represent Victoria he would need at least three other States to agree to his transfer. I knew for certain that South Australia would not be one of them.

There was much huffing and puffing between the various parties, with talk of Darren being restricted to playing club cricket in Melbourne if his transfer from South Australia to Victoria was not approved. As far as the Australian Cricket Board was concerned, there was no impediment to Darren playing for Carlton while still being eligible to represent SA in the Sheffield Shield competition; he was even available for Test selection if required.

There was even a suggestion that if South Australia blocked Lehmann's transfer, we ran the risk of facing an action for breach of the Trade Practices Act. Fortunately it never got to that. Eventually the VCA lodged the appropriate transfer form with the ACB and the other States, requesting approval for Darren to play for Victoria. I was quick to return the form, making it clear that South Australia did not support the application. But the cricket grapevine indicated that Victoria and one other State had already approved the transfer.

At this stage the ACB stepped in, with all parties agreeing that the common sense move would be to have the matter resolved by the full Board at a meeting that was imminent. The end result was that Lehmann was cleared to play for Victoria by a majority vote.

What I didn't know then, but certainly did later on, was that the initial approach to Darren *did* come from a VCA official, who was in turn negotiating with Carlton. Ken Jacobs told me at the time that he had no knowledge of any such approach and I accept that, but the facts are that it was one of his staff who made the first telephone call, not the Carlton Cricket and Football Social Club.

In the climate that prevailed at that time, with players migrating all over Australia and the ACB transfer rules being blatantly flouted, I doubt that knowing of a VCA official's direct involvement would have made any difference to the final outcome. I say this as, incredibly, the rules contained no financial or any other type of penalty in the event that one State or club didn't advise another State or club of its intentions.

At the end of the day the reality was that Darren Lehmann had signed a contract with Carlton and he was going to play for that club for at least the next three years. He was lost to South Australian cricket for the time being, which was a huge blow to a State team that had not enjoyed much success in recent years but looked ready to turn that around.

It is extremely frustrating to sit by and watch, virtually helpless, as a brilliant young cricketer who has come right through a concentrated local development program gets picked off by another State just when he is beginning to realise his full potential.

In response to the raid on Lehmann, the SACA straight away set about putting in place a defensive strategy aimed at ensuring that no more of our emerging talent was 'kidnapped'. The first part of this plan was to introduce a tiered system of contracts for members of the State training squad, guaranteeing players an agreed level of minimum yearly income in return for an option over their services for the next season.

Player contracts had never been tried before at Sheffield Shield level and, while they achieved the objective of ensuring that players could not just take off to another State if the money was right, there were a few teething problems in the early days. These revolved mainly around the selectors' classification of players into the various minimum payment levels, and also to the method and timing of payments. The individual contract amount was supposed to be confidential between SACA and the player, but the inevitable comparing of notes got a few noses out of joint.

Another problem arose among players who were not working, or did not want to work. A few of them sought a part, or even all, of their guaranteed amount as an up-front payment, some wanting their payment even before the season had begun. There was the real potential for these cricketers to be playing for nothing later on in the year, depending on how many games they took part in.

For my own part, I made a mental note that Darren Lehmann's three-year contract would run out in 1993, by which time he would still be only 23. Come hell or high water, I vowed that I would do whatever I could to bring 'Boof' back to Adelaide – eventually.

By the start of the 1991/92 season the ACB had further tightened the player transfer rules, with the onus being placed squarely on State associations to ensure that its clubs followed the proper procedures. Importantly a financial penalty of $5000 was introduced for non-compliance, payable by the offending State body. Subsequently that penalty rose to $50,000 for a first offence and an even higher amount for a second or subsequent breach, to be determined by the Board.

To the best of my knowledge, in the decade since there has not been a single instance of a financial penalty being imposed on a State for a breach of the player-transfer rules. I would like to be able to say that this has been brought about by the tougher stance taken by the ACB in relation to penalties, as well as by the States doing the right thing. Unfortunately that is not necessarily the case, although the thought of a $50,000 fine hanging over your head must surely act as some sort of disincentive.

There have been numerous instances over the years where the spirit and the wording of the player-transfer rules have been blatantly disregarded and no action has been taken. I suspect that the majority of senior cricket administrators around Australia, if they are honest with themselves, will admit to some knowledge of this occurring.

Even though I am not directly involved in State cricket administration these days, I do have my ear close enough to the ground to know that players are still being sounded out about moving interstate without too much regard for the transfer rules – or action taken to enforce them.

Darren Lehmann enjoyed success with his newly adopted State, but didn't reach the heights of his fabulous summer of 1989/90 with South Australia. He averaged over 42 in his three seasons across the border. Most players would have been satisfied with this sort of result, but not Lehmann. He knew that he had not done enough to attract the attention of the national selectors.

Years later I was talking on the record to Darren about his time in Victoria. He said:

> As far as the life experience I had over there for those three years, I have to say it was the right decision. I grew up a lot as a person, which helped me develop my game and learn my game. Playing alongside players like Merv Hughes and Dean Jones was great experience, it was something I will never forget. As for my career path in cricket, it might have even put me back a little bit, who knows. It is something I will never know, only the people who select the sides I suppose know that.

Looking back on his international career it seems as though Lehmann had an inkling then about what lay ahead of him.

It just so happened that I received a timely message from a very reliable source late in 1992, when Darren was into the last year of his contract with Carlton. My information was that he wasn't at all happy in the Victorian team environment. Immediately I thought to myself that this could be the opportunity.

At very short notice I quietly slipped into Melbourne, but not before ringing Darren to let him know I would be coming over. He was happy to catch up with me for a chat about old times, so we arranged to meet at his home the next morning. When we got together it didn't take very long for me to get the impression from some of the things he said in passing that there was a very real chance of 'Boof' coming back to Adelaide at the end of the season. If it was going to happen, I had to act quickly, and covertly, as he was still contracted and I was going with my gut feeling.

Darren may have been disenchanted with some aspects of Victorian cricket but his major employer Carlton, which had been good to him, was keen to sign him to a new long-term contract. Still I had the feeling that money wasn't going to be Lehmann's only consideration in deciding whether to stay in Melbourne.

I returned to Adelaide with a dilemma on my hands – how on earth do I quickly and quietly put together a deal that is attractive enough to compete with the substantial resources of both the Carlton Cricket and Football Social Club and the Victorian Cricket Association.

Darren had mentioned that he would be in Adelaide for a few days over Christmas to see his family. This was the opportunity I needed. It would be my one shot at pulling off a deal that was of critical importance to South Australian cricket – getting Darren Lehmann back home where he belonged.

I knew enough about Darren's package in Victoria to understand what sort of ballpark figure would be of interest to him, bearing in mind Carlton wanted to keep him at Princes Park. The hard part was pulling it all together, particularly as I had a board to report to, a yearly budget to operate within and knowing how imperative it was to keep negotiations confidential for the time being.

With time ticking away I spoke in very general terms to a couple of key members of the SACA board about an 'interesting project' I was working on which, if it came off, would bring both decided financial advantages to the Association, and more on-field success. The board members encouraged me to continue with the project and assured me that I would have their full support.

So there I was, out on a limb, knowing this just had to be done. I think the people from Nike would have liked the scenario.

Darren came to see me in Adelaide shortly afterwards, and around my living-room table we talked frankly about him coming back to South Australia. By then I was in a position to put a satisfactory proposal in front of him; he liked the look of what I put on the table so we shook hands on it, agreeing to keep the details of our meeting between the two of us.

I then got busy and prepared a letter of offer, which I hand wrote, such was the secrecy involved. Shortly afterward I got the word from Lehmann that we had a deal, which pleased me no end. My only problem was that I couldn't tell anyone about it until the timing was right by him, as he still had the remainder of the season to complete in Victoria. Eventually it was all systems go. Darren came back to Adelaide and was welcomed home like the prodigal son.

Lehmann's batting hadn't suffered during his three years in Victoria. If anything he had tightened up his technique while playing on pitches in Melbourne that were not as true as Adelaide Oval's. Not that Adelaide's pitches were now the same batting paradises 'Boof' had grown up on. They had changed, and very much for the better.

Les Burdett, SACA's oval manager, had decided that the time had come to lay down new turf on the four central strips of the wicket block. I think he was sick of journalists, and some players, calling his pitches 'roads', and was conscious of the feeling that there had been too many drawn matches, particularly in Tests, on his beloved oval. Now there is more bounce and carry for the fast bowlers early, as well as turn for the spinners later in the game.

These changes didn't impact on Darren's ability to score lots of runs, quickly. If anything the new pitches helped him, as the ball was coming on to the bat faster, which meant that it was leaving it faster if you were in touch – which is nearly all the time as far as Lehmann is concerned.

'Boof' peeled off over 1000 runs in 1993/94, his first season back. Then came a total of 1104 in 1994/95 and a massive 1237 the following year. There had never been any doubt in my mind about the critical importance of having Darren back playing for South Australia if we were to achieve consistent success on the field. This came when the SA team went from second last to runners up and then Sheffield Shield champions in the space of those three years.

Gaining international recognition has been a far more difficult task for Lehmann. After being twelfth man in 1989 he had to wait until March 1998 to make his Test debut, against India at Bangalore. He followed this up with two Tests in Pakistan later that year and two more against England in Australia during the 1998/99 season, taking his total to five Tests – where it has remained. For several seasons he was an automatic choice in the one-day team, playing in over 60 matches – including the memorable World Cup final at Lord's against Pakistan in 1999, when he hit the winning run – but in recent times he has been overlooked for the Australian team in both forms of the game. This is one of those mysteries that occur around the selection table and which defy statistics and logic.

I am sure by now it is clearly evident that I have a very high regard for Darren Lehmann, both as a cricketer and a person. A measure of that esteem can be gauged from a comment I made when I announced my retirement as SACA chief executive in 1996. In an interview published in the Adelaide *Advertiser* at the time, I was asked to list some of the highlights during my nine years in the job. High up there was securing the return of 'Boof' to Adelaide, which I said was: 'A very significant decision and a long story. It had to be done, and it was.'

Darren is already a sporting icon in a State with a very long and proud cricketing tradition. His contribution to the game in South Australia simply cannot be measured by mere statistics, as impressive as they are. Inevitably history will place him among the greats who have walked through the player's gate at Adelaide Oval.

14

DAVID GOWER AND THOSE FLYING MACHINES

David Gower is one of the most delightful cricketers I have met. He played cricket for enjoyment, the way it should be played, and in the process brought pleasure to countless thousands of spectators across the world. David is articulate, urbane and possessed of a wonderful sense of humour. He is one of the few England players to become a genuine favourite with Australian crowds.

For years I had delighted in watching Gower bat but it was a famous – or infamous – off-field escapade that eventually resulted in me getting to know him well personally.

England was playing Queensland during 1990/91 at Carrara, a town inland from the Gold Coast tourist strip and 80 kilometres south of Brisbane, when David became intrigued by the sight of old Tiger Moth biplanes taking off on joy flights from a nearby airport. He and fellow batsman John Morris had been dismissed early in the day and it appears that they decided that flying around in a Tiger Moth had more appeal than watching Allan Lamb and Robin Smith flay the Queensland attack before a small crowd in a stadium built to accommodate about 30,000 people.

So, without informing their captain Graham Gooch, they trotted off to the airport, donned leather helmets and flying goggles, climbed into separate aircraft and proceeded to enjoy a little low flying over the cricket ground. This display of aeronautics was met by curiosity from the spectators, amusement by the few players who thought they recognised those on board and, ultimately, the wrath of the England team management.

Unfortunately I wasn't at Carrara that day. I was, however, on the spot a couple of days later in Adelaide, England's next stop, when the inevitable backlash occurred.

I had an interest in Carrara from my merchant banking days with CitiNational Limited. In 1983 I had been involved in syndicating the $110 million financing arrangement for the construction of Jupiters Casino and the Conrad International Hotel complex at nearby Broadbeach on the Gold Coast.

Jupiters Trust, which was awarded the Casino licence by the Queensland government, had agreed that it would assist financially with a number of community projects in the local government areas. One of these was a cricket and football ground at Carrara that was to be developed into an arena with a playing surface about the same size as the Melbourne Cricket Ground.

Several times I was taken to Carrara to see the work in progress at the ground, mainly I suspect because of my position as the Australian Cricket Board's Code of Behaviour Commissioner. The upgrading work always looked impressive, but I suspected that located where it was, inland from Broadbeach heading towards the hinterland, there wasn't likely to be much major sport played there.

Little did I know then that Carrara would become the home ground for the Brisbane Bears in 1987, the Queensland team's first season in the expanded Victorian Football League, now the AFL. As it turned out the Bears moved to Brisbane a few years later. Rugby League came to, and went from, Carrara, confirming my initial thought that the place might be a white elephant.

As for Tiger Moths, I have had a love affair with these delightful planes since 1959 when I was Secretary of the Royal Victorian Aero Club at Melbourne's Moorabbin airport. In those days I held a student flying licence and whenever the opportunity presented itself I would get some time in the log book by flying in the old Tigers, which were still being used as a basic training aircraft.

A leather helmet, goggles and other warm protective clothing – especially in Melbourne – were absolute necessities in Tiger Moths, with their two open cockpits, one astern of the other. They were an ideal aircraft in which to learn the rudiments of flying, forgiving of heavy-handed trainees like me who didn't always know how far below the ground was when landing.

The combination of an unusual headline sports story featuring a batsman whom I could watch in action all day, a sporting arena near the Gold Coast in Queensland that I had some involvement with and a little aeroplane I have an absolute passion for had me eagerly awaiting the England team's arrival in Adelaide so that I could compare notes with Gower and Morris.

As the SACA chief executive it was always my custom to meet and welcome international teams at the airport. This was a common courtesy that Jack Ledward, a wonderful administrator of the 1950s and '60s who managed to be secretary of both the Victorian Cricket Association and the Australian Board of Control, had impressed on me.

By the time the England party got to Adelaide, the Tiger Moth incident was big sporting news and naturally journalists were at the airport in droves. The manager of the England team, Peter Lush, had let it be known that he had met with Gower and Morris before they left Queensland and that consideration was being given to what action should be taken.

Shortly after arriving in Adelaide Lush announced that the intrepid pair had been fined £1000 each. That would have equated to about A$3000, which was a lot of money for a cricketer then. David tried to make light of it by telling the media that he thought £1000 was a scandalous amount to pay for 20 minutes in the air, especially now that the industry was de-regulated!

I eventually got the chance to have a chat with Gower about Tiger Moths and other matters. He was livid at the attitude of the team management, particularly as it had come on the eve of a vital Test match that England had to win to keep the series alive. As someone experienced in issues of player discipline and penalties, I have to say I agreed with David that the fines were way over the top. The joy flight was a harmless prank as far as he was concerned.

Gower, or 'Lubo', as his team-mates called him, now became known as 'Biggles', after the heroic fictional World War 1 aviator created by Captain W.E. Johns. The name seemed apt given David's panache and derring-do.

I have a most vivid recollection of David standing alone in the middle of Adelaide Oval on the day before the Test match long after an England team practice session had concluded. He was leaning on his bat, St Peters

Cathedral and the old scoreboard as a backdrop, soaking up the sun, scenery and atmosphere. I wandered out to the middle where Gower stood. He talked to me for a few minutes about how much enjoyment he had derived from playing at this beautiful place and how he was going to miss it; then I left him alone with his thoughts. This great cricketer was quietly saying goodbye to Adelaide Oval in his own way, in his own time.

The Test match was drawn, which meant that Australia retained the Ashes. After making centuries in the previous two Tests in Melbourne and Sydney, Gower scored just 11 and 16. While David would not be seen again in a Test at Adelaide Oval, Mark Waugh on debut made a superb 138. It was as if the cricketing gods had elected to incarnate the rare talents of Gower in the person of the younger of the Waugh twins, such was Mark's grace and elegance.

Off the field, the highlight was the mysterious appearance of a light aircraft towing a banner in close proximity to Adelaide Oval that proclaimed: GOWER AND MORRIS ARE INNOCENT — OK. As far as I know no one has admitted to arranging this aerial display, but there was speculation that Gower's good mate Geoff Merrill, a prominent South Australian winemaker and cricket buff, may well have been responsible. He has denied any involvement.

On the last day of the Test I was sitting in the match office seeking inspiration about what we could do to show our appreciation to David for the enjoyment he had given spectators at Adelaide Oval over the last twelve years. My view was that the gesture should be appropriate to the man, which meant out of the ordinary, and the presentation made in a manner he would be happy with – which gave us plenty of scope.

Our discussion in that small office, the nerve centre during Tests at Adelaide Oval, went something like: 'Come on guys, what can we do for "Biggles" to send him away from here with memories he will not forget in a hurry?' Needless to say there were a number of outrageous suggestions, some of which even D. Gower might have shuddered at.

Out of the blue I thought of it. 'Why don't we get hold of a copy of that song, *Those Magnificent Men in their Flying Machines*, and play it over the public address system at an appropriate time?' I asked out loud. Everyone agreed this was the way to go – but how to find a copy of the song on tape or CD at such short notice? It was already after lunch on the final day's play.

The SACA marketing manager, John Leak, was assigned the task of tracking down the song. He tried just about every music store in Adelaide without success, which wasn't surprising as this song from the sixties was hardly on the current hit parade.

'What about the radio stations?' someone suggested. They were quickly contacted and – jackpot! – one of the easy-listening stations, 5AD, had the song and, yes, they could run us off an audio tape and deliver it within 30 minutes.

Now for the next major decision – when should we give it an airing? *Those Magnificent Men in their Flying Machines,* would be heard belting out at not only Adelaide Oval, but in parts of surrounding North Adelaide, not to mention the radio and television coverage effects microphones.

David walked out to bat nearing afternoon tea with England needing more than 200 runs to win but with plenty of wickets in hand. The match was as good as dead. I toyed, very briefly, with the idea of welcoming him with our surprise song, but dismissed the notion on the basis that if he happened to score a duck all hell would break loose – in my direction.

A better time to surprise our celebrity batsman, we figured, might be when he was walking off Adelaide Oval for the last time. We all hoped that by then he would have a reasonable total alongside his name and maybe even a not out to boot.

Like most best-laid plans, this one went astray. Gower was given out lbw to Merv Hughes for 16 in a decision that clearly displeased him. This was the second England wicket to fall at 287, much to the glee of the Australians. Perhaps the game was alive now? Very definitely it was not a good time to play *Those Magnificent Men.*

Our song finally played as the players left the ground at the end of the match, much to the amusement of not-out England batsman Robin Smith who, while batting at Carrara, had aimed his bat at Gower's Tiger Moth as if attempting to shoot it down.

In the England dressing room I presented David with the tape, which he assured me would be put to good use. Walking past the dressing rooms a little while later I couldn't help but hear *Those Magnificent Men* booming out from the England room via the team ghetto blaster. Obviously those players in the visiting team who liked to stay behind in the rooms to relax for a while could see the humour of our present to 'Biggles'.

At the end of each Adelaide Oval Test the SACA staff used to get together for a drink out on the lawn at the back of the members' stand among marquees that dispense champagne and chicken, lobster and lager. For hours after play has ended each day, hundreds of people converge 'out the back' to party on. There is even a jazz band on hand to keep the patrons in the right frame of mind. The ambience of Adelaide Oval at Test match time is unequalled at any ground I have visited in the world.

After the 1991 Test the SACA 'choir', led by impresario John Leak, regaled the willing throng with boisterous renditions of *Those Magnificent Men*. A new tradition was born and for years afterwards staff celebrated the end of each Adelaide Test by singing the song out the back near the Chappell Bar. I remember at least one time when 'Biggles' Gower, now a media commentator, stood watching with a quiet smile.

David was not selected at home in 1991 against the West Indies and it looked like the end of the road for him as a Test player. But after he was passed over for the first two Tests of the next season's home series against Pakistan, Gower was included for the third at Old Trafford. I sent him a congratulatory fax and was pleased to receive a prompt response:

> THANKS FOR THE MESSAGE; IT LOOKS LIKE I'VE GOT TO TAKE LIFE SERIOUSLY AGAIN NOW! MUST GET IT RIGHT THIS TIME. REGARDS TO ALL. BIGGLES.

And get it right he did. In England's only innings of a drawn match, David scored 73 to become its highest Test run-scorer. But, thank goodness, he still doesn't seem to take life *too* seriously.

15

NEIL HAWKE: MIRACLE MAN

By way of background, I need to explain that Neil Hawke and I had formed a strong friendship since first meeting in Brisbane in 1961. We invariably got together for a beer and a chat after stumps when the South Australian cricket team came north to play at the Gabba.

Over the years we had often joked about the only century he made in his long first-class cricket career, a milestone I remember well. It happened in a Sheffield Shield match between South Australia and Queensland at Adelaide Oval in December 1964.

I was the Queensland team manager on its southern tour, which during that era comprised four matches on the road in Melbourne, Perth, Adelaide and Sydney. I was still playing district cricket in Brisbane when I could find the time, and was able to help out as a net bowler while we were on tour.

Neil made a duck in the South Australian first innings. He reckoned that he had been 'done' by Wally Grout and Ross Duncan, who had their very confident appeal for caught behind upheld although 'Hawkeye' maintained he missed the ball by a couple of inches. That left SA really struggling at 7/86, chasing Queensland's first innings of 464.

Hawke didn't even take the pads off when he returned to the dressing room, heading straight to the practice nets at the back of the grandstand. Even though I was the Queensland manager, Neil asked if I would mind bowling to him for a while, which I was happy to do. That's what friends are for.

South Australia was asked to follow and in the second innings Hawke hammered the Queensland attack to all parts of Adelaide Oval, scoring 141 not out as the home team forced a draw. While we were having our customary beer after the match, I congratulated Neil on his century and he in turn thanked me for my help. 'Gibbsy, after facing that stuff of yours in the nets for a while I found my confidence growing by the minute. When

I went out in the middle again, the ball was as big as a football and batting was a breeze, mate.' He grinned from ear to ear.

I have a letter from Neil Hawke that I read when in need of inspiration. Written in October 1990 from the Royal Adelaide Hospital, where he lay desperately ill, Neil's note included the following words:

> Still got a tenuous hold on life and am back 'home' searching for an answer to assist me in an unwinnable struggle. Would you please convey my appreciation to the SACA for their support in the Testimonial dinner. The objective was attained. Should I be well enough I hope to see my many friends at the Oval.

Behind this short message, penned in very shaky handwriting, lies a remarkable story of courage, love, friendship, the will to survive and, above all, faith. That part of the Neil Hawke story began in Adelaide in 1980, when the handsome former Australian Test cricketer and Australian Rules footballer for Western Australia and South Australia headed off to Adelaide's Cheltenham Park for a day at the races.

Hawke, at 40 years of age, was then in the prime of his life. With 27 Test matches, nearly two decades of Sheffield Shield cricket for three States and a highly decorated football career behind him, this strapping athlete had the world at his feet.

At the races that day Neil met an attractive young lady by the name of Beverley Holmes. He didn't know it at the time, but that meeting was to change his life completely. For now, the pair fell in love and started seeing each other regularly.

A few months later Neil entered an Adelaide suburban hospital for what was expected to be routine operation to clear a blockage in the bowel, a legacy of an earlier appendix operation gone wrong. He had undergone a similar operation at the Burnley hospital when living in England in the 1970s after playing many years of Lancashire league cricket.

On that occasion doctors found that Hawke's problem had been caused by his obsession for chewing peanuts. He simply could not digest them as some internal adhesions, sustained after the appendectomy, had gradually been strangling his intestines. The earlier blockage was duly cleared but, unknown to anyone, another problem had occurred while he was being stitched up at Burnley; some of his internal working parts had become attached to the stomach wall. And no one had thought to tell him that he should not eat peanuts any more.

In Adelaide during 1980, a straightforward surgical procedure became a living nightmare for Hawke as his doctors quickly discovered the abnormality resulting from his Burnley operation. They also found in the region an infected abscess that was literally poisoning him. The infection raced through his system, bringing on septicemia, which in turn knocked his kidneys and liver out of action.

Neil's condition grew critical. The doctors decided to rush him by ambulance to the intensive care unit at Royal Adelaide Hospital. They had doubts that he would last even that short distance. Hawke did make it to the Royal Adelaide, where he began a life-or-death struggle with the same courage and determination he had shown as one of South Australia's greatest sportsmen.

One of the doctors on duty 'comforted' him by saying that they worked as a team at the RAH and would do everything they possibly could to save him. Later Neil recalled his reaction: 'I've got to be dreaming, it isn't happening. You start to think that you are indestructible; but we're not. You say, Why me? Straight away you think, Why not me?'

For three months Neil drifted in an out of consciousness while he underwent operations that were performed in his nook in intensive care; he was too ill to be taken to the operating theatre. During one of these, when his life hung in the balance, he had an experience that altered his outlook completely. Years later he told me about it:

> I woke up in the middle of an operation. I couldn't move, but my eyes were wide-awake. Suddenly there were seven other pairs of eyes staring at mine and my eyes were sparkling. Whatever it was, there was a voice that had spoken to me and said: 'Neil, in all your life it's been a question of winning or losing; I decide whether you win or lose, whether you live or die.'
>
> At the time Bev, everyone, was concerned whether I was going to get through it, including myself. From the time I heard that voice, all fears went. For the rest of my stay I knew that I was in good hands.

That was the first of several spiritual experiences. Neil and Bev referred to them as 'God's intervention'. Each served to strengthen Neil's new-found Christian faith as he defied the known boundaries of medical science on the long road to health. Throughout, Bev maintained a vigil at his bedside from early morning until late in the evening.

Time after time Hawke overcame setbacks that his weakened body had no right to survive. He survived 13 cardiac arrests in one day. Medical staff were confounded by his will – and ability – to live and eventually he was sent home for a period to prepare for his next lot of operations.

Going home meant that Bev became his full-time carer. Day and night she changed the intravenous drips that fed him; dressed the massive open wound that still left his innards partially exposed; bathed him; and did whatever was humanly possible to help her man. She was a guardian angel.

One night the IV drip sounded an alarm that normally indicated it was blocked, or some other minor problem. Usually Bev would wake in an instant and fix the problem, but on this rare occasion she didn't hear the alarm and Neil, who could hear it, was powerless to do anything about his plight.

> About six in the morning the machine is going beep, beep, beep and Bev gets to hear it. She pushes the button, but it is still going beep, beep,' Neil remembered. 'The bag had emptied and an air bubble could have got straight into my bloodstream and killed me if she hadn't changed it in a matter of seconds. Bev reckons it was as though God was telling her 'Listen now, I think you had better wake up, and quickly'.

Thanks to these and similar experiences during those dark days in 1980, Neil concluded that his time just wasn't up, whether through fate or divine intervention.

Neil was in and out of hospital for about nine months. Now began another battle – the long haul back to a normal existence. In 1982 Neil and Bev married, formalising the partnership they had forged during adversity. The traditional marriage vows they exchanged had more than the usual significance.

After a period of rest Bev and Neil felt, as part of their Church work, they would be able to assist others by telling their story. They travelled

Australia, as Neil put it, 'not preaching, but talking about the experiences that I'd had'. One of these engagements was at the Entertainment Centre in Sydney where 8000 people came to hear speakers including the Hawkes.

A videotape produced from these appearances was much in demand. Requests came to visit Christian functions at which Neil would tell cricketing yarns with his characteristic dry humour, mostly against himself. Then he would talk about the miraculous happenings that occurred while he was so desperately ill.

For the best part of a decade after his horrific experiences of 1980, Hawke was able to lead a fairly normal existence. Importantly, Neil was able to resume writing cricket and football for the *News* in Adelaide as he had been doing since about 1960 when he returned home from Perth. He had got the job after being interviewed by Rupert Murdoch, then the proprietor of the Adelaide afternoon tabloid that launched Murdoch's global entertainment and communications empire.

In his sports' reporting Hawke drew on his vast cricket and football playing experience to give readers a unique perspective on what was taking place both on the field and behind the scenes.

By 1990 Neil's health had again deteriorated. The telltale signs that all was not well manifested themselves in a feeling of disorientation, particularly in his work at the *News*. This got steadily worse, resulting in Hawke being referred to a neurologist who carried out numerous tests, including what Neil called 'the idiot test', presumably to see if he still had all his marbles.

Eventually he was diagnosed as having acute liver disease, which he believed came about through dietary deficiencies and general physical deterioration, although the condition was almost certainly brought on by the extensive surgery and other medical treatment he had undergone a decade earlier. Next stop was another specialist so that he could be assessed for suitability for a liver transplant, a procedure that, by now, was being carried out in Adelaide with a reasonable degree of success.

After a week in the Flinders Medical Centre, Neil was told that as the supply of donated livers for transplants was in short supply, it was felt that younger people than Hawke, by now in his fifties, should take precedence. He was also told that he may not survive the operation and if he did his weakened body might well reject the transplant. In short, the medical opinion was that he was not the ideal candidate for such a delicate operation, especially as there was no certainty that it would improve his quality of life.

Neil left the hospital with a philosophical attitude: 'Let's forget about worries, let's take each day at a time and view it as a bonus.' Before long he was back in the Royal Adelaide Hospital. The prognosis was not good. For the second time, the Hawkes had to face up to the possibility of Neil dying in the near future.

His greatest concern at that time was to ensure that he left behind enough money for Bev to get by on and to allow for his own burial 'with a bit of dignity'. Neil's many friends, Peg and I included, rallied around and a gala dinner was held at Adelaide's Hilton Hotel in August 1990 to help ease the Hawkes financial plight.

Over 500 people attended the dinner to pay tribute to a great Australian sportsman and, quite possibly, to say farewell. Former Australian captain Ian Chappell and legendary England fast bowler Freddie Trueman were among those who donated items to be auctioned. The highlight, however, was the introduction of Neil and Bev to the audience.

Neil had been allowed out of hospital for the evening and, when the couple were presented to the crowd, they received an emotion-charged standing ovation. Bev spoke with feeling about the courage of her man, reducing the audience to tears. It was one of the most memorable functions I have ever attended.

After that it was back to the RAH for 'Hawkeye' to continue to search for answers in his struggle to live. He also had another unexpected problem to contend with.

Neil had accumulated memorabilia from his days as a Test and Sheffield Shield cricketer, including Australian and South Australian blazers, caps, signed team photographs and books. All of these he decided to sell to raise money. An acquaintance, Chris Harte, an Englishman who had been living in Australia for a number of years, convinced Hawke that the items would realise considerably more if they were offered for sale in England, where there was a much larger market.

The arrangement was that Harte, the president of the South Australian branch of the Australian Cricket Society, and an author and cricket historian, would ship the items to England, where he was returning to live. When he got there he would sell them, paying 80 per cent of any proceeds to Neil and Bev back in Australia.

This seemed to be a reasonable proposition to the ailing Hawke, who wasn't in any condition to be concerned about formal documentation. The two had met on many occasions and Harte appeared to be well respected, having been commissioned by the South Australian Cricket Association to write a book on the history of the SACA, a project he had recently completed. Hawke relied on Harte's word.

Harte came out to the Hawkes' home to go through the memorabilia. Neil had an appointment later in the day with a specialist physician and, as Harte was still ruffling through the items, the historian was left there alone. Harte had said that there was so much material to go through he would still be working at it when Neil and Bev got home. But when Neil and Bev returned, Harte had gone and so had most of Neil's cricket possessions.

Because of the problems associated with his illness, Hawke could not recall all the items that had been taken by Harte to be sold. Neil accepted his word that they would be packed in trunks and shipped to England in a container.

Several months later Neil, having survived a second near-death experience, had heard nothing from Harte about the sale of any goods. He rang Harte at his home in Kent, only to be told a hard-luck story: the goods inside the container had either been lost or irreparably damaged in transit. There had also, supposedly, been continual problems with the insurance company, which had held up payment for the loss and damage.

Shortly afterward, just when Neil was becoming resigned to the fact that he was not going to get any money at all, he received a letter from an English collector asking for a letter of authenticity for an Australian blazer of Hawke's that he had purchased from Harte for $1250. As proof of the purchase, the collector in England sent Neil a copy of the cheque he had given Harte.

The cat was out of the bag. Neil spoke again to Harte in England, only to receive a flat denial that he had sold any of the items. Despite the proof he had to the contrary, there was really nothing Neil could do. While he was disappointed at being taken for a ride by a man he had trusted, Hawke was remarkably tolerant, saying: 'Harte has lost more than I have, he has to live with his conscience.'

At about the time all this was going on I received a telephone call from Bob Radford, the Chief Executive of the New South Wales Cricket Association and himself an avid cricket memorabilia collector. Radford had just received a cricket auction catalogue from a London dealer that listed original minutes of South Australian Cricket Association meetings held in the 1920s.

My ears pricked up. There had to be something wrong here. All of the old SACA minute books and useful items of correspondence had been deposited with the public Mortlock Library of South Australiana. I checked through the records on file and found a letter from the Mortlock Library confirming that the minutes Radford mentioned had indeed been handed over to its custody.

Armed with the appropriate letter of authority that I had signed as SACA chief executive, Ray Sutton and John Leak from the Association's office staff joined me in conducting a thorough inspection of the old minute books at the library. Sure enough, when we got to the 1920s there were a number of pages missing, especially at the end of the minutes where the chairman of the meeting signed to confirm their correctness. Closer inspection revealed that the chairman of one or two of these meetings was the great left-handed batsman Clem Hill.

The plot thickened. The minutes themselves were probably not of much significance, but signed as chairman by a cricketer of Clem Hill's eminence they assumed greater value, both historically and financially. It was interesting that the minute books had been lodged with the Mortlock Library on behalf of the SACA by none other than one Chris Harte, after he had finished researching them for the commissioned SACA history.

Next we carried out a detailed examination of all the SACA minutes at the Mortlock Library as well as those still held in the Association's offices. We were concerned that other pages also might be missing, particularly those from the period 1965 to 1973 when Sir Donald Bradman was president. Any records of meetings signed personally by Sir Donald would have brought a price at the premium end of the lucrative English market. Fortunately the search revealed that all the minutes from Bradman's era as president were intact.

Nevertheless, we decided to report the matter of the missing minutes to the police. Detective-sergeant Bob Lindner and Detective John Schrader came to Adelaide Oval to get the details from me and, from that point on, Schrader pursued the matters that arose with thorough determination and success.

There was no evidence that Chris Harte was responsible for removing the minutes, although he would have to have had ample opportunity to do so during the years of access he had to them while writing *The History of the South Australian Cricket Association*. But no charges were ever laid in that regard. Ironically that book was eventually published in 1990, at about the same time as its author left Australia to return to England to live, taking with him Neil Hawke's cricket memorabilia.

During my discussions with John Schrader I mentioned the problems that Neil Hawke was having in his dealings with Harte. Schrader visited Hawke and took a detailed statement, but there seemed little prospect of any satisfactory resolution to the matter now Harte was not in Australia.

Fate intervened to change all that when I received a letter in September 1991 from the owner of a photograph of the 1928/29 England touring team in Australia that had been forwarded to the SACA office a year earlier along with a request for Sir Donald Bradman to sign it. Already all that England team, including Douglas Jardine and Harold Larwood, two key figures of the infamous 'Bodyline' series, had signed it. The owner had been advised following a previous inquiry to SACA that the photograph had been signed by Sir Donald and sent back. But it had never turned up. While this was unusual, perhaps the photo had gone astray in the mail.

Around the same time I had a telephone call from Noel Gorman, a cricket memorabilia collector from Brisbane whom I knew from when I lived there. Noel had read of the problems Neil Hawke had experienced with Harte. The affair by now had received coverage in Australian and English newspapers, *People* newspaper in England publishing an article describing Harte as a cruel con-man and dubbing him 'Rat of the Week'.

Gorman had purchased more than 40 photographs from Harte in good faith at a supposed charity auction at the Queensland Cricketers' Club in 1990 and now, understandably, was concerned about where they had come from. He also had a catalogue from a similar auction that Harte had conducted at Chinchilla in western Queensland. There, listed among the items being offered for sale, was a photograph of the 1928/29 England team that had been autographed by all the players *and* Sir Donald Bradman!

Well, what a coincidence. Chris Harte had spent many hours in the exact part of the SACA administration building where an identical photograph had been kept for a time. Inquiries revealed that the licensee of the Club Hotel in Chinchilla had purchased the photo from Harte for $500.

Noel Gorman was embarrassed that he may have unwittingly bought items from Harte that belonged to someone else. Although he had paid Harte good money, Noel readily offered to hand back any of the memorabilia that hadn't been Harte's to sell.

From there events moved quickly, with John Schrader travelling to Queensland to investigate. He returned with the photographs that Gorman had purchased from Harte, as well as the one from Chinchilla's Club Hotel.

Meanwhile David Frith, editor of *Wisden Cricket Monthly*, contacted me from London to let me know that Harte had offered him a number of old cricket films. David had good reason to believe these were the property of the SACA, so he wisely took possession of them for the time being. I then made arrangements through the South Australian Government for the films to be collected from Frith by the Agent-General in London, who air freighted them to Adelaide.

When all this material arrived, it had to be identified as either belonging to the South Australian Cricket Association or having been there for the purpose of being signed by Sir Donald Bradman at some time. Sir Donald kindly agreed to visit Adelaide Oval, where he went through the items in the company of Ray Sutton, John Schrader from the CIB and me.

We were able to confirm that the majority of the items were the property of the Association, including 19 of the photographs Noel Gorman had purchased from Harte and the cricket films David Frith had located in London. The autographed 1928/29 English tour portrait that had spent some time hanging up in a Chinchilla hotel was also identified by Sir Donald as the one he had signed many months earlier.

The list of missing property grew. We had received reports that Harte had been offering copies of *The History of the South Australian Cricket Association* for sale before he had left Australia hurriedly late in 1990. To my knowledge he had not purchased any of the books and initially it was thought that he may have obtained a few of the 5000 print run from the publishers for his own personal use.

In the process of carrying the annual audit of the Association's accounts, a stocktake was done on the books still on hand, which revealed that 1000 copies were missing. Enquiries were made with the printers, who advised us that Harte had instructed them to deliver 4000 books only to Adelaide Oval, the remaining 1000 being consigned to his home in North Adelaide.

By this time there was compelling evidence that Harte, while in a position of trust, had stolen goods worth many thousands of dollars from the South Australian Cricket Association. No-one will ever know the full extent of his theft as no meaningful inventory existed at that time of the vast amount of cricket memorabilia that had been accumulated by the SACA over 120 years.

There was little doubt that Harte had also obtained Neil Hawke's belongings by false pretences, and sold them for personal gain.

In the wake of media publicity it came to light that Barbara Fishpool, a member of the Australian Cricket Society along with her late husband Gerald, had been persuaded by Harte to allow him to take away for valuation a large collection of ties, autograph sheets and other items shortly after Gerald had died in 1989. That was the last she ever saw of the collection.

Warrants were soon issued by the police for Harte's arrest on various charges of larceny and false pretences. But there was little more that anyone could do to advance the cause of justice, as Harte was living in England. The only real possibility of him facing the charges lay in the unlikely event that he should return to Australia.

Detective Schrader had taken the precaution of issuing an alert with the Commonwealth immigration department in relation to the outstanding warrants against Harte. This meant that if he did come back to Australia, immigration would immediately notify State and Federal police.

Then, out of the blue, in June 1993 I received a call from John Schrader at home one evening to tell me Harte had returned unexpectedly to

Australia to promote a new book he had written. He had been arrested by Schrader after an immigration alert and was now in custody at the Adelaide Remand Centre. I didn't know whether Harte had been stupid, naive or just plain arrogant in coming back to Australia – but I was extremely happy to hear the news.

Harte appeared in the Adelaide Magistrates Court the next day on a number of charges and was granted temporary bail under strict conditions, including that he should not contact Neil Hawke or go near Adelaide Oval.

Obviously Harte was having second thoughts about the wisdom of returning to Australia to promote his book. In October 1993 he was back in the Adelaide Remand Centre and then the Magistrates Court, this time on a charge of intending to abscond. He had been stopped by Federal Police after clearing immigration at Adelaide Airport just as he was about to board a flight to London.

Christopher John Harte eventually appeared before Magistrate Jacynth Sanders in November 1993. The charge of False Pretences against Neil Hawke was withdrawn, as was the charge of Larceny against Barbara Fishpool, both upon full compensation being paid to each victim by Harte. This compensation was paid.

After a trial before Magistrate Sanders, the court found Harte guilty of False Pretences involving 1009 copies of the book *The History of the South Australian Cricket Association* that he caused to be delivered to his home address at North Adelaide.

Harte pleaded guilty to charges of larceny of 20 historical cricket photographs from the South Australian Cricket Association during the time he was researching and completing the SACA book. Nineteen of these photographs were among the 47 he sold to Noel Gorman in Brisbane, the other was the one returned by the licensee of the Chinchilla Hotel in Queensland. Harte also pleaded guilty of larceny of ten historical cricket films from the SACA.

Magistrate Sanders sentenced Harte to ten months' imprisonment, which was suspended upon him entering a good behaviour bond. He was ordered to pay compensation of nearly $20,000 to the SACA within two years, and $500 compensation to the Chinchilla publican. For theft of the films, he was fined $1000.

The magistrate didn't mince words. She told Harte he had 'abused' his professional relationship with the SACA and that: 'You no longer enjoy a reputation of professional integrity and honesty.'

Shortly after the trial Harte went back to England, this time carrying no ill-gotten goods, simply a criminal record and an order to pay compensation of $20,000 to his victims. As I write, that compensation still has not been paid – despite correspondence from the Adelaide Magistrates Court requesting him to do so. The costs to SACA of initiating civil action against Harte in the United Kingdom would almost certainly be more than the amount he was ordered to pay, so this is unlikely to occur.

The main positive result from the court proceedings was that Neil Hawke and Barbara Fishpool were compensated in full for the loss of their belongings, without the need to be involved in court proceedings.

Hawke was able to return to work at the *News,* but not for very long. The newspaper went the way of most afternoon dailies in Australia, ceasing publication 1992. This left Neil, along with many others, out of a job. He was immensely disappointed by the closure of the *News.* What concerned him particularly, he wrote in a letter to me at the time, was 'losing the avenue to project the welfare of cricket, and in particular South Australian cricket, which has brought me much pleasure over the past thirty years'.

Neil's health remained reasonably good for about five years after he had gone into involuntary retirement. He was able to indulge his passion for fishing, dangling his line over the side of the jetties dotted along Adelaide's beachside suburbs.

In 1997 Bev had a visit from a young woman she knew. The visitor was the mother of a baby boy who was going through a bad time and simply couldn't take care of the child. She asked Bev if anyone at her Church might be prepared to give the baby a foster home for a while.

The Hawkes took the baby into their home to give the young mother some breathing space. This would be a short-term arrangement, or so they thought. The inevitable happened, of course. After a period caring for the baby Bev and Neil discovered that a strong bond had been forged between the three of them. The Hawkes became the legal guardians of the little one.

Now think about this for a minute. Both of the Hawkes already had children of their own. Neil was a doting grandfather to his daughter Janet's two young sons; he had somehow managed to reach 60 years of age although he was supposed to have died in 1980 and again in 1990. Bev, although younger than Neil, led a very active life which included looking after her husband's needs and attending to her Church activities. But still this couple willingly found the time, and the love, to give a little boy in need a caring home.

Neil had several more brushes with death. The first of these began during a trip to Cairns. He told me later:

> I was walking around shopping centres and it was almost as though I wasn't on the planet. People were rushing past and I felt as though I was going to collide with everyone.
>
> I felt as though I was on my way out so they dashed me back to Adelaide by aeroplane. Two days later I was at my daughter's place and I lost my balance, knocking over a tray of ornaments. They got me into bed where I collapsed and woke up in the Royal Adelaide Hospital. I had a few days there, then asked Bev to come and pick me up as I didn't want to die in hospital.

They took Neil back to his daughter's home to wait for the end. But, incredibly, for the third time he pulled through.

A year later Hawke once more became desperately ill. His mind began playing tricks on him again. He later described the experience to me as 'reverting to his childhood times and having a feeling in my mind like a corkscrew drawing me into a deep tunnel, at the bottom of which was a big camera lens without a shutter'.

Bev was woken up at three in the morning by the sound of Neil's television set. He had somehow managed to turn it up to its highest volume. She rushed into the room to see her husband in a dreadful state, pale grey and apparently about to die. All she could do was pray for him as he went to meet his maker.

But Neil still wasn't ready to go. Within two days he was talking coherently and his colour gradually returned. Before too long he was back dangling a fishing line and even getting a few nibbles.

I visited Neil and Bev at their home about three months later. Physically and mentally Neil appeared to me to be as well as I had seen him for seven or eight years. His eyes sparkled and his mind was sharp as we talked for two hours.

After all that he had been through during the previous 20 years, Hawke was philosophical about life. 'At the moment Bev and I are enjoying the bonus time. Bev says I have to stick around for a while anyway to guide the little boy,' he told me in the voice of a contented man.

Neil spoke with typically dry humour about what the future might hold for him: 'The experience I had recently suggested that where I am going is not a place to fear – I never got singed.'

In October 2000 Neil was once more admitted to hospital in a critical condition. Many of the symptoms of his past illnesses began to re-appear and the prognosis was bad. In November he was transferred to the Mary Potter Hospice in North Adelaide. Surely this was the point of no return? Yet again this seemingly invincible man began to rally. I visited him often in what he described as his 'six-star hotel'. At times he was sitting up in bed and conversing quite lucidly, and even began to talk about going home.

Sure enough, after nearly a month he was discharged to the care of his family. He was so proud of making it home; his smiling face when I went to visit him there lives in my memory. But it quickly became apparent that it was not possible for Bev to give Neil the specialised nursing attention his worn-out body demanded.

Within a few days 'Hawkeye' was back in Mary Potter Hospice, where he began to lapse in and out of consciousness. Two days before Christmas Bev rang me to tell me that it looked as though Neil only had hours to live and asked if I would like to see him. I went in straight away. He was sleeping peacefully as I said goodbye.

On Christmas Day 2000 Bev rang again with the news that her husband had passed away. Neil Hawke was no longer searching for an answer to assist him in the unwinnable struggle. He told me in a private moment before he died: 'I am at peace.'

Neil Hawke: For the Record

- Played in 27 Test matches for Australia from 1962 to 1968, taking 91 wickets.
- Played in 69 first class matches for Western Australia, South Australia and Tasmania, taking 220 wickets and scoring 2300 runs, including one century.
- Played in a career total of 145 first class matches, taking 458 wickets and scoring 3383 runs.
- Represented Western Australia in interstate Australian Rules football.
- Represented South Australia in interstate Australian Rules football and was a member of the legendary 1963 SA team which defeated Victoria at the Melbourne Cricket Ground.
- Played league football in Adelaide for Port Adelaide and West Torrens.
- Played league football in Perth for East Perth.

16

SHEDDING LIGHT ON ADELAIDE OVAL

I doubt that any decision to floodlight a sporting venue has led to such controversy as the lighting of Adelaide Oval. What seemed like a perfect solution to sensitive heritage and environmental issues became a nightmare for those of us who were closely involved. The magnificent old oval now, following a seven-year struggle, has permanent lighting. These present lights are very different from the ground-breaking retractable system that was originally planned, but the end result is brilliant, dimming the anguish and frustration caused by seemingly endless delays.

There is no doubt Adelaide Oval has the capacity to inflame the passions of people, especially when it comes to making changes to this most beautiful of cricket grounds. The installation of fixed light towers, as necessary as they became, unleashed a lot of that fervour.

The project finally cost many millions of dollars. Just how much money was spent to fix the problems, and who footed the bill, is a closely guarded secret. So too are the terms of the settlement reached after a lengthy commercial dispute involving the South Australian Cricket Association, builders, Baulderstone Hornibrook Engineering Pty Ltd and designers, Dare Sutton Clarke Pty Ltd.

This dispute was before the Supreme Court of South Australia from 1996 until 2000. It was also the subject of court-assisted mediation discussions on two occasions. Documents lodged with the court reveal claims by Baulderstone Hornibrook Engineering against Dare Sutton Clarke for additional costs incurred of some $11 million over and above the original tender amount of about $6 million. If these numbers reflect the true cost of the completed job, I think we can conclude that the lighting of Adelaide Oval may well have turned out to be the most expensive project of its type ever undertaken.

While the total end-cost of the lights is the subject of conjecture, the audited accounts of the SACA are not. Its last published balance sheet shows that the amount of debt owing for the lights actually *reduced* by $250,000 in the year to 30 June 2001. This indicates that the cost of the lights to SACA didn't escalate dramatically from the original contract sum of about $6 million. There are good reasons for the satisfactory position SACA enjoys in this regard, and I will deal with them later.

Now that the oval lights are finally bringing their spectacular new dimension to sports viewing in Adelaide, I believe the time has come to set the record straight on some of the negative, ill-informed comment that has surrounded the project for so long. To me, a lot of this criticism is symptomatic of the 'tall poppy' syndrome that seems to flourish in South Australia – and believe me, Adelaide Oval is considered fair game in this regard. SACA should be lauded, not lampooned, for having the courage to try something new by taking on the concept of building a retractable lighting system. It was a genuine attempt to preserve the unique ambience of this beautiful ground.

The saga began with a meeting of a small group of SACA officials at the home of committee member Ian McLachlan one Saturday early in 1993. On top of the list of topics for discussion was: 'How do we achieve greater utilisation of Adelaide Oval?' This question was posed against a scenario of dramatically declining attendances at South Australian National Football League matches following the admission of the Adelaide Crows into the national Australian Football League competition two years earlier.

The SANFL was the sole winter tenant at Adelaide Oval. The SANFL competition, now a local league, was no longer the 'big time' of South Australian football. To the group that met at the McLachlan home that day it was obvious that, if SACA was to remain viable in the long term, it needed to bring winter sport that would attract large crowds back to the oval.

The existing agreement between SACA and SANFL gave the football league the right to program matches at Adelaide Oval on Saturdays, Sundays and public holidays. When the deal had been done a number of years earlier this was fine for both parties as SANFL was then the premier football league in the State. Now that AFL football had finally arrived in Adelaide, the situation had changed altogether.

The agreement had the potential to block any other form of winter sport, particularly AFL matches and their large crowds, from being played at Adelaide Oval. There was only one year of the agreement to run and we were in the process of negotiating a new one with the football league.

High on our list of priorities was the need to keep as many future programming options open as possible. Besides our desire one day to host AFL matches – then and still the sole privilege in Adelaide of suburban Football Park, built by SANFL and opened in 1974 – we had been impressed by the New South Wales Rugby League's success in staging two 'home' night matches involving the famous St. George Rugby League club under temporary lights at Adelaide Oval. Crowds of 20,000 attended each game, even though rugby league has never been prominent in SA football culture.

The prospect of regular rugby league matches was an attractive one. SACA would benefit financially by hiring out the ground and gathering catering revenue, and SACA members and the public would be offered alternative, high-quality football. But we knew that the NSWRL would not continue meeting the high costs of erecting temporary lighting. If we wanted rugby league to continue at Adelaide Oval as part of an expanded national competition, our venue needed permanent lighting.

Adelaide was also missing out on the marvellous spectacle and revenue-earning potential of day/night international cricket. It was patently obvious to the group who met at Ian McLachlan's home in 1993 that night cricket and football equated to greater venue utilisation. Clearly night sport was the way of the future and the lighting of Adelaide Oval was essential.

Identifying these needs was easy enough, but clearing the obstacles in the way would be difficult. SACA leases the oval from the Adelaide City Council, which in turn would have to grant its approval before we began formally planning the lights. Our discussions with Council members over the years had left us in no doubt that we would be wasting our time even making an application if we had permanent light towers in mind.

A second problem was money to pay for lights. SACA had borrowed nine million dollars to finance the construction of the Sir Donald Bradman grandstand that had been completed four years earlier. We could meet the repayments on this loan comfortably, but they still represented a significant outlay. The prospect of taking on further debt for a lighting project, without a long-term major winter tenant to provide increased revenue, was not one the traditionally conservative committee was likely to embrace with enthusiasm.

Then there was the moral dilemma. Should we allow intrusive light towers to disturb Adelaide Oval's grandeur? The oval's reputation as one of the most beautiful in the world had been earned thanks to the work and foresight of generations of administrators. Those of us in office at SACA felt that we were the custodians of a trust passed down, one that needed to be carefully guarded.

Against this background the full SACA Ground and Finance Committee began to consider the whole question of lighting the oval, eventually deciding to proceed with inquiries about the availability of portable lights. This was but the first tentative step. It didn't mean that the committee had given its approval to install lights on this or any other basis, but the process had begun.

The 'think tank' chaired by Ian McLachlan that had been established to look at increased utilisation of the oval cranked itself up again and came up with a few ideas. Perhaps we could hire giant drive-in cranes to support banks of lights to do the job? The cranes would be driven in a day or so before an event and then taken away the next day. As for the lights, they could be stored away off site when not in use and Adelaide Oval would not be visually compromised.

We discovered that there were plenty of cranes available to do the job. The cost of hiring them, while high, was not so great as to make the exercise uneconomical. The banks of lights, which SACA would also have to pay for, could be assembled locally at a reasonable price.

Then we received technical advice that this form of lighting would not be up to the standard required for regularly telecasting sporting events, mainly due to movement of the head-frames in windy conditions. For cricket in particular, drive-in lights would not stand high enough to ensure the players always could sight the ball clearly.

Another bright idea was the erection of FAVCO-type cranes as commonly used in the construction industry. These cranes, which look like giant meccano pieces, could be erected and dismantled quickly, were rigid enough to eliminate head-frame movement, could rise easily high enough to mount lights for the telecasting of night cricket matches and, when not required, could be stored away. But we found out these 'extending' cranes had to be attached to a solid structure of about the same height. There were no buildings 60 metres high at Adelaide Oval. Back to the drawing board.

We didn't know it at the time, but as a result of the enquiries we had been making about drive-in cranes there were other interested people who had been busy thinking about ways of lighting the oval without building permanent towers. One of them was Mike Dare, managing director of local engineering firm Dare Sutton Clarke, who approached us in April 1993 with an imaginative concept to build retractable lights. Dare's idea was that the towers would be lowered into huge silo-like structures below ground when they were not in use, completely out of sight.

This sounded interesting indeed, even more so when Dare Sutton Clarke said it was willing to do the preliminary design work at its own expense so that we could assess the merits of the proposal.

SACA gave Dare the green light to proceed on this basis and he soon provided drawings and simulated photographs of how the lights would look if they were installed at Adelaide Oval. Then, in June 1993, DSC submitted a report on their engineering investigation into the provision of lighting at Adelaide Oval.

By August we had gathered enough information to put a detailed proposal before the SACA controlling body, the Ground and Finance Committee, which approved continued discussions with Dare Sutton Clarke. The committee also allocated a small budget for professional fees to enable the concept to be developed to a stage where it could be considered in greater detail.

The next step would be to present the plans informally to the Adelaide City Council as part of the process of seeking planning approval. While all these developments were encouraging, the SACA committee was still a long way from making a decision as to whether lights should be installed.

In the meantime a new five-year agreement had been concluded with the South Australian National Football League. During negotiations, I had suggested that we should perhaps make provision for the possibility of staging some AFL matches at the oval in the future. SANFL president Max Basheer was quick to respond that AFL matches would *never* be played at Adelaide Oval. Here's an interesting challenge, I thought to myself. Little did I know how interesting it would turn out to be.

The new arrangement with SANFL allowed for the football league to program matches on Saturdays only. Sundays and public holidays, as well as Friday nights, were now available to other potential winter tenants such as the NSW Rugby League and, fingers crossed, AFL clubs.

The signing of this agreement had brought the issue of lighting Adelaide Oval into sharper focus, particularly now that SACA had gained greater flexibility in being able to negotiate dates for matches with other sporting bodies during the winter season.

The SACA committee decided that the time was right to test the waters with the Adelaide City Council and to go public on the concept of retractable lights. A written explanation of the proposal was submitted to each Council member and at about the same time the Adelaide *Advertiser* ran a front-page story, written by chief cricket writer Alan Shiell, proclaiming in bold headlines: 'Radical lights plan for Adelaide Oval'. The story was accompanied by an artist's impression of how the lights would look.

A delegation from SACA presented full details of the proposal to a meeting of Council early in September 1993 and followed up a few weeks later with a formal planning application for the retractable lights. After further discussions and briefing sessions with members of Council, planning approval was granted before the end of the year.

This was a breakthrough, but we knew well that it didn't mean final building consent would be automatically forthcoming.

Interestingly, there appeared to be almost complete public support for the project. One Adelaide City Councillor, Francene Connor, door-knocked the residents of the Council Ward she represented to find out if they had any concerns about the lights. She received only one objection. The North Adelaide Society, an influential local residents' group, said it had no problems with the concept after Mike Dare and I met with members to explain the plans and answer questions.

Now it was crunch time for SACA. In January 1994 the Ground and Finance Committee gave conditional approval for the project to proceed, subject to the engineering specifications being verified and the estimated completion cost being an amount acceptable to the committee.

For the next few months staff at Dare Sutton Clarke were busy with the task of completing a more detailed preliminary design and the preparation of cost estimates, which SACA thought, based on our earlier discussions, would be about $4.5 million.

By now the question of lighting Adelaide Oval had become extremely time-consuming and complex for the SACA committee and management. To streamline the process the committee decided to appoint an outside consultant to help with lighting matters as they arose. In July 1994 John Goodman, a successful businessman with a great deal of experience in the construction industry, agreed to take on the role.

Goodman soon arranged a briefing meeting with Mike Dare and me. Come the day, Dare arrived shaken and late after writing off his car in an accident on the way to Adelaide Oval, while just prior to our scheduled meeting I received news that my stepfather had died that morning in Geelong. By the time Mike got to the oval I was about to rush out the door to catch a plane to Melbourne, leaving Dare and Goodman to talk about the project without me.

SACA and Dare Sutton Clarke formalised their arrangement in August by signing an agreement, a section of which gave the Association an entitlement to future royalties from any other retractable lighting projects that DSC may be involved in as a result of an international patent application it had lodged. Even after this agreement had been signed, SACA still was not obliged to proceed with the Adelaide Oval lights.

The prospect of future royalties for SA cricket was most attractive. Shortly after the media publicised the possibility of Adelaide Oval being floodlit, I received approaches from sporting-venue managers in Australia and overseas seeking information on the revolutionary retractable lighting system.

Among them were Subiaco Oval in Perth, the Brisbane Cricket Ground, the Tasmanian Football League, Bruce Stadium in Canberra, Eden Park in New Zealand, Kingsmead Oval in South Africa and the Durham County Cricket Ground in England. Some of these venues had environmental, regulatory, space or community difficulties that would have to be overcome if lights were ever to be installed. The retractable concept looked very much like a solution to these problems.

And the interest didn't come only from sporting venues. One enquiry, for instance, was about the possible use of towers to light up an ancient building in Europe at night and then be lowered below ground, out of sight, during the day. The potential impact on tourism in any number of places across the world was interesting to contemplate.

South Australia had long been an innovator in technology; here was another opportunity to show the way. In order to tap into the sporting-venue and tourism market, both SACA and DSC realised we needed one set of retractable lights to be operating efficiently as a sort of outdoor showroom. What better place to do that than Adelaide Oval? We were excited by the prospect.

One of John Goodman's main concerns was the most appropriate method of tendering for the work to be carried out in the event of SACA giving the project the final go-ahead. He believed strongly that it should be tendered as a total 'design and construct' package, in which tenderers are required to finalise the preliminary design and to complete the construction at a fixed price. This would place the responsibility for satisfactory completion of the design squarely on the successful tenderer, eliminating any risk to SACA in this regard.

Eventually the necessary agreements and documentation were in place and in September 1994 the Ground and Finance Committee gave its approval for the project to proceed to tender in the way John Goodman had recommended. This decision, together with the manner in which the contract documentation was prepared by our solicitors, Finlaysons, would prove one of the most important decisions the South Australian Cricket Association has ever made.

Negotiations with the selected tenderers were long and complex, due in part to the unusual nature of the project which, to our knowledge, was a world first. It took until May 1995 for Baulderstone Hornibrook Engineering, which had earlier been identified as the preferred tenderer, and SACA to sign the agreement for the construction of the lights.

Work began almost immediately, with the planned practical completion date set for November 1995. If all went according to plan the lights would be ready for use during two day/night World Series Cup matches involving Australia, West Indies and Sri Lanka in mid-December.

While all this activity had been going on over two years, SACA had been busy promoting the possibility of a second, as yet unnamed, South Australian team competing in the AFL competition and playing its home games at Adelaide Oval.

Port Adelaide and Norwood appeared to be the front-runners to get the go-ahead from the South Australian National Football League and the AFL as SA's second team. From there, it would be up to the SANFL to decide where the new team played. Obviously the SANFL's first choice would be its own ground, Football Park at West Lakes, where the Adelaide Crows had been drawing crowds of 40,000 to each match.

To succeed in having the second team play at Adelaide Oval, SACA would need to convince the SANFL hierarchy, and the AFL, that basing the new team there would deliver significant advantages as compared to having both teams play at Football Park. As one of the main reasons Football Park was established in 1974 was that SACA and SANFL had been unable to reach agreement on the continuing use of Adelaide Oval as the headquarters of football after nearly 100 years, we knew that we had a big job ahead of us.

The parting of the ways between South Australia's two premier sporting bodies had been acrimonious and, while relations were on a better footing 20 years on, the wounds still had not healed. Perhaps they never will.

During the time SACA was endeavouring to secure some AFL football at Adelaide Oval, I discovered first-hand something of the residual deep-seated bitterness that existed between the peak cricket and football organisations in South Australia. But coming to Adelaide from interstate, as I did in 1988, I also found that not carrying any baggage from the past could to be useful. I felt I could look at the issues objectively without having them clouded by history.

SACA went ahead and developed a detailed business plan for the use of Adelaide Oval by the recipient of the second SA-based AFL licence. The plan was submitted to the SANFL in April 1994 after preliminary discussions with the football league's general manager, Leigh Whicker.

The proposal envisaged the building of a new grandstand on the eastern side of the oval that, along with other new spectator facilities, would initially take total seating availability up to 28,000, while the capacity of the ground would rise to 48,000.

Based on average attendances of 35,000, we calculated that the incremental revenue in the first ten years, above that which could be derived from the same number of matches at Football Park, would be more than $100 million.

Market research conducted by an independent body demonstrated that the majority of South Australians preferred the near-city Adelaide Oval to Football Park as SA's second team's home ground. Both these projections gave SACA reason for cautious optimism that the SANFL might look favourably on our proposal.

The ball was in SANFL's court. It came back like a Lleyton Hewitt rocket. Within hours of our initial discussions with him, Leigh Whicker told the public that Football Park was the home of football and the second South Australian AFL team *would* play there.

SANFL's knee-jerk response was predictable; we knew their policy on the matter. But we at SACA still hoped that our proposal, with its impressive, water-tight business plan, would change the SANFL's conventional way of thinking. The league assured us that our proposal would be considered on its merits. The parties met within days for the first of a series of discussions, which culminated in SACA officials making a detailed presentation to the SANFL Commission. Outwardly at least, the business plan appeared to have been well received

The SANFL decided that our proposal should be referred to an independent firm of accountants for evaluation and told us that the findings would be made available to us. In August 1994 representatives of SANFL, SACA and accountants Arthur Andersen and Company gathered together so that we could all learn the outcome.

At that meeting we were told that our figures didn't stack up. There was said to be a significant financial shortfall in our proposal for using Adelaide Oval as compared to Football Park. Unfortunately SACA didn't get to find out just where this shortfall lay; the independent findings were never made available for our scrutiny. The reason for this, we were told, was the highly confidential nature of some of the information submitted by the SANFL to the accounting firm.

At SANFL's suggestion we agreed to revisit our calculations and come back with figures based on a 'best-case' scenario. In other words we were looking to see if there was any more money available for football. As we didn't have the details of the accountancy firms' comparison of the original SACA numbers with those of the SANFL, this was no easy task. We had to compare apples with oranges.

A few weeks later, after some number-crunching by our advisers Capital Strategies, a revised set of financial projections was provided to SANFL. These showed an additional million dollars per year being available to football. We had been told of the need to demonstrate increased revenues but we didn't know how *much* extra would be needed to win the day. We knew we had to jump, but no one would tell us how high.

In November 1994 the SANFL advised SACA that it was still no go, as the revised business plan was not considered to be financially viable. Again, the precise reasons were never explained to us. This meant that there would be no AFL football at Adelaide Oval in the foreseeable future and the second SA team in the national league – by now announced as Port Adelaide – would play its home matches at Football Park.

In a last-ditch effort we asked the SANFL one more time to reconsider its position and, as a sweetener, offered an even more attractive financial package to back up our request. This brought no response at all, and with time dragging on it was becoming obvious that we needed a new strategy.

By January 1995 we decided that it was time to put 'Plan B' in operation; we would make public the details of our extended discussions with the SANFL. With this strategy at least we knew that football followers would be fully informed about the merits of our proposal. Perhaps the weight of public opinion might convince football's decision-makers to change their mind.

The campaign was timed to commence during an Ashes Test match between Australia and England when Adelaide Oval would be the focus of international attention. It began publicly on Saturday 28 January 1995 when the 200,000 plus people who bought the Adelaide *Advertiser* were greeted with a front-page story about SACA's 'bold new plans to attract AFL football to Adelaide Oval'.

Spectators that day were offered a brochure on the way into the ground. It included an artist's impression of a packed Adelaide Oval, incorporating the proposed new eastern grandstand and additional seating, and a questionnaire that invited comments about AFL football at the oval.

Our campaign triggered a huge local reaction. Suddenly the possibility of Adelaide Oval becoming an AFL venue, an issue that was supposed to be dead and buried, was sharing the headlines with the action from a gripping Test match. Predictably it also sparked off a war of words between SACA and SANFL in the media.

Within a few days the SANFL called a major press conference. The league's directors, members of its commission, club general managers and senior staff were all requested to attend. SANFL president Max Basheer read from an 11-page media release to announce that the league had rejected, once and for all, any move to play AFL football at Adelaide Oval.

Basheer used some colourful language while launching a bitter attack on the SACA for what he described as 'an indulgent, emotional and self-serving publicity campaign that does not stand up to critical analysis'. There was no mention of the fact that the critical analysis had never been released to us for scrutiny.

Max, really wound up, said that: 'Despite all of the pompous and patronising comments flowing from the SACA, the association has only one reason for wanting football at Adelaide Oval – a selfish push to fund its expansion plans, which are in the interests of cricket, not football.'

This statement was wrong. The 'expansion plans' were improvements that would be made to accommodate AFL football; without AFL football at the oval, the work would not need to be done. In any event, based on our calculations and the information we had available, grass-roots football in South Australia would be much better off financially with Port Adelaide playing at Adelaide Oval, even if the costly improvements did go ahead.

The SANFL president went on to claim that 'SACA's action in lobbying the AFL direct is impertinent, insulting and unprofessional'. How the SANFL expected us to provide an informed best-case scenario for consideration – as we had been asked us to do – without obtaining vital information from the AFL on elements of a soundly based proposal, I do not know.

Importantly, approaches about the availability of Adelaide Oval had been coming *to* SACA from senior AFL officials for five years, as well as from a number of Melbourne-based clubs.

Basheer concluded by saying that: 'As far as we are concerned the matter is closed. Finished.' Six years later, much the same comments are still being made by the SANFL.

I was aware that the SANFL media conference was being held and had asked journalists to ring me with updates. Later in the afternoon I saw vision of this event for the first time when I agreed to do a live cross with Channel 10 sports presenter Peter Marker during the station's evening news service. A monitor had been set up in the middle of Adelaide Oval enabling me to view what was going to air.

What I saw was rows of stern football officials sitting alongside and behind Max Basheer as he solemnly read out parts of the release. Some of the men in the room that day later told me they were uncomfortable about having to be there at all. That was plainly evident in their body language.

Asked by Peter Marker to comment as I stood out on an empty Adelaide Oval, my first words were: 'I've got to say I feel a bit lonely out here on my own after viewing all that fanfare at Football Park'.

As far as SACA was concerned the matter of AFL football at Adelaide Oval was not finished. Far from it. Now, more than ever, the completion of the retractable lighting project became an urgent imperative.

Baulderstone Hornibrook and its sub-contractors were soon working flat out completing the design work and manufacturing the components. During the second half of 1995 Adelaide Oval resembled a heavy engineering storage depot as massive pieces of machinery were lifted into place before the intricate assembly work began.

SACA staff looked out on giant steel-liner sleeves waiting to be lowered below ground, pieces of the tower columns, massive drive units and lighting head-frames that were temporarily positioned in the car parks, by the bowling greens, behind the Sir Donald Bradman Stand and out near the Victor Richardson Gates. The scene was like a colossal jigsaw puzzle. Excitement was in the air as the pieces began to come together.

But there were surprises in store as the construction proceeded. We had expected to encounter underground water given that the oval is so close to the River Torrens, but hadn't suspected that in the northwest corner, near the beautiful old Moreton Bay fig trees, the contractors would strike a thick seam of coal. This was no real inconvenience, but it did arouse some geological and historical interest. Apparently in the very early days of settlement, coal had been extracted from that area of North Adelaide as fuel.

Digging also revealed 20 metres below the surface fossilised rocks. They contained various types of marine life. On reflection it might have been a good idea to have an archaeologist on hand while this work was going on, particularly when the rear of the mounds on the eastern side of the ground had to be partly excavated to accommodate the light towers on that side of the ground. This work exposed the gradual building up of these mounds, covering a period of more than 100 years. Fortunately I took some photographs of this excavation work.

The practical completion date for the lights was still November 1995, in time for the international one-day matches. As this date grew nearer, I – and other SACA staff – began to have concerns about whether the job would be completed on time.

SACA continued to receive work-in-progress schedules from Baulderstone Hornibrook Engineering that showed the work would be finished by the practical completion date, but the Adelaide Oval 'grapevine' was telling us that a number of construction problems were being experienced that would most likely result in substantial delays.

I had accepted an invitation to be guest speaker at the SACA President's lunch on 12 October 1995 to talk about the lighting project. I knew the rumours, of course, but was given formal assurances from Baulderstone Hornibrook that the lights *would* be ready in time for the one-day internationals, so I spoke accordingly at the lunch. The designer of the lights, Mike Dare, was present, as were representatives of Baulderstone Hornibrook and various sub-contractors engaged on the job. So too were members of the media, which had shown enormous interest in the project from the day it was first suggested in 1993.

Only weeks after I had spoken so enthusiastically at that lunch, SACA was advised by Baulderstone Hornibrook Engineering that, due to technical difficulties, the practical completion date would have to be put back about a month. This cast immediate doubts about the lights being available for the internationals, leaving the Australian Cricket Board no alternative other than to re-schedule them as day fixtures. As a result, SACA and the ACB had to revise – downwards – their match-revenue projections.

As if it was not bad enough, the delay in the project also wrecked delicate confidential negotiations we were having with interstate parties extremely interested in playing AFL matches at Adelaide Oval.

In addition, a 'Super League' Rugby competition had been formed by interests associated with News Limited, and we had reached in-principal agreement with them that an Adelaide-based team would play its home games at Adelaide Oval – mainly under lights. AFL football and NSW Rugby League matches were both being played regularly at the WACA ground in Perth. I had gone to WA specifically to look at the way the two codes co-existed and was confident that there would be no difficulties in Adelaide Oval doing the same. So was Les Burdett who had seen the Western Reds Rugby League set-up at the WACA.

While AFL footy at Adelaide Oval looked a dead duck for the time being, on the Super League front things were looking good. Early in December 1995 urgent meetings were held between Ian McLachlan, Jack Clarke and me from SACA and Lachlan Murdoch, John Ribot and Julian Swinstead representing Super League, together with our legal advisers. These culminated in the signing of a Heads of Agreement document by the two parties, whereby the new Adelaide Rams would play at Adelaide Oval for five years from the start of the 1996 season.

A few weeks later SACA received more bad news about the lights. Early in January 1996 Baulderstone Hornibrook Engineering revealed that it had experienced significant problems in raising and lowering the lights. At subsequent meetings we learned more about these problems which, we were advised, would necessitate an extensive engineering review of a number of aspects of the design.

This in turn meant an extended delay to the practical completion date – with the Super League competition due to start within two months. It also put a dampener on our hopes of deriving any royalties from future sales of retractable-lighting technology by Dare Sutton Clarke.

The Super League problem was overcome for the time being when Baulderstone Hornibrook erected temporary lights that enabled SACA to meet its obligations to the Adelaide Rams. To do this, the company fixed the top half of the retractable towers and the lighting head-frames in the positions where the retractable lights were to be located. These temporary lights were about 35 metres high, adequate for rugby league, a game played mainly at ground level, but nowhere near tall enough for cricket or Australian Rules football.

The temporary lights were switched on for the first time on 20 March 1996 – and looked fantastic. Adelaide Oval took on an even more serene appearance. Three years almost to the day since SACA identified the need for lights back in 1993, the oval was finally floodlit, even if the light towers themselves were at half-mast.

The lights shone on Adelaide Oval, but dark clouds hung over the world of rugby league. The Australian Rugby League, the game's controlling body, secured orders from the Federal Court in Sydney prohibiting the kick-off of the Super League competition. The Adelaide Rams, one of two teams custom-made to take part in Super League, suddenly didn't have a competition to play in.

The Rams had a full complement of players and an army of support staff, had sold season tickets, had met the costs of erecting a temporary grandstand on the eastern side of the oval and installing additional corporate entertaining facilities to meet the anticipated demand – and now they were told they couldn't play. It was gut-wrenching stuff for all concerned, including SACA and me personally.

SACA's five-year deal had been conditional on Super League actually getting going in 1996; we were facing loss of both revenue and oval usage.

By now, in our view and that of our legal advisors, Baulderstone Hornibrook was in breach of contract. In accordance with the dispute resolution clauses of the contract, John Goodman formally notified BHE in June 1996 that a dispute existed between the two parties. We were unable to resolve the matter between ourselves, which led to SACA initiating legal action against BHE in the Supreme Court of South Australia.

The Supreme Court agreed to hear the matter urgently in the public interest and it was first listed on 13 September 1996. After several appearances in court Judge John Perry ordered both parties to appear before him two weeks later to discuss the feasibility of a 'Court-controlled alternative dispute resolution process'. SACA and BHE each came to the conclusion that this matter might be resolved by mediation, so wheels were put in motion. Sir Laurence Street, a former Chief Justice of the Supreme Court of New South Wales, agreed to act as mediator.

A meeting between the two parties, their legal teams and Sir Laurence took place in Sydney on 21 October 1996. It was a fascinating and productive experience; in a single day we settled our differences, reaching agreement on this very complex matter that had been the subject of legal proceedings for nearly four months.

A part of the agreement was that the terms of settlement were to remain confidential, which precludes me from giving any insight about what happened behind closed doors that day. Suffice to say that the three SACA representatives present – board members Ian McLachlan and Creagh O'Connor, and I – were satisfied with the outcome.

For me this was a significant moment. A few months earlier I had told the Board of the South Australian Cricket Association – as the former Ground and Finance Committee had recently become with the adoption of a new constitution – that I intended to retire from my position as chief executive early in 1997. Now I could do so in the knowledge that the lights would be substantially completed by that time. Or so I thought.

Work commenced on the installation of the substantially re-designed lights in November 1996, the scheduled completion date now being 30 June 1997. Before that date arrived my retirement from SACA became effective, allowing Peg and I to travel to South Africa for a month when the Australian cricket team was touring there.

It was great to link up with the same Australian cricketers who had given me a champagne and beer drenched send-off in the Adelaide Oval dressing room a few weeks earlier. They were out to make sure I wouldn't forget the last Test match I was to be involved in as an administrator.

Weeks after we returned to Australia, Mike Deare, who had succeeded me as SACA chief executive, had to announce that the practical completion date for the lights had been put back a month or so to allow for some fine-tuning. He had received assurances, he said, that they would be ready in time for the cricket season. This sounds familiar, I thought. At least I wasn't the man in the hot seat any more.

Further delays caused by problems during the tower-erection work later put the practical completion date back to 31 October 1997, meaning that the first day/night Sheffield Shield match scheduled for Adelaide Oval, set down for mid-November, had to be played as a day game. The Australian Cricket Board and SACA could not take the risk of even a small additional delay.

These technical problems were overcome in time for the one-day international matches involving Australia, South Africa and New Zealand a month later. Finally the retractable lighting system was used for the first time in the New Zealand v South Africa day/night match on 6 December 1997.

A ceremony had been arranged to 'launch' the lights during the break between innings. The Premier of South Australia, John Olsen, SACA board members Ian McLachlan and Creagh O'Connor, the managing director of Baulderstone Hornibrook Engineering, Hedley Davis, and I were to turn on the lights from the middle of the Oval.

We gathered in the SACA committee room waiting for the break in play scheduled for 5.30 pm. The day was overcast, with heavy clouds building up during the afternoon. Under the playing conditions for one-day international matches, the umpires could request that available artificial lighting be used at any time during play if the natural light deteriorated to an unfit level.

It started to get dark out in the middle at around 4.30, prompting umpires Steve Davis and Ross Emerson to ask for the lights to be turned on. While this made it easier for the players in the middle to see the white ball, it rendered pointless the ceremony that was due to take place in about an hour. Nevertheless we went ahead with a shortened version of the launch. Premier Olsen said a few words but the symbolic flicking of switches and drum roll were, well, given the flick. What an anti-climax after four years of drama.

I recall thinking how strange it was that artificial lights should be needed on a summer afternoon in the driest State of the driest continent on the planet, particularly with daylight saving in operation.

When the sun had set behind the clouds and twilight faded, the floodlit scene of Adelaide Oval at night with a cricket match in progress was simply magnificent. Unfortunately there were less than 10,000 people there to witness this historic occasion.

The next day Australia played New Zealand in another day/night match before a crowd of more than 30,000, and Mark Waugh scored a superb century. Altogether it was a happier day.

I was a guest in one of the corporate hospitality suites high up in the Sir Donald Bradman Stand for the second match. After play I lingered for a while outside the suite to soak up the atmosphere and reflect on all that had happened in the lead-up to this long awaited first weekend of day/night cricket. A man in the seats in front of the corporate box next door called me over to where he was standing and said: 'I just want to thank you for the part you have played in making this possible. I know something about what you have been through and you have every right to be proud of what you have done for the people of South Australia.'

I thanked this stranger sincerely and turned back with a lump in my throat to savour again the sight of the most beautiful cricket ground in the world, which had become even more majestic. It was a very proud moment for me.

Just three months later, on 17 March 1998 – St Patrick's Day – the number two tower collapsed without warning into the concrete pit that housed it while routine maintenance was being done.

Two workmen, Peter Cousins and Trevor Bickle, who were carrying out adjustments at the top of the light tower from a 'cherry picker', were injured when the eight-metre-square lighting head-frame careered downwards, striking the platform they were on. They were left dangling from the crane high above the ground in their safety harnesses. The two were rescued when the crane was lowered and they were rushed to nearby Royal Adelaide Hospital.

I was driving to Adelaide Oval to attend a function when I heard a news flash on the car radio. By the time I arrived the injured workmen had been taken to hospital and the area cordoned off. The sight of that shattered light tower lying crudely in its pit is seared in my memory. Amid all the highs and lows the lights had given me I had experienced nothing like the despair I felt that day. The thought of two men lying in hospital was devastating.

Channel 7 captured images of the two workmen hanging from their safety harnesses. They were shown around the world that night. Next day the *Advertiser* front page featured a picture from the footage of the men suspended mid-air. Even now I get an eerie feeling when I look at that photograph.

The Department of Industrial Affairs and Baulderstone Hornibrook Engineering each launched inquiries into the collapse. These investigations had to be carried out, but it was obvious that the days of the retractable lights were numbered.

Nearly three years since construction work commenced on a lighting project that was to be completed in six months, the only sporting action Adelaide Oval had seen under the fully erected lights was two one-day international cricket matches in December 1997. A lighting tower lay in a crumbled mess and no one really knew why.

To enable SACA to provide lighting for the 1998/99 cricket season, the Adelaide City Council approved the temporary installation of a disused radio mast in the Creswell Gardens on the eastern side of Adelaide Oval. The other three retractable towers remained securely locked in the 'up' position until further notice.

The Baulderstone Hornibrook report into the collapse was completed by November 1998 and a copy eventually given to SACA in January 1999, on the basis that the contents remained confidential. Meanwhile speculation was mounting that it might take until at least September 1999 before the retractable system was fully functional again, if it ever would be.

Not until February 1999 did the State Government release any details of its own investigation. That report uncovered 'deficiencies in installation and management' of the project and as a result warning letters were sent to SACA and BHE.

Meanwhile proceedings continued in the Supreme Court before Justice Perry in February 1999. Earlier Baulderstone Hornibrook Engineering had, with the court's consent, become the plaintiff in the case, replacing SACA, while Dare Sutton Clarke was listed as the sole defendant. In an 85-page statement of claim Baulderstone Hornibrook sought damages of more than $11 million from Dare Sutton Clarke for alleged design faults.

The BHE investigation report into the collapse of light tower number two was thrust into the spotlight during these court proceedings. In response to a statement by Dare Sutton Clarke that it believed the report could help it defend a statement of claim for damages first lodged in 1996, Justice Perry ordered BHE to hand over relevant documents to the court within three days. While the damages claim and the tower collapse were separate matters, it was starting to look inevitable that the two would become linked together in the future.

Dare Sutton Clarke showed that it was clearly ready to defend the allegations made by Baulderstone Hornibrook in its statement of claim, filing a detailed 104-page response. There were claims and counter-claims going in all directions in the Supreme Court, but on the surface at least, there was nothing much happening about making the Adelaide Oval lights fully operative again.

Almost exactly a year after light tower number two had collapsed, SACA announced that it was considering abandoning the retractable system if no engineering solution could be found to the problems. Frustrated by the lack of action on several fronts and the State Government's requirement that lights remain up due to safety concerns, SACA indicated that it was looking at a number of other options, including permanent light towers.

Baulderstone Hornibrook continued to try and find an acceptable engineering solution to the preferred option of retractable light towers, but without success. With no other practical alternative, SACA announced in September 1999 that planning approval would be sought for permanent light towers and made public the design of the proposed new lights.

The announcement brought an immediate, predictable response from interests opposed to such a concept, including the North Adelaide Society. This was always going to be a head-on clash.

SACA, on the one hand, had done everything it could to ensure that the ambience of Adelaide Oval had not been compromised in its attempts to light the venue. This had come at a cost of $6 million for lights that didn't work and an additional $1.4 million in lost revenue and legal fees.

The North Adelaide Society had been opposed to permanent lights from day one. It had given the retractable lights the thumbs-up after protracted consultation, but there was no way that this influential residents' group would embrace a project that it believed would permanently mar the landscape of the beautiful suburbs around Adelaide Oval.

Adelaide City Council decided that it needed an independent engineering report on the failure of the retractable lights before it could consider the merits of the new SACA proposal. There were already two reports in existence and this third one, commissioned at a cost of a reported $117,000, was destined to remain confidential like the other two.

SACA's new proposal gained momentum early in October 1999 when agreement was reached with Baulderstone Hornibrook Engineering that the construction company would pay the full $6.6 million cost of replacing the retractable lights with four fixed towers. The necessary development application was lodged with Adelaide City Council seeking approval to build towers that would be 64 metres tall, cylindrical in shape instead of square, and measure 2.5 metres in diameter at the base.

Adelaide City Council considered the development application at a meeting on 13 December 1999, springing a surprise when it voted 5-4 against the application, but leaving the door ajar by requesting SACA to submit a fresh application that took into account Council concerns about the design of the light heads and thickness of the towers.

The decision created more headlines as Councillor Michael Harbison, who supported the SACA proposal, accused colleagues who voted against the permanent towers of being 'very foolish', adding: 'It is time that this Council woke up to itself.' The North Adelaide Society maintained its stance that the fixed towers would ruin the skyline and reiterated its support for retractable lights only.

The president of the South Australian Cricket Association, Ian McLachlan, stated publicly the next day that he was furious and incredulous at the Council's vote. I'm sure he spoke for SACA generally and a lot of people in South Australia, as it was clear SACA had done everything it possibly could to install non-intrusive lights at Adelaide Oval before reluctantly resorting to the permanent tower option.

Fortunately the Adelaide City Council's decision was short-lived. Just 24 hours later it was reversed at a meeting specially convened by Michael Harbison to give another chance to Councillors who were 'embarrassed and remorseful' about their original vote. This time the voting was 6-2 in favour of the SACA application.

Adelaide's Lord Mayor at the time, Jane Lomax-Smith, who voted against the proposal the day before, summed the situation up when she said: 'These are the lights we had to have. Probably we have reached the end of the line, this is the best that is humanly possible.'

Nearly two years after the collapse of LT2, it appeared that the last obstacle had been cleared and Adelaide Oval would finally get its lights. Wrong! Three days later an Adelaide businessman, Theo Maras, signalled his intention to lodge a court challenge to block the permanent lights on behalf of a community group, reportedly comprising mainly North Adelaide residents, opposed to fixed towers.

The story ran in the media for the next few days as SACA officials and those North Adelaide residents who didn't want permanent lights at any price engaged in a public war of words. The possibility was raised of the State Government being asked to proclaim the lights as a 'major project.' This status would allow an application for fixed towers to short-circuit planning objections and bypass developmental and environmental regulations. SACA chief executive Michael Deare played down this possibility, saying that the State Government would be asked to intervene only as a last resort.

The row subsided over Christmas but erupted again early in January 2000 when the North Adelaide Society launched an action with the Environment, Resources and Development Court aimed at preventing installation of permanent lights. The society appeal against the ACC's decision was heard less than three weeks after it was lodged, and dismissed the next day.

The North Adelaide Society pulled another rabbit from the hat when its chairman, Ed Briedis, announced members were considering a further appeal, this time to the Supreme Court of South Australia.

The deadline for lodging an appeal – 17 February 2000 – passed and no appeal materialised. But was it really all over? Not according to the North Adelaide Society, which was reported as saying it was now exploring new legal avenues to block the towers, including the possibility of seeking a judicial review by the Supreme Court to prevent permanent lights being installed at Adelaide Oval. Fortunately we heard no more about that proposed course of action.

At last work could go ahead without the threat of legal action. This time construction proceeded smoothly, with the practical completion date scheduled for November 2000. The three remaining retractable towers were dismantled and removed from Adelaide Oval by the end of August.

Meanwhile ASC Engineering, a subsidiary of the Australian Submarine Corporation, was fabricating the new steel towers. Access to the bank of floodlights for maintenance work would be gained by climbing internal stairwells. The four below-ground 'silos' were filled in with concrete, forming the base on which the permanent towers could be erected, with this work to start in September.

The head-frames from the original design were re-used on the permanent fixtures, with modifications that provided improved lighting at ground level. SACA, conscious of the need to make the lights as aesthetically pleasing as possible, considered five alternatives before choosing a design that included an oblique 'spire' at the top in sympathy with the spires of nearby St Peter's Cathedral.

Progressing more slowly were the Supreme Court proceedings in which Baulderstone Hornibrook Engineering was seeking damages of $11 million from Dare Sutton Clarke for alleged design problems.

The court appointed Sir Laurence Street mediator in an attempt to settle the long-running dispute before it went to trial in February 2001. The two main parties and three third parties involved met in Adelaide but failed to resolve the dispute after a full day of mediation in early August 2000. The Supreme Court later heard that Dare Sutton Clarke had reached agreements with two of the third parties but that the remaining third party, the plaintiff Baulderstone Hornibrook Engineering and the defendant could not agree. The good news was that negotiations would continue in an attempt to broker a settlement.

Persistence finally paid off when, on 30 October 2000, Supreme Court Justice John Perry was notified that a confidential settlement had been reached between BHE and DSC.

At last, six years after SACA had decided to put the lighting project out to tender and four years since it first took action against Baulderstone Hornibrook Engineering in the Supreme Court, the decks had been cleared on all fronts.

By early November installation of the four permanent light towers was completed and the delicate job of lifting the headframes into place was about to begin. The sight of the towers brought mixed reactions.

Ed Briedis from the North Adelaide Society said that the towers 'turned out even bigger than I expected. They will only look taller when the light heads go on'. Theo Maris reckoned that the poles 'desecrate the view from Montefiore Hill and Light's Vision.'

Kim Bonython, patron of the arts, war hero and South Australian icon, raised a few eyebrows when he wrote to the *Advertiser*:

> Today, and perhaps in perpetuity, the venue that was for so long the envy of all other cricketing countries of this world now looks more like a stark memorial to a horrendous European crematorium than the hallowed playing fields bequeathed to us by our forebears.

SACA's chief executive Mike Deare responded that the headframes would improve the towers' appearance. 'They will add something special and any judgment about the towers should wait until they are finished.'

A few days later the first of the new-look 17-tonne headframes was lifted into position by a giant crane, bringing smiles of approval from members of a tour group who were watching proceedings from Light's Vision on Montefiore Hill, the spot overlooking Adelaide Oval from which Colonel William Light planned the City of Adelaide in the 1830s.

The last of the four headframes was in position by mid November in the southwest corner of the oval at the back of the Bradman Stand and alongside the century-old bowling greens. In that tight part of Adelaide Oval, the 400-tonne crane could not be driven in; it had to be dismantled and re-assembled to enable the job to be done.

This time round the project was completed on schedule and the new lights were tested for the first time late in the evening of 29 November 2000. Adelaide Oval is one of the few stadiums where you can feel the atmosphere without a crowd and a game going on. That night, with only a few workmen, staff, officials and curious onlookers present, the near-empty oval was simply spine-tingling.

A few days later lights were used in a Test match at Adelaide Oval for the first time. On day three of the Australia versus West Indies match an Adelaide heat wave was broken by rain, which caused the umpires to request the lights to be turned on, as the tour playing conditions sensibly permitted.

The first scheduled match at Adelaide Oval under the new lights was West Indies versus Australia 'A' in a day/night match on 9 January 2001. More than 12,000 people turned up to see the West Indies cruise home to an easy victory, so easy that it was just about finished before the lights were needed.

Later that month two one-day internationals, West Indies playing Zimbabwe and Australia taking on the West Indies, marked the official beginning of recognised international cricket under the re-designed lights. The lights passed the test with flying colours.

More than seven years after the possibility of lighting up Adelaide Oval was first made public the lights had finally arrived. In that time a revolutionary retractable system turned out to be unworkable, there were four years of wrangling in the Supreme Court, two mediation hearings chaired by Sir Laurence Street took place, the Adelaide Rams and the Super League competition came and went, approximately $20 million was spent on fixing the lighting problems, no AFL football was played at Adelaide Oval, South Australia finally won the Sheffield Shield after a 14-year drought and the SACA chief executive who was in the chair when it all started retired to write his memoirs.

17

JOE SCUDERI'S CRICKETING ODYSSEY

I first saw Joe Scuderi playing cricket during the Australian under-19 championships in Brisbane early in 1988. Joe had just turned nineteen but, being born in late December, was still eligible to play for his home State Queensland in the under-age competition.

Scuderi was one of many promising players taking part in this annual competition. It was the pathway to the Australian Youth Team, and in 1988 there was greater incentive for players to impress the selectors than ever before. The first Youth World Cup was to be staged in South Australia in March, and there was also the prospect of being offered a scholarship at the new Commonwealth Bank Cricket Academy, then being established.

Joe, who came from Ingham in sugar-cane country about 1500 kilometres north of Brisbane, had caught the eye of astute judges early in his cricket career, being selected in the Queensland under-19 team for the first time when he was still sixteen. For three successive years he played in the under-19 championships, a unique achievement for any young cricketer and an outstanding one for a teenager from a small country town in north Queensland.

Joe's father, Enrico, was born in Australia to a couple who migrated to Australia from Italy after the Second World War; his mother, Nelda, came to Australia from Italy when she was 12 years old. Enrico and Nelda married and lived on a cane farm in the Ingam area, raising two sons, Sam and Joe, whom they hoped would be able to continue working the farm. Sadly, Enrico died after a long illness in 1976 when Sam was 17 and Joe just eight.

It was hard going for the Scuderi family and eventually the property was sold in 1988. The sugar industry was depressed in those years and, with both of the Scuderi boys displaying exceptional talent at cricket, the sale made sense in that Sam and Joe would be able to play in Brisbane.

Queensland won the 1988 under-19 tournament and Joe was picked in the Australian team that won the 1988 Youth World Cup. Then he was chosen as one of the initial Commonwealth Bank Cricket Academy scholarship holders. To top off a big year, he was later selected to play for South Australia in their Sheffield Shield team. In less than twelve months the youngster from Ingham had gone from being a Queensland under-19 representative to playing first-class cricket for South Australia.

Joe's selection in the SA team came about as a result of the Sheffield Shield rules as they related to Academy scholarship-holders in those early days. These gave the home States first option on scholars' services, but allowed them to play for SA if they were not picked by their home State. Before the 1988/89 season began Joe made enquiries at the Queensland Cricket Association and discovered that he didn't feature in its immediate plans for the State side, so he made himself available to play for SA.

The Sheffield Shield rules also permitted a scholarship-holder to play for both his home State and South Australia in a given season, but once he had played three or more first-class matches for either his home State or South Australia, he had to finish the season with that State.

After Joe had played his second Sheffield Shield match for South Australia, he suddenly became the centre of attention back home. Queensland coach John Bell knew that if the young all-rounder was not picked for Queensland before he played another match for South Australia, he could not be called on for the rest of the season.

Queensland was scheduled to play two one-day matches against the touring Pakistan team, conveniently before South Australia's next Sheffield Shield match. While these didn't count as far as Sheffield Shield eligibility was concerned, Queensland's selectors wasted no time in naming Scuderi in their team for the Pakistan matches, giving them an opportunity to have a proper look at him.

While he was back in his home State, officials put pressure on the young man to make himself available to play for Queensland over the remainder of the season. Joe, who was disenchanted by the early lack of interest, told the QCA that he wanted to continue to play for South Australia, which had shown faith in him.

This triggered a tug-of-war between the two States for Scuderi's services, accompanied by a verbal joust in the media between Bell and SA coach Barry Richards. John Bell wasn't at all happy about Joe's decision and made some inflammatory remarks in a TV interview for Channel 7 in Brisbane about the way SACA had handled the matter. Barry and I went to the Channel 7 studios in Adelaide to see the Bell interview before responding to it. Both of us were unhappy about what he said and set the record straight during interviews we did for that the evening's news – Richards in particular going on the attack about what the Queensland coach had inferred.

In the end Scuderi chose South Australia which, by a quirk of fate, played their next match against Queensland at the Gabba, where Joe rubbed salt into the wound by collecting five Maroon wickets in an innings.

South Australia ended the season in second place on the Sheffield Shield ladder, which put them into the Sheffield Shield final against Western Australia at the WACA Ground. Joe played in the SA team in a match that saw WA win the Shield for the third successive season. By then Joe had become an established first-class cricketer with a promising future ahead of him, having taken 33 wickets and making 309 runs in nine matches in his debut season.

The Australian selectors were about to pick a 17-man squad for the 1989 tour of England, and there were reports that Joe would be included in the touring party. In the end he didn't make it, missing out on the last spot, according to some experts, to Greg Campbell.

Joe went back home to Ingham for a couple of months to contemplate his future. Despite his success with South Australia, the young all-rounder was still tied to Queensland residentially, so he had some serious thinking to do.

I had got to know Joe well during his first year in Adelaide. We had both come to live in Adelaide from Queensland early in 1988 and both of us had played cricket in Townsville – though Scuderi played 20 years after I did, and with a lot more success!

The indoor centre at Adelaide Oval is located behind the first floor of the SACA administration building, adjoining where my office was. The Academy players spent a lot of time in that centre, particularly during the winter, and some of them were frequent visitors to the SACA offices next door. By far the most regular of these was Joe Scuderi, who would materialise at my door just for a chat and occasionally seeking advice. I guess I became a surrogate father for a while to this likeable young man.

From our discussions I knew that he was keen to return to South Australia to continue his cricket career, but the interest in him back home had changed dramatically; now he was much in demand. But, although he was selected in an end-of-season match for Queensland against England county champions Worcestershire, he had decided already that his cricketing future would be better served by playing in South Australia.

So it was back to Adelaide again for Joe, even though he knew that he would have to go through the Sheffield Shield player transfer procedures, which involved obtaining the approval of a majority of the States. Eventually, after another tug-of-war over his services, the necessary approvals came through and the Australian Cricket Board approved the transfer. Scuderi was now a South Australian player with no strings attached.

In the 1989/90 season Joe continued to impress, scoring 434 runs and taking 27 wickets. These were good figures, but of some concern was the fact that his bowling average of 33 was higher than his batting average of 28, not the hallmark of a Test-quality all-rounder.

Hidden in those statistics was one incredible performance with the ball against Western Australia at the batsman-friendly Adelaide Oval. Scuderi took 6/6 from 5.3 overs in the WA first innings total of just 41, their lowest score ever and also the lowest total against South Australia in Sheffield Shield cricket.

There is a story behind that story. I know Tony Mann and Terry Jenner won't mind me telling it. Mann, a former Test leg spinner, was managing the WA team. 'Rocket', as he is known, was a great mate of Jenner, another Test leg spinner who hailed from Perth.

Terry was a guest of Her Majesty the Queen at Yatala Prison at the time, having pleaded guilty to three charges of embezzlement. Mann wanted to visit 'TJ', who was about to be paroled, to see how he was going, and had waited until Mike Veletta and Mark McPhee opened the batting for WA. Tony reckoned he wouldn't be away from the ground for very long, nor miss too much cricket.

When 'Rocket' returned to Adelaide Oval later in the afternoon he glanced up at the scoreboard and was pleased to see Veletta and McPhee still at the crease. Then he looked at the score and observed they had only put on a handful of runs. Either they were batting slowly indeed or there had been a rain delay, Tony thought to himself.

On closer scrutiny of the scoreboard Mann was shocked to see that this was Western Australia's *second* innings. He had missed the whole of the WA first innings in the time it took him to drive out to pay a short visit to Terry Jenner and then drive back to Adelaide Oval.

By season's end Joe Scuderi was looking to broaden his cricketing horizons and began to entertain the prospect of becoming a full-time professional cricketer. Previously he had resisted lucrative offers to play Lancashire League cricket, preferring to spend time at home in Ingham with his family and mates in between Australian seasons.

But selection in the Australian team began to look less likely after a merely handy year with South Australia in 1990/91. Once again he finished with a batting average lower than his bowling average and, after three full seasons of first-class cricket, he still hadn't made a century. This time he accepted an offer to play in the Lancashire League as the professional with Nelson Cricket Club and South Australia saw a far more mature Joe Scuderi in 1991/92. He was mentally tougher, technically more correct and, importantly, displayed concentration and consistency that had been missing from his game. He finally scored his maiden first-class century, 125 against the strong Western Australia attack.

In the next match Joe took a career best seven-wicket haul against New South Wales in their first innings. He followed this up with his second century and then took three more NSW wickets in the second innings, to make it ten for the match. The last South Australian player to make a century and take ten wickets in one match was the legendary George Giffen, nearly 100 years earlier.

Back in the frame for international honours, Joe was selected in the initial 20-man Australian squad for the World Cup to be held later in the season. Although his name was missing from the final 14 it looked as though the 23 year old was about to fulfil the great promise he had shown since emerging as a country schoolboy prodigy seven years earlier. By the end of the season he had scored over 500 runs from nine matches and taken

28 wickets – and his batting average was higher than his bowling average.

Although no one realised it at the time, unfortunately for Joe and the South Australian team he had reached his peak as a Sheffield Shield cricketer. Now that he was playing cricket year round, becoming the regular professional at Nelson in the northern summer, perhaps the continual grind of the game was taking its toll.

Whatever the reason, before long the name Scuderi could no longer be written down automatically when the State selectors sat down to choose their team. He managed only eight matches in 1992/93 and took just nine wickets – one less than he had taken in a single match the previous season. Next season he managed just three games. It looked as though he would be tossed on the cricketing scrap heap at the age of 25 after playing 51 first-class matches for his adopted State.

Then fate intervened. He was having a chat with Queensland player Geoff Foley, and one of the topics that cropped up was the difficulty of getting a work permit to play Lancashire League cricket each year. Foley suggested that Joe might be able to overcome this problem if he was eligible for an Italian passport.

The theory was that the holder of an Italian passport would, naturally, be a citizen of the European Union and as such could be employed in the United Kingdom, or any other EU country, without the need for a work permit.

Joe, who had no idea whether he could get an Italian passport, made enquiries and soon discovered that he had been entitled to one all his life as his mother was born in Italy and his father's parents were Italian citizens at the time Joe was born at Ingham on 24 December 1968.

Scuderi went on to have a sensational season for Nelson in 1994, his contribution being vital in the team's first Lancashire League championship since 1986, and Joe returned to Adelaide determined to win back a place in the South Australian team. The selectors didn't see it that way, however, and he played no first-class cricket at all in 1994/95, even though he was a regular member of SA's one-day combination that lost the final to Victoria at the MCG.

Disillusioned, Joe began to look elsewhere to secure his cricketing future. After discarding some offers from other States in Australia, he decided that, technically being an Italian citizen, he should make himself available to play for the Italian national team. Italy competes in the European championships and plays regular matches against nearby countries such as Holland and Denmark.

A relaxed young man, Joe finally got around to securing an Italian passport in 1995. From then on all he had to do on arrival in England from Australia to play in the Lancashire League was show his Italian passport at customs. He was free to come and go – and work – as he pleased.

In 1995/96 he was again frustrated in his attempts to regain a place in the Sheffield Shield team. This was particularly galling for Joe as South Australia captured the Shield for the first time in 14 years. He was, however, still a permanent fixture in the State's one-day team.

The three-way cricketing commitment Scuderi had with Nelson, Italy and South Australia continued for another year. He arrived back in Adelaide for the 1996/97 season and this time the selectors told the 28 year-old he was in their plans for the Sheffield Shield team. He repaid their confidence, topping the bowling averages, and scoring 352 runs at 30. He had now taken 154 first class wickets, lifting him into the top-20 all-time wicket takers for South Australia.

After six successful seasons with Nelson, Joe decided to take a spell from the Lancashire League and the year-round cricket treadmill. For the first time in eight years he was able to spend months at home in Ingham with his family, fishing with friends and enjoying the sub-tropical north Queensland winter.

His wiry body rested and enthusiasm for cricket rekindled, Joe embarked on pre-season training with the South Australian squad enthusiastically in 1997. But he missed selection in the SA team for its first three Sheffield Shield matches of the season and had to wait until the fourth, when Greg Blewett was absent on Test duties, before he was picked. He failed to take a wicket and batted at number nine for probably the only time in his career.

Two matches against Queensland late in the season took his appearances for the season to three. As he walked off the Adelaide Oval on 8 March 1998, he probably guessed that it would be his last appearance for South Australia nearly ten years after making his debut.

Joe now re-arranged his cricketing priorities, signing up with Colne in the Lancashire League for the 1998 season and committing himself to play for Italy. His contract with Colne allowed him to take time off when required to represent Italy, which he did during a short tour of Holland and in a couple of matches against other European countries at home.

Under the guidance of its energetic president, Simone Gambino, the Italian Cricket Federation had set its sights on competing in the World Cup in 2003. The mission was possible, but everything would have to go right during the qualifying tournaments over the next four years. Joe Scuderi was seen as a key factor.

Following discussions with his friend Gambino, Joe started to think seriously about playing county cricket in England. As an Australian citizen he could only do this as an overseas player. Under the rules of the competition, each county could have only one overseas player, which didn't leave much scope for Joe. Test players across the world line up for lucrative county contracts.

Joe enquired of the England and Wales Cricket Board (ECB) about his standing in county cricket as an Italian passport holder, only to be told that the rules were the same for European Union citizens as they were for Australian ones.

Not convinced that what the ECB had said was fair and just, he headed back to Adelaide for his eleventh season in South Australia. This time round, Joe's expectations were not high. He was captain of grade club East Torrens, which was delighted to have him back, but he was no longer a contracted State player.

He played a single one-day Mercantile Mutual Cup match early in the season and then was dropped again. It seemed certain that there would be no more South Australian representative cricket for Joe Scuderi. He decided that his cricketing days in Australia were over and he announced that he would not be coming back for the 1999/2000 season.

Scuderi's cricketing goals now became helping Italy qualify to play in the 2003 World Cup and securing eligibility to play county cricket. Back in England he again represented Colne in the Lancashire League, and was available for Italy when required.

Joe wrote to the ECB, pointing out that as a European Union citizen he didn't need a work permit to play in the Lancashire League and that he could live freely in England if he chose to do so. Weren't the ECB's rules on county cricket eligibility at odds with EU law?

The ECB responded that their rules stipulated he could not play county cricket for a number of reasons, one of them being that he was ineligible as he was not *born* in an EU country. Another was a rule that said that if a cricketer had played first-class cricket in another country, a seven-year residential qualification had to be fulfilled.

All this was like waving a red rag in front of a bull. Scuderi, by nature a laid-back individual, is also very determined when he puts his mind to pursuing a cause he believes in. Joe knew that he had the full entitlements of an EU citizen – and one of these was a right to free trade, his trade being that of a professional cricketer. As for the residential qualification, he likened it to saying that if he was an accountant and wanted to come from Italy to England to live and work, there would be a wait of seven years before he could take on an accountancy job.

The position adopted by the ECB was clearly out of line with the charter of the European Union and there was no doubt in Joe's mind that the ECB rules should be challenged on the basis of his fundamental rights. Simone Gambino supported his stance fully.

Anyone who knows Joe Scuderi would never have expected him to become a trail-blazing pioneer who would rock cricket's establishment, but that is exactly what he did when he took on the ECB.

To show that he was serious Joe, at his own expense, engaged a solicitor to act on his behalf, encouraged by the fact that just about everyone he spoke to felt that in court he would be likely to win. The solicitor said in a letter he sent to the ECB that the laws of freedom of movement within the EU permitted Joe to play county cricket, placing emphasis on the critical aspect of restraint of trade.

The argument about restraint of trade is not new to sport, having been used successfully a lot over the years – notably by Kerry Packer in the days of World Series Cricket, and more recently by Paul Nobes, the South Australian batsman, when he challenged the Australian Cricket Board's interstate player-transfer rules in the Supreme Court of Victoria to secure approval to play for Victoria in 1991. Joe explained it bluntly to me later on:

It was basically a polite letter, inferring that the ECB had better be very careful in handling the matter. The inference was there that my solicitor and I were prepared to take them to court without actually making that threat. I reckon that the ECB knew it was on shaky ground and was hoping we would just go away. The thing was that I knew my rights as far as the EU law was concerned.

There were many precedents in other sports for what Joe was attempting to achieve. In British soccer, in particular, players often move back and forth between England and other countries. After the dust had settled Joe told me: 'It was staggering to think that you could have the other major sports doing the right thing as far as the EU law goes and then cricket having their own set of rules. It obviously wasn't right.'

The matter never got to court. Late in 1999 the ECB dropped its opposition to Scuderi's application to be struck off the overseas quota as far as county cricket was concerned. He was now free to play with Lancashire, which signed him to a two-year contract. Joe was about to become the first dual-citizen Italian to play county cricket.

The ECB has since made a change in the eligibility regulations. Now, if a cricketer has played at the first-class level in another country during the preceding 12 months, he is ineligible to play in the county competition. Scuderi believes that even that restriction could be challenged in a court of law: 'At the end of the day, if you are an EU citizen then you are an EU citizen; whether you have played cricket in another country is irrelevant.'

Joe understands that the ECB is trying to stop first-class cricketers who have dual passports, for example Australian and British, playing 12 months of the year with a county in England and then in the Australian domestic competition. The current quota of one overseas player to a county is designed to allow a limited number of players to do that.

Apart from playing for Lancashire for the past two seasons Joe has been proud, as a European citizen, to represent Italy, the country of his ancestors, when the rule-makers at the International Cricket Council allow it – even if he is a fair-dinkum Aussie. He certainly has no intention of becoming a 12-month-a-year cricketing journeyman again.

The year 2001 started out to be a promising one for Scuderi but with Lancashire 'releasing' him, as they politely put it, and the International

Cricket Council ruling him ineligible to represent Italy in the ICC Trophy in Canada as it strived to make the 2003 World Cup, it ended in a disappointing way.

The ICC trophy is contested by the 24 countries who are Associate members of the International Cricket Council. With the two finalists and the winner of the play-off for third place earning automatic berths to the 2003 World Cup in South Africa, Joe was to be the big gun in Italy's 14-man squad. But at the last minute he was told that he couldn't play in the ICC Trophy in Toronto during June and July 2001. The eligibility rules for the trophy had been changed – now a player needed to have resided in a country for at least 240 days in each year of the *five* years leading up to the tournament in order to be allowed to represent that nation.

That rule change left Italy without four of its best players, causing Gambino and the Italian Cricket Federation to withdraw from the competition. This tough stance may be altered for the next ICC Trophy series in 2005, but only time will tell.

I spoke to Joe after he had been told by Lancashire that they were releasing him. He told me:

> It came as a complete surprise. I know that Bob Simpson had put in a strong recommendation to the committee that I be offered a new contract and that the captain, John Crawley, wanted me in the team, but for some reason the committee decided differently.

Joe Scuderi is disappointed, but philosophical. He is now free to look at other county cricket opportunities; maybe go back to Lancashire League cricket – where he would be snapped up by several clubs – or perhaps spend some more time promoting and helping develop the game in Italy, as he has been doing. He reckons that he has two or three good years left in him and is keen to make the most of them. Joe nearly made it to the World Cup with the Australian team in 1992. He had a chance of possibly playing in the World Cup for Italy in 2003 but now will probably have to wait until 2007 – if everything falls into place.

If Joe does get to play in the World Cup he will be 39. It would top off a remarkable career, one that started in Ingham, began to take off with his selection in the winning Australian Youth World Cup team in 1988, included ten years of first-class cricket with South Australia, eight years in the Lancashire League, international cricket for Italy and, against the odds, county cricket with Lancashire.

Nelda Scuderi is justifiably proud of her youngest son. His father, Enrico, is probably looking down from above nodding his approval. Joe never got around to running that sugar-cane farm with his brother Sam, but Enrico won't mind a bit as Joe Scuderi continues his remarkable cricketing odyssey.

18

SPORTING PEOPLE, PLACES AND PASSIONS

The Centenary Test: Melbourne Cricket Ground March 1977

Mention the 1977 Centenary Test in my home and it will spark off mixed reactions. Talk about David Hookes' blazing 56 in Australia's second innings and it is likely that the subject will be changed, very quickly. You see, David's little gem is like a bad dream to me. I was at the MCG when he took five fours in succession off Tony Greig but didn't get to see a ball of his now famous innings. Instead, I heard it from the car park!

My wife Peg and I intended to get to the ground in plenty of time to see the new South Australian batting sensation at the crease. Our departure from home, however, got slowed down and let me just leave it at that – but I was definitely ready first! On the way to the MCG we missed every light, traffic was heavy and vehicles were lined up at the car park in droves. But we were able to keep in touch with the action inside the ground courtesy of the ABC radio coverage. Hookes was batting well – let's just get there.

After what seemed an eternity we got into the car park where, to our horror, we were bluffly directed to the furthermost point of Jolimont Park, about a kilometre from the entrance gate. I turned the ignition off, locked the car and started striding briskly towards the ground with Peg already trailing behind. Immediately my anticipation was aroused by a roar from the stadium. It definitely wasn't an 'out' noise – the crowd was cheering. A few seconds later, there was an even louder roar followed shortly by a third, then a noisier fourth. By this stage I was just about running with the good lady racing to catch up.

Then came an eruption that I can compare only with the fantastic sound that echoes around the MCG when the mighty Blues burst onto the arena on grand final day. By this stage I was jiggling our tickets at the entrance gate, impatiently waiting for Peg. No problems, I thought, no 'out' noise, so Hookesy must still be at the crease.

As we made our way to our seats through the maze of stairs, there was a groan – now that *was* the reaction of the crowd to an Aussie batsman getting out. Sure enough, we reached our seats just in time to see Hookes trudging off to a standing ovation – out for 56, caught Fletcher bowled Underwood. Then emptiness and frustration took over – to think that I was actually there and still managed to miss one of the great little innings in a century of Test-match cricket.

Every time I see a replay of the young David Hookes flaying the England captain to all parts of the MCG, I get this sinking feeling. I can't possibly blame my dear wife for wanting to look her best for a day at the cricket – but that parking attendant sure has a hell of a lot to answer for.

Victoria Park, Melbourne: Saturday 6 July 1974

Robert Rose, son of Collingwood football legend Bob Rose, is slowly recovering from a horrific motor vehicle accident he was involved in five months ago that left him a quadriplegic. He is now well enough to report on sporting events for the Melbourne *Sunday Press.* Today he returns to Victoria Park, the home of the famous Magpies, for the first time since the crash.

With 26 VFL games behind him at Collingwood and Footscray, a regular place as a top-order batsman in the Victorian Sheffield Shield cricket team and talk of being close to Australian selection, young Rose clearly had a lot going for him before fate intervened. He was then just 22.

I was working part time as a freelance cricket and football writer on the *Sunday Press.* My assignment this day was to 'ghost' Robert in his coverage of the Collingwood v Fitzroy match and to do whatever I could to guide him through a day that was always going to be very tough for him.

Victoria Park lies in the heart of working-class, inner-suburban Melbourne. As you walk from your car, you pass rows of cottages, big and small factories and corner pubs, all of which look as though they have jumped from the pages of Frank Hardy's novel *Power Without Glory.*

Entering Victoria Park as an outsider you can feel the hostility. The Magpie faithful are there, all family together in their traditional black and white. I have always looked upon Collingwood's headquarters as the most intimidating football ground anywhere. The only one that runs close is Brisbane's Lang Park, known as the 'cauldron'.

This day is different at Victoria Park. I feel almost comfortable when I meet Robert as arranged. He is already settled into his wheelchair and we make our way up to the committee area on the second floor of the bustling Collingwood Social Club. Fortunately there is a lift to get us up from the ground floor – not that it would have been the first time I carried this smiling, courageous, young man from here to there.

A crowd of 18,000 watch the Magpies win by 31 points in a match they never look like losing. The faithful are buoyant as we head off to the Collingwood dressing rooms 100 metres away underneath the ageing members' reserve on the northern wing.

Wheel-chair access is not a high priority at Victoria Park. There are steps to be negotiated, tight corners to get around, spectators heading out of the ground to push against and well-wishers to greet. It hits home to me: Robert can't sign autographs any more.

We eventually get inside the holy of holies. To a man – from the president of the club to the superstars like Peter McKenna, Len Thompson and Wayne Richardson, through to the doorkeeper who calls the shots about who gets inside – the Magpies give Robert a welcome which brings tears to his eyes.

After magical moments we must take our leave as there is a newspaper deadline to meet. Throughout the afternoon Robert and I have been comparing notes. Apart from the usual match report, he has been asked to put together a short piece summing up his thoughts on his 'homecoming'. This is what Robert has to say in the next day's *Sunday Press*:

> My visit to Victoria Park yesterday was a day I will never forget. It was simply great to be back in football in some capacity.
>
> I was overwhelmed by the kindness of the supporters, players and officials who made me feel so welcome back at my old home ground.

I was worried about going into the Collingwood rooms after the game as I wasn't sure how I would react to being exposed to the unique atmosphere there.

As it turned out, there was no reason to be concerned. The boys made me feel as though I was still a part of Collingwood.

I must confess to a king-sized lump in my throat when Collingwood president, Mr Tom Sherrin, introduced me after the game.

The spontaneous, genuine cheers they gave me touched me deeply. That was a moment I will never forget.

Yes it is great to be back. Thanks everyone for what you did for me yesterday. It made me feel fabulous.

That day was very important to Robert in many ways. He had shown great courage, which is very much a Rose family trait, to come this far in his fierce desire to lead a life that was as normal as possible under the circumstances he found himself in.

For the next 25 years that determination didn't leave him.

Wednesday 12 May 1999. Robert Rose dies in the Austin Hospital, Melbourne, at the age of 47. His funeral service is held on Friday 14 May 1999 after which his family and friends gather, appropriately, at Victoria Park, on the second floor of the Collingwood Football Club. They remember, and salute, a young man who dealt with adversity in such a way that he gave inspiration to those around him.

Saturday 15 May 1999. Collingwood wins against Fremantle, breaking an all-time record losing streak of 13 matches, which had lasted 301 days.

Saturday 28 August 1999. Collingwood are beaten by the Brisbane Lions in their last-ever match at Victoria Park. The Lions are coached by Leigh Matthews, who steered Collingwood to their last premiership, in 1990, the only pennant the Magpies have won in 46 years.

Chris Chataway Comes to Dinner at the MCG

Melbourne Cricket Ground: 10 June 1986

I have attended hundreds of functions at the Melbourne Cricket Ground, but this one is special. The occasion is a dinner given by my employers, Capel Court Investment Bank, for Christopher Chataway, vice-chairman of London based Orion Royal Bank Limited.

Chataway is better known for the role he played, along with Chris Brasher, in the world's first sub-four-minute-mile run by Roger Bannister at Oxford in May 1954, and for setting a new world record for 5000 metres while defeating the great Russian, Vladimir Kuts, at London's White City stadium a few months later.

It is thirty years since Chris has been to the MCG, the previous occasion being when he represented Great Britain in the 5000 metres at the 1956 Melbourne Olympic Games. Kuts won the gold medal while Chataway, battling stomach cramps during the race, finished out of a place.

The dinner is the idea of Brian Watson, a director of Capel Court Investment Bank and a member of the Melbourne Cricket Club committee, with some help from me, a general manager of Capel Court, which has headquarters in Melbourne. Chris's employer, Orion Royal Bank, is a member of the Royal Bank of Canada group, while Capel Court is a member of the National Mutual group. The Royal Bank of Canada and National Mutual are the two shareholders in a new bank in Australia, National Mutual Royal Bank Limited, which also employs both of us.

Brian Watson, known to all as 'Watto', is a dear friend of mine and a long-time merchant banking colleague. We have each had a long and continual involvement with cricket. Sadly, 'Watto' has been diagnosed with a malignant brain tumour that has necessitated operations. These have affected his speech, but have not diminished his boundless enthusiasm.

The Rt Hon. Christopher Chataway PC, honours graduate from Oxford University in Politics, Philosophy and Economics, formerly a Conservative Party member of parliament and British Government cabinet minister, chairman of British Telecommunications Systems, champion athlete and now highly successful international banker, is in Australia to address a conference in Sydney on company takeovers.

Chris is to spend three days in Melbourne meeting with as many leaders of industry and commerce as we can arrange. In the main these discussions are to be held during visits to companies or at boardroom luncheons. All of this looks very stiff to 'Watto', who decides to turn what is listed on Chataway's itinerary as 'Dinner with Capel Court Executives' into a night to remember.

We have put our heads together and come up with a list of prominent sporting identities who are also successful in business, and decide to invite them to the dinner. The venue, appropriately, is the Cuthbert Room at the Melbourne Cricket Ground, named in honour of the Australian runner Betty Cuthbert, who won three gold medals at the 1956 Olympic Games.

Chris Chataway knows nothing of these arrangements, other than that I will pick him up at his hotel and take him to the MCG for a low-key dinner where he can meet senior Melbourne-based Capel Court personnel. I can imagine the thoughts running through his mind at the prospect – surely he'd prefer a rare free night of relaxation.

When we arrive at the Cuthbert Room, high up in the Olympic Stand overlooking a floodlit, hauntingly beautiful Melbourne Cricket Ground, Chris gets a wonderful surprise. Rising in a spontaneous welcome are some sporting – and business – legends.

Among them are Herb Elliott, the greatest mile and 1500 metres runner the world has known, general manager of Puma Australia; Peter Bartels, Olympic cyclist, managing director of Carlton & United Breweries Limited; Derek Clayton, world marathon record holder; Merv Lincoln, one of the first mile runners in Australia to break the four minute barrier, former head of the Melbourne University MBA course; Tony Ryan, Australian Davis Cup tennis selector, commercial sales manager of Pacific Dunlop Limited; Dr Don Cordner, Brownlow medallist and former captain of the Melbourne Football Club, president of the Melbourne Cricket Club; Ron Evans, champion Essendon full forward who kicked over 100 goals in a VFL season, director of administration, Spotless Limited; Colin McDonald, former Australian opening batsman who played in 47 Tests, executive director of the Lawn Tennis Association of Australia; Dr John Lill, former South Australian top order batsman, secretary of the Melbourne

Cricket Club; John Hasker, former champion athlete, managing director of F.H. Faulding and Company Limited.

The dinner is an enormous success. The guest of honour is delighted and stories are told well into the night. Just when it seems the surprises for the night are over, 'Watto' announces that he has been able to locate an old film of the 1956 Olympic Games 5000-metre race. We watch it on monitors in the room and on the MCG's giant screen.

Considering the end result, I don't think that this, of all the races he had run in, is the one Chris would most like to watch. Quite possibly he has never seen it before. But his words as he takes us through the tortuous 5000 metres thirty years earlier are genuine and moving.

All too soon this magical evening comes to an end. It is time to prepare for another round of meetings the next day, which will include a reunion, after 20 years, between Chris and the legendary Austrian coach Franz Stampfl, who was the mentor of Bannister, Brasher and Chataway in the mid 1950s.

26 June 1986

A letter arrives at Capel Court for Brian Watson and me from Chris Chataway, now back at Orion Royal Bank headquarters:

> Having now recovered from the surprise of the dinner at the Melbourne Cricket Club, I am writing to thank you for such a delightful evening.
>
> As you gather the 1956 Olympics and its venue had been firmly pushed to the back of my mind. After a two-year spell of unbroken wins at 5000 metres I had gone there hoping that I might finish my athletic career with a gold medal. To fail so badly was a great disappointment and I went on to other things without trying too hard to remember the occasion. Last week's dinner at length made it all worthwhile! To see the ground and stadium in such magnificent condition and suddenly to be confronted with old friends after such a long time was a real joy.

20 February 1987

Brian Watson dies today, aged 52. The brain tumour he has battled so long cannot be denied. Those of us who have been witness to Brian's continuing passion for life in the face of the certain knowledge that his own was about to be cut short can only draw inspiration from his example.

Christopher Chataway, who knows a lot about guts and determination, will be saluting 'Watto' today.

The Loneliness of a Long Distance Carlton Supporter

Adelaide, Saturday 25 September 1999

9 am: This is the last day of one of the longest weeks of my life. It is that day in September, my beloved Carlton are playing in the AFL grand final against the Kangaroos at the MCG, and here I am sitting at the computer in my office at home in Adelaide. Something has to be wrong – after all I have been at every grand final Carlton has played in since the Second World War, starting with the 1945 'Blood Bath' against South Melbourne at Princes Park.

An eerie feeling this. No huge hangover from the famous Vingt Cinq Club lunch the day before, although I do confess to feeling fuzzy in the head after going in search of some grand-final atmosphere yesterday with a couple of mates. Sadly we failed – there is simply no grand final feeling in the air in Adelaide, not this year, as the city laments that the Crows are not in the big one following their great wins in 1997 and 1998. We did find a good pub though and took solace from a few beers, a big steak and a top red.

I have only myself to blame for my predicament. Late last Saturday afternoon, in the euphoria that prevailed in the Gibbs' household after Carlton's one-point win against Essendon in the preliminary final, nothing was going to stop me being at the MCG today to watch the mighty Blues.

Come Sunday morning in the cold light of day it gradually entered my head that my unbroken 50-plus year run of Carlton grand finals might be coming to an end. I have been retired for more than two years now and have a significantly reduced disposable income. With this in mind I checked how many frequent flier points I had left. There were enough to get to Melbourne and back but the bad news was I had to allow 14 days for processing of the tickets and the grand final was only six days away. I rang the airline and was told I could get a return ticket to Melbourne but it would cost me over five hundred dollars. Not too bad, I thought, if I really want to be there.

Next problem. Where do I stay? I would just *have* to be at the Vingt Cinq Club lunch the day before, having been a proud member of that club for over 30 years now. I lived in Melbourne for the greater part of my life and know plenty of people who could give me a bed to doss down on. Or do I, after an absence of nearly 12 years?

I start ringing around only to find out what I should have known anyway. Most people have their own family and football commitments at grand-final time and taking in an unexpected house guest, particularly at short notice, really doesn't fit the plan.

No matter, I have almost always stayed at a hotel in the city when I have come from interstate to see the Blues in action, so why should I do it any differently now? But getting accommodation in Melbourne at this time of the year isn't exactly an easy assignment. Before retirement I had access to people in the right places who could create a hotel vacancy with a phone call, and at the right price too. Sadly I can't do that these days, so I start ringing hotels direct and soon find out – surprise, surprise – that Melbourne is 'sold out' and has been for months. There may be the chance of a room in the event of a cancellation, but I am looking at between $250 and $400 a night.

The penny finally starts to drop. I am trying to live in the past. This little trip will cost me well over a grand even before I begin the usual grand-final feasting and drinking. I can't justify it in my own mind so, for once, I make the big sacrifice and decide to stay put in Adelaide and watch the game on television.

To console myself I remember how lucky I have been to watch Carlton win the most VFL/AFL premierships of any club since the war. Had my Dad not got back from the war in time for the 1945 flag there is no way that, as a 12-year-old boarding-school pupil in suburban Melbourne, I could have been among the 62,000 people who crammed into Princes Park that day.

Back at the MCG in 1947, provided you got to the ground early enough you could buy a standing-room-only ticket – thank goodness I was a tall lad. The same applied in 1949 except that this time Carlton lost. Still, I saw a football genius in Essendon's John Coleman kick his 100th goal for the season.

That was the start of a long Carlton premiership drought. It lasted until 1968 when my employers had the foresight to transfer me from Townsville back to Melbourne only months before the Blues pipped Essendon by three points. For the next 15 years Carlton were *the* team in the competition, playing in a further seven grand finals and winning another five flags, all of which I was able to watch from the comfort of the MCG press box as one of the *Sporting Globe* team.

After three years of making up the numbers in the final five from 1983 to 1985, the Blues reached the grand final in 1986 but were not good enough to beat Hawthorn.

By 1987 I had been transferred in my job to Brisbane. Fortunately getting to the grand final posed no difficulty thanks to some kind assistance from the Australian Cricket Board, which was happy to help out its honorary Code of Behaviour Commissioner at a time of need. Not only did I see Carlton turn the tables and beat Hawthorn in a classic encounter, as a bonus I was able to sit in the Victorian Cricket Association enclosure with the Australian cricket team that was leaving the next day for the World Cup campaign in India and Pakistan.

After six more years the Blues again contested a grand final in 1993, this time against the old foe Essendon. By now we were living in Adelaide, where I was chief executive of the South Australian Cricket Association. New South Wales Rugby League matches were being staged once a year at Adelaide Oval, with St George opting to forego one of their home matches and move it to Adelaide to assist the NSWRL push towards a national competition.

I had been invited to Sydney as a guest to watch the rugby league grand final at the Sydney Football Stadium on the day after the AFL grand final. The timing was right, so I stopped off in Melbourne and watched Essendon win a one-sided match that turned out to be the Michael Long show. I enjoyed the hospitality of the Melbourne Cricket Club, but not the contest.

Then it was straight to the airport and on to Sydney to see St George tackle the Brisbane Broncos. I had played cricket with St George many years before and, as they were Adelaide Oval's adopted rugby league team, I was supporting the Saints. But they too got belted, so it was a pretty ordinary weekend.

Two years later in 1995, Carlton was clearly the best team in the competition, finishing the regular season on top of the ladder after stringing together 14 successive wins. I simply had to be there and gladly booked my flights and accommodation, watching the Blues thrash Geelong to win a record 16th premiership.

A combination of being in the right place at the right time and a dash of good fortune had resulted in my attendance at 50 years of Carlton grand finals. Now all that was about to come to an end.

As the weekend drew nearer and the media build-up grew, I suffered grand-final withdrawal symptoms. It was strange not being able to experience that wonderful atmosphere in Melbourne before the grand final, especially when your team is playing in it. Peg suffered my twitchiness in silence, as she knew better than anyone how badly I wanted to be at the MCG.

Now the big day is here I am fairly philosophical. The Kangaroos are red-hot favourites. Only Robert Walls reckons Carlton can win – but he would, having played in and coached Carlton premiership teams.

There are absolutely no good vibes in the air about the game. This morning's newspaper even has a front-page picture of tennis players. Adelaide's paper seems to regard yesterday's start of the Davis Cup semi-final with Russia – which, of all places, is being played on a Rugby League ground in Brisbane – as bigger news than the AFL grand final. Sacrilege!

11 am: It dawns on Peg and me that today, for the first time in over 46 years of marriage, we are actually going to sit down and watch our first Carlton grand final *together* on TV. That's a good reason to make it a special occasion, so I head down to Samtass Seafood for a supply of cooked prawns, grab a couple of bottles of cold bubbly from Fred Hamood's bottle shop on the way back and we have a party for two before the game gets under way.

2 pm: The pre-match entertainment is in full swing and as the cameras pan around the MCG and peek into the Carlton dressing rooms I have a lump in my throat. I wish I was there. But too late now and besides, when you have been married as long as we have and can still get excited about doing something new together, *and* actually get genuinely excited about doing it, what does being at a footy match really matter?

5 pm: The game is over, Kangaroos too good, no excuses. I have had a top day despite the loss and am nowhere near as light in the pocket as I would have been if I'd flitted off to Melbourne. I know now that being at a Carlton grand final isn't a matter of life and death after all. But I also know that the 800 kilometres between Adelaide and Melbourne can be a long, long way!

7 pm: It has just hit me. I have *still* seen all of Carlton's *winning* grand finals since 1945. Carn the Blues!

Wasim Akram Runs Hot in the Desert

Alice Springs: 6 December 1992

I have come up to Alice Springs from Adelaide to act as referee for a one-day cricket match between Pakistan and a Northern Territory Invitation Xl at Traeger Park. Pakistan is in Australia to take part in the three-nation World Series Cup competition along with Australia and the West Indies.

Pakistan's opening WSC match was against the West Indies in Perth two days earlier and their next is against Australia in Hobart on 10 December. They have dropped in at Alice Springs to get some match practice and promote cricket in the Red Centre.

The Northern Territory Xl is made up of a number of first-class cricketers from the Sheffield Shield States and a few players from 'The Alice' and Darwin, where there are flourishing cricket competitions. One of the interstate players is New South Wales fast bowler Wayne Holdsworth.

Pakistan, captained by great all-rounder Wasim Akram, bats first and they make 273 from 50 overs Wasim smashes a quick 50. Like most of the NT Invitation Xl bowlers, 'Cracker' Holdsworth gets some rough treatment from the batsmen.

Holdsworth isn't happy about being carted around Traeger Park late in his 10 over spell; the faster he gets the harder they hit him. The 'chat' in the middle makes me sit up and take notice. This is supposed to be a friendly match, but if there is any untoward incident, I'll have to put on my referees hat and deal with it.

With Wasim Akram on strike, Holdsworth, a genuinely quick bowler, fires a bouncer past the Pakistan captain's nose. Umpire Daryl Harper immediately calls 'no ball'. One run to the Pakistan total and the bowler has to expend more energy in the stifling heat. From the gesturing going on in the middle, there is never any doubt that Akram will return the favour if 'Cracker' later comes to the crease.

Wayne does get his chance to bat and, sure enough, the Pakistan captain brings himself on to bowl – and marks out his long run.

Wasim Akram has this uncanny ability to bowl very fast off a short run. When he goes back to the long run he looks absolutely terrifying, particularly if, like Holdsworth, you are not a recognised batsman. The left-handed Wasim is able to dip the ball in to a right handed batsman more sharply than any bowler I have ever seen.

The first ball is a roaring bouncer that has 'Cracker' ducking from the moment it leaves Akram's hand. The resultant no-ball call doesn't prevent another short-pitched delivery straight away, this one aimed at the throat. Fortunately for Wayne it misses him by a centimetre.

Wasim grabs the ball, wheels around from the short run and lets go the perfect in-swinging yorker. It hits the base of off stump before Holdsworth can lift his bat. Wayne looks happy to head off to the safety of the dressing room.

By this time the Invitation XI is eight wickets down and 100 runs behind. Next batsman is South Australian opening bowler Damian Reeves. First ball is another lethal in-swinging yorker. Reeves doesn't see it before it crashes into off stump. Last batsman in is Darwin-based Greg Connors. He takes guard, looks around the field nervously and another unplayable in-swinging yorker cannons into that battered off stump. Game over. Akram has taken the most astonishing 'hat trick' I have ever seen, hitting the same stump, in the same spot, with three successive balls, all delivered with blinding speed off the short run.

19

THE CHANGING FACE OF CRICKET ADMINISTRATION

Cricket administration today is vastly different from 40 years ago when I first became involved full-time. This has been brought about mainly by the need to keep pace with the evolution of the sport at the elite playing level as it moved to increasing professionalism. It has also been necessary to make up for the years when administrators were not as progressive as they are now, running the game more-or-less in the past without paying too much attention to the future.

Administration of first-class cricket in Australia in the early 1960s was, I suspect, little different from the 1920s. When I took on the job as secretary of the Queensland Cricket Association in 1961, it was still emerging from a period of domination by two strong-minded individuals, Jack Hutcheon and Roger Hartigan. They had ruled the game, and the Gabba, with an iron fist for decades. Until not long before my appointment the secretary was not full-time and his role was essentially to keep the minutes and carry out the specific instructions of the committee. To illustrate how much things have changed, when I started work at the QCA the full-time staff was two and total revenue for the year was $80,000. By 2001 the staff at the QCA had grown to 37 and annual revenue escalated to $10 million.

In 1961 the Australian Board of Control for International Cricket, as it was known then, did what its name implied – controlled international cricket in this country. The Sheffield Shield competition and matches involving non-Sheffield Shield States were the responsibility of the Interstate Conference that met at the same time as the Board of Control.

The secretary of the Board of Control and the Interstate Conference was also the secretary of one of the three 'founder' State Cricket Associations – New South Wales, Victoria and South Australia. Those three States, which first played for the Sheffield Shield when the competition commenced in 1892, had three delegates each to the Board, Queensland had two, and Western Australia and Tasmania one each. Alan Barnes from New South Wales was the Board secretary in 1961, having just taken over from Jack Ledward, the Victorian Cricket Association secretary. Bill Jeanes, the long-serving South Australian Cricket Association secretary, carried out the role as ACB secretary for 27 years.

The Interstate Conference has long since disappeared, with the Australian Cricket Board now overseeing both interstate and international cricket. The representation from the States to the ACB hasn't changed much at all with NSW, Victoria and SA still having three directors on the Board and Queensland two. Western Australia now has two directors, while Tasmania remains at one. This leaves a lot of power with the 'big three' who, if they vote in block, have the numbers required to carry a vote around the table.

Interestingly, the distribution of the Board's surplus income each year until around 1990 was based on the number of directors each State had. The cake was carved up so that New South Wales, Victoria and South Australia each received three-fourteenths of the pool, Queensland and Western Australia two and Tasmania one.

The inequity of this method was eventually acknowledged, and changed in 1990, so that each State on the mainland was allocated one-sixth of the surplus with Tasmania receiving half of that amount. The balance was retained by the ACB to go towards its administrative costs. A further refinement to this formula occurred in 1998 when Tasmania was granted the same financial status as the other States.

This meant that all States were equal financial stakeholders, but the representation around the Board table remains the same as it was when Western Australia gained a second director in 1973.

To illustrate where the power base lies within the ACB, the chairman of the Board came from New South Wales, Victoria or South Australia for 70 years until Tasmania's Denis Rogers was appointed to the position in 1995. Rogers remained chairman for six years until 2001, necessitating a change in the Board's constitution in 1998 to remove the previous limit of a maximum three consecutive years in that post.

Victoria's Bob Merriman became ACB chairman in September 2001. From a personal perspective I will find it interesting to observe what happens in the future, particularly as to whether the 'founder' States try to get back to the unofficial rotation of the chairmanship that existed before Denis Rogers' appointment.

While the composition of the Australian Cricket Board at director (or delegate) level has changed little during the last 40 years, the Board's administrative staff has grown enormously. From operating with a part-time secretary, the Board now has 50 full-time employees. That growth started following the appointment of David Richards in 1980 to the position as the Board's first full-time chief executive, based in Melbourne. This, significantly, was soon after the upheaval of Kerry Packer's World Series Cricket.

Richards held the post until 1993 when he was appointed as the first chief executive of the International Cricket Council, whose offices are situated at Lord's ground in London. Graham Halbish, the ACB's general manager, took over from Richards as ACB chief executive before leaving in 1997. That brought Malcolm Speed to the job before he also headed off to London in 2001 to replace David Richards as CEO of the International Cricket Council. James Sutherland succeeded Speed at the ACB in 2001. Sutherland now oversees an operation that had revenue of $60 million in the last financial year, of which $42 million came from media rights and sponsorship.

Since 1980 there has been a significant shift in the day-to-day control of the way the Board operates. Where previously there were sub-committees of ACB directors who administered various aspects of the game, such as marketing, coaching, development, player contracts, future tours, cricket operations, programming and tour playing and financial conditions, these are now essentially management functions performed by the permanent staff, with the Board determining policy. In other words the Board is being run as a business.

This is further reflected by the fact that the full Board now meets monthly, whereas it used to convene only three or four times a year, relying on an executive committee comprising of a representative from each State with delegated power to act between meetings of the Board.

Over the years there has been discussion among ACB directors about the possibility of having equal representation from States on the Board. This would have resulted in each of the 'founding' States reducing its directors from three to two; Queensland and Western Australia remaining at two and Tasmania increasing by one. The fact that this equalisation hasn't happened is probably an indication that New South Wales, Victoria and South Australia, or some of those States, were not keen on losing a place around the Board table after all these years. Financial equality is obviously fine, but giving up a seat of power – that is a different matter.

At the State administration level there have been similar changes in recent years. For instance the South Australian Cricket Association operated with a committee and sub-committee system for the best part of a century until it introduced a completely new constitution in 1996. This gave the day-to-day operational responsibility to the chief executive and his staff, reporting to a Board of Management that determines policy matters.

On the topic of administration of cricket at the State level, I doubt that it is generally understood how much the responsibilities differ between States. The South Australian Cricket Association is unique in that, apart from administering and developing cricket in the State, it also runs the Adelaide Oval, which it leases from the Adelaide City Council. As a consequence SACA is a major sporting venue operator with an obligation to meet the cost of all capital improvements at the oval, including large projects such as the Sir Donald Bradman stand and the lights. In addition it operates its own large in-house function and catering division.

SACA controls all activities at Adelaide Oval, including the staging of Test and one-day international matches on behalf of the Australian Cricket Board. It currently generates revenue of over $14 million a year.

Western Australia has a similar structure to South Australia, with the exception that the WACA Ground is on freehold land but its catering operation is outsourced, not managed internally.

The Victorian, New South Wales and Queensland Cricket Association's hire the Melbourne Cricket Ground, Sydney Cricket Ground and Brisbane Cricket Ground (or Gabba), from the respective Government trusts that control them. This leaves those States free to concentrate on the administration, development and coaching aspects of cricket. They do stage Tests and one-day internationals for the ACB, but do not have the responsibility of actually managing major sporting complexes.

The QCA has recently developed its own ground, Allan Border Field, that has hosted first-class matches but the Gabba remains the home of Test and one-day international fixtures in Brisbane.

Tasmania is largely in control of its own destiny, playing its international matches at Bellerive Oval in Hobart, which it leases from the local Council. In that respect, it functions in a similar manner to South Australia, but on a smaller scale.

Cricket in this country has responded well to all this change. That much is evidenced by the dominant position the Australian teams currently enjoy in world cricket – that didn't just happen – it is the result of a lot of hard work and planning, on and off the field.

20

A TRILOGY OF CLASSIC MATCHES

Any sport in which a contest can continue for five days without a result, but retains the capacity to enthrall you right down to the last ball, has to be unique. Cricket can be a nail-biting struggle between two fierce combatants, ultimately being decided by a solitary run when a thousand or more have already been scored. Or the grand old game can be a test of character, endurance and courage against the odds, making it possible for heroes to emerge and the seemingly impossible to be achieved.

Thanks to my job, in the space of just four years I was able to see close-up three first-class matches that encompassed at some stage all the qualities I have mentioned. To make my joy even greater, each was played at the most delightful cricket ground in the world, Adelaide Oval.

One of those matches was a win, another a loss and the third a draw. These are my recollections of those three classic matches.

Only 506 Runs to Go!

In February 1992 a confident and talented Queensland side took the field against South Australia at full strength. The Maroons' line-up included current international players Allan Border, Ian Healy, Craig McDermott and Peter Taylor alongside past and future Test players Carl Rackemann, Dirk Wellham, Matthew Hayden and Stuart Law.

South Australia, which featured internationals Jamie Siddons, Andrew Hilditch, Tim May, David Hookes, Peter Sleep and Greg Blewett, also had a fair team, but there was not a current Test player among them. Man for man, the Queenslanders appeared far stronger. South Australia was in last place on the Sheffield Shield table while Queensland was ready to grab top spot if it won.

Ex-Victorian Jamie Siddons, who was in his first season as captain of South Australia, won the toss and surprised his counterpart Carl Rackemann by inviting the visitors to bat on a pitch that looked a bit greener than usual. Jamie knew how dangerous Rackemann and McDermott could be with the new ball on a track with some grass on it, particularly in the first session.

At the end of the first day honours were even with Queensland on 9/313 after recovering from 4/92. They took this up to 334 next day, thanks to an unlikely 52-run last-wicket partnership between Greg Rowell and Rackemann during which the latter scored his first runs of the season after six consecutive ducks.

On a second-day Adelaide pitch you would normally think that 335 was a 'gettable' total to take the first innings points. Wrong! South Australia was bundled out for 130 in less than three hours. Craig McDermott did the damage, taking 6/58 with superb fast bowling.

Now it was decision time for big Carl, a veteran cricketer but a rookie captain. Should he enforce the follow on, or have a couple of sessions at the crease to set the home team a big target to chase on the last day?

His decision was to bat again and set SA a target, which put Rackemann at odds with his coach, fast bowling legend Jeff Thomson. Thommo later said publicly that he was 'shocked' by the decision. On the other hand Jamie Siddons and his fellow South Australian batsmen were happy not to face the music again straight away.

Matthew Hayden and Trevor Barsby got Queensland off to a good start, putting on 143 in smart time for the first wicket. Their lead was stretched to 505 just after lunch on day three when Rackemann declared the innings closed at 4/301.

For South Australia to win they would have to create history by scoring a massive 506 runs. No team had ever successfully chased a fourth innings total of over 500 in a first-class match in Australia. The nearest was New South Wales' total of 446 against South Australia at Adelaide Oval in 1926/27. In fact there had only been one bigger winning target achieved in first class cricket anywhere in the world. Cambridge University scored 7/507 against the Marylebone Cricket Club at Lord's in 1896.

With a Test-class pace attack at its disposal, 500 runs up their sleeve and nearly five sessions left to play, Queensland rightly fancied its chances.

The Maroons had plenty of incentive, including the prospect of playing in a home final and, perhaps, winning the Sheffield Shield for the first time after more than 60 years.

On the other hand, Jamie Siddons had said to me he felt that the pitch was getting better for batting as the game progressed. He believed, quietly, that a draw was possible if his team batted sensibly. With this in mind it was a fair bet that there would be no easy wickets for the Queensland bowlers.

The real wild card was a simple arithmetic calculation that showed South Australia needed to score at less than four runs an over to win the match. But surely no one thought that a win to the home team was possible when Andrew Hilditch and Greg Blewett went out to open the batting just after lunch on day three.

At the tea break the two openers were still together with the run-rate ticking along. So far so good, but there were still four sessions remaining. At stumps veteran Hilditch and young star Blewett were unconquered, having put on an opening stand of 204 runs.

Now the target had been reduced to 302 with all ten wickets intact and a minimum of 96 overs to be bowled on the last day. In one-day cricket parlance the equation was 3.16 runs per over, or about one every two balls. Indeed the game had now taken on the cast of an elongated one-day contest and that is precisely the way the South Australians approached it.

They had milestones to reach, the first having been achieved by not losing a wicket before stumps on day three. From now on it was either side's game though it swung Queensland's way when Blewett was out early next day for 98.

James Brayshaw joined Hilditch. The pair consolidated and moved the score to 1/281 at lunch. SA had wickets in hand and were well over half way towards achieving their target with 65 overs remaining and a required run rate of 3.4 an over.

After lunch South Australia lost 4/40 in an hour as Brayshaw, Hilditch, David Hookes and Joe Scuderi departed, the last three wickets adding just nine runs. At 5/316 nearing the half way mark of the day, it looked as though Queensland had the game in their keeping.

By the tea break Siddons and the laconic Peter Sleep had steadied the ship. At 5/354 the required run rate had moved out to four an over – but was still achievable while the aggressive Jamie Siddons was at the crease.

Siddons and Sleep went on the attack, posting a partnership of 152 in 157 minutes before the captain was bowled by Rackemann for a brilliant 87. South Australia were now just 38 runs behind with eight overs remaining, and victory was well within reach.

Tim Nielsen, a good man in a crisis, joined Sleep. By now the crowd had swelled to 5000 from a few hundred and the spectators began counting down the runs. 35 off seven overs, 28 off six, 22 off five, 16 off four, 12 off three, nine off two and then, after eight runs came from the penultimate over, just one run was needed off the last over with four wickets in hand. Up in the match office where I was nervously watching, you could feel the tension ease around the ground.

Peter Sleep, who had scored 96 of the finest runs he had made in a long, illustrious career for SA, had strike. Carl Rackemann, trying his heart out as usual for his beloved Queensland, bowled the final over of the match, his 33rd of the innings.

Sleep played the first three deliveries without ever looking like scoring; it was almost as though he was brushing up on his defensive technique. There he was, needing a single to give his team an incredible win and just a boundary away from a century, looking as though he didn't have a care in the world. At the non-striker's end Tim Nielsen, the fastest man between wickets in the team by far, was edgy.

The fourth ball of big Carl's over was a short one that 'Sounda' somehow got an edge on, deflecting it behind square leg. While Ian Healy desperately ran from behind the stumps to do the fielding, Nielsen scampered off like a hare and Sleep instinctively responded to his call. They made it home for the single and clinched a famous victory to South Australia. The scoreboard clock showed that it was 6.16 pm.

I will never forget the sight of 'Sounda' Sleep, arms raised above his head, a cheeky grin from ear to ear, standing in the middle of Adelaide Oval and looking up triumphantly towards his ecstatic team mates in the dressing room after he had scrambled that winning run.

It was the stuff that dreams are made of.

One Lousy Run

The gripping Test match between Australia and the West Indies played at Adelaide Oval in January 1993 has become a part of cricketing folklore.

When the captains, Allan Border and Richie Richardson, went out to toss before the start of the 51st Test played at Adelaide Oval, Australia was on the threshold of regaining the Frank Worrell Trophy after 15 years. One up after winning the Melbourne Test and drawing the matches in Brisbane and Sydney, a win in Adelaide would give the Aussies the trophy, but a loss would see the series all square and the fifth Test on the bouncy Perth track in a week's time would be the decider.

The drama began the day before the match when young Western Australian batsman Damien Martyn suffered a freak injury to his left eye in the last minute of Australia's rigorous fielding drill. At the precise moment that coach Bob Simpson raised his arms to call a halt to the session Martyn, who was backing up a throw from Tim May, ran into Simpson's thumb, cutting the surface of the eye. He was rushed to hospital and ruled out of the Test match.

The Australian selectors hurriedly called up another young Western Australian, left-handed batsman Justin Langer, as Martyn's replacement. Justin had about an hour to catch a plane from Perth to Adelaide, where he would be making his Test debut and taking on the awesome West Indies pace attack of Curtly Ambrose, Courtney Walsh, Ian Bishop and Ken Benjamin.

Langer was in good form and raring to go. He had earned a reputation as a tough little competitor. If Justin had any concerns they were for his good friend Martyn, who had played in the first three Tests of the series only to lose his hard-earned spot in the Australian team as a result of a million-to-one accident.

Richardson won the toss and had no hesitation in batting. An hour before stumps on day one the West Indies were all out for a modest 252, Merv Hughes taking 5/64 with a typical sustained burst of pace and hostility.

Australian openers Mark Taylor and David Boon walked out to negotiate a nasty session of less than an hour before stumps in deteriorating light.

Both knew from experience there would be no holding back by the West Indies pace attack. And they were right.

Taylor was out for one. To the surprise of many people, this brought Justin Langer to the crease in the first over of the Australian innings in his Test debut. The number three spot had been occupied by Steve Waugh in the earlier Tests, but captain Border and the selectors obviously thought that Langer had what it takes to fill that pivotal role.

Immediately Justin was on the receiving end of a fierce welcome from frighteningly fast Ian Bishop. Two short deliveries from Bishop to end the over were followed by a brutish ball at the start of his next that struck Langer on the back of the helmet with a thud you could hear in the grandstand. He wobbled on his feet like a boxer about to go down for the count.

Play was held up while physiotherapist Errol Alcott examined Langer, fearing that he might be concussed. Despite a cracked helmet that had to be replaced and a cut at the back of his head, the little Western Australian, one of the toughest players in the game, insisted that he was fit to continue batting. Alcott would have needed to drag him off the ground. Justin shook his head to clear it, put a new helmet on, took block again and prepared to face some more 'chin music'.

No prizes for guessing what came next – another rearing delivery from the big West Indian fast bowler. Two deliveries later Langer, uncharacteristically, backed away as Bishop was about to run in. Was he suffering delayed shock? Alcott and SACA medical officer Dr Don Beard rushed out to the middle to check him out but soon discovered that Justin was definitely *not* about to retire hurt.

With ten minutes left to play umpires Darrell Hair and Len King offered the light to the batsmen, who headed straight to the dressing room. Langer had toughed it out for 26 minutes and still hadn't scored his first Test match run. Boon, one of the fiercest competitors in world cricket, would have liked the look of what he had seen from the other end.

Boon and Langer resumed the combat next morning in unseasonally gloomy conditions. Justin was struck another blow, this time in the stomach while attempting to hook. Again he batted on. Boon too was in the wars, being hit on the left elbow by a searing Curtly Ambrose delivery. The blow left the Australian opener with no feeling in the forearm and hand, and no option other than to leave the field so that he could be taken to hospital for X-rays.

Mark Waugh came and went without troubling the scorers, leaving Australia at a perilous 2/16 with one man on the way to hospital. This brought Steve Waugh to the crease to join Langer, who was out late in the morning session for a heroic 20. He departed the scene to a standing ovation. It was 3/46 when Allan Border came in to embark on yet another rescue mission.

There was added pressure on the Australian captain as he was only 71 away from surpassing Sunil Gavaskar's Test record aggregate of 10,122 runs. Steve Waugh and Border remained together in the face of a West Indies fast bowling assault, as well as rain interruptions and bad light, to take the score to a respectable 3/100 when stumps were drawn.

Waugh's hands had taken a pounding while he was fending off the short-pitched bowling, leaving him with severe bruising to the fingers on both hands. The good news on the injury front was that David Boon's X-rays revealed no broken bones in his elbow. Having regained the feeling in his arm, the plucky Tasmanian had declared he would bat the next day.

Day three dawned like a typical Adelaide summer after more than four hours play had been lost earlier in the match as a result of bad weather. Normally at Adelaide Oval conditions for batting on the third day are as good as it gets anywhere in the world and so the day promised many Aussie runs.

But 3/100 soon became 4/108 when Border was caught in the slips off the hostile Curtly Ambrose, who was clearly a man on a mission. Ian Healy came and went quickly, bringing the gallant Boon back to the crease to confront a crisis for his team. Four runs later Steve Waugh too fell victim to Ambrose, and the giant Antiguan had claimed three wickets for three runs in nine balls.

Merv Hughes, who clearly has a sense of occasion, responded to the challenge Ambrose had laid down by scoring 43 of a 69-run partnership with Boon before he was out to the off-spin of Carl Hooper. Big Merv was looming as Man of the Match following his five-wicket haul in the West Indies first innings and now top scoring for his team.

After Shane Warne went lbw to Hooper for a duck Australia was in big trouble at 8/181. Tim May stuck around with Boon for a while before he became Ambrose's fifth victim and then Craig McDermott showed a lot of courage under fire, making 14 before Curtly struck again to finish with 6/74 in an awesome display of fast bowling.

Australia had struggled to 213 after losing 7/113 in a session and a bit, leaving them 39 runs behind the West Indies.

The wounded David Boon was stranded at the non-striker's end, unbeaten on 39. He had opened the innings, spent time in hospital during it and was still there at the finish. Boon batted for over three hours, most of that time with an elbow injury that would have stopped lesser mortals in their tracks.

The West Indies began their second innings half way through day three with plenty of time to build their slender lead to a total that would make life difficult for Australia, which would have to bat last on a wearing pitch.

The Australian bowlers soon showed that runs would be hard to earn. A fired-up Craig McDermott got rid of the dangerous Desmond Haynes in his third over, and followed that up with the wicket of Phil Simmons. Then Merv Hughes had Brian Lara well caught by Steve Waugh and McDermott bowled Keith Arthurton for a duck. The West Indies were on the back foot at 4/65.

Richie Richardson and Carl Hooper managed a partnership of 59 before Tim May began one of the most astonishing spells of spin bowling I have seen. It started when May had Hooper caught at deep square leg for 25 when the total was 5/124. From there, it was a procession. Junior Murray was May's second victim, caught at bat-pad by Mark Waugh without scoring and then Warne had Richardson caught behind for a belligerent 72 from only 106 balls. The West Indies were reeling at 7/145.

In quick succession May dismissed Curtly Ambrose, Ken Benjamin and Ian Bishop with the addition of just one more run. Incredibly the West Indies was all out just before stumps for 146, having lost 6/25 in a dramatic collapse. Tim May had the remarkable figures of 5/9 from 6.5 overs of off-spin bowling, taking 5/5 from his last 32 balls.

Unbelievably 17 wickets had fallen during the day while 259 runs were scored. Australia needed 186 runs to win the match and regain the

Frank Worrell Trophy with two full days remaining. On the other hand the West Indies speed machine had all that time to bowl Australia out and keep the series alive.

Day four was 26 January, Australia Day. It was also Tim May's 31st birthday. With the weather fine and clear it looked certain that this enthralling contest would be decided with a day to spare. If Australia was to win it needed to score at about two runs an over and keep some wickets intact. The West Indies needed to take ten wickets, or one every nine overs on average, while restricting the scoring to less than two an over. If none of this worked out there was always tomorrow.

Ambrose trapped Boon lbw without scoring and Australia was 1/5. With the score on 16 Mark Taylor edged one to the keeper off Benjamin and Australia had both openers back in the dressing room. Mark Waugh avoided a 'pair' then put on 38 runs with Justin Langer before Waugh was out to a Courtney Walsh lifter just before lunch. Australia had tumbled to 3/54.

Steve Waugh was dismissed first ball after lunch for 4, falling victim to Ambrose for the second time in the match and the sixth occasion so far in the series. Allan Border then got a ball from Ambrose that rose sharply off a good length. He succeeded only in fending it off from the front of his nose into the hands of Desmond Haynes. At 5/72 only the tenacious Langer remained of the recognised batsmen.

The situation became desperate when Ian Healy edged a Walsh delivery onto his stumps to complete a 'pair' and Merv Hughes went lbw to Ambrose in the next over. Ambrose had taken ten wickets for the match, leaving Australia facing defeat. The score was 7/74, and the Aussies had lost 4/16 in 30 minutes.

Langer, again showing courage under fire, had moved his score along to 25 while he watched six of his team-mates depart. But Australia needed 112 runs for victory, with just Warne, May and McDermott to support Langer. I doubt there was a single person at Adelaide Oval who thought the home team could truly win.

Warne and Langer stopped the rot, or rout if you like, by adding 28 before Warne went. Australia was 8/102, the deficit 84.

Tim May had put his team back in the match with his great bowling the previous day; now he had to get his head down and apply his batting skills to the task of staying out in the middle with Langer. May did that job to perfection, sustaining a number of blows to the body and fingers but continually getting right behind the ball against Ambrose, Walsh, Bishop and Benjamin.

Both players played their natural game, dispatching the odd loose delivery to the boundary and taking any runs that were on offer. Langer reached a courageous 50 to sustained applause from the crowd who were beginning to sense that Australia just might be in with a chance of snatching an improbable victory.

Then Langer's innings came to an unexpected end on 54, caught by wicketkeeper Junior Murray attempting to hook a short delivery from Bishop. Australia was now on the brink of defeat at 9/144, still requiring 42 to win. The young Western Australian was angry with himself, but he had shown he has what it takes.

Now it was down to Tim May and Craig McDermott. May had played more like a top-order batsman than a number ten while McDermott had looked composed in the first innings. He also had something to prove – the West Indies fast bowlers had claimed he backed away when the going got tough. But 42 runs?

May was cool in the crisis while McDermott moved his feet in the right direction, getting his bat and body behind anything pitched near the line of the stumps, standing up to the short deliveries and sending a message to the West Indies camp that he would not be intimidated.

Run by run these two reduced the deficit as the tension mounted. The crowd was rapt. *Waltzing Matilda* and *Come on, Aussie, Come on* echoed across the ground from the scoreboard bar.

Up in the match office where I was watching, strict instructions were issued that no one was allowed to move and nothing was to be said about the state of play. These superstitions, borrowed from the players' dressing rooms, had become a part of our way of doing things during tight finishes.

A run here, a couple there, the odd no-ball and leg bye kept the score ticking towards that magical total of 186 required for an Australian victory. Every run brought thunderous applause and a burst of singing. Soon the 42 deficit was reduced to 14 as May and McDermott played sensibly.

You could have cut the air with a knife as Richie Richardson called up his big guns, Curtly Ambrose and Courtney Walsh, for a final assault. Three runs off Walsh reduced the target to 11, two off Ambrose, and then another four conceded by Walsh made it five to win.

Ambrose steamed in for his 26th over of the day, but he could not make the break and two more runs were added to the total. Walsh bowled again with Australia needing just three runs to pinch the match. May took a single putting McDermott on strike with two runs to get. The last delivery of the over was the Courtney Walsh 'change up' ball, one that has caught many a batsman unprepared for the extra pace. This one was no exception. Short of a length, it lifted awkwardly in at McDermott, who pulled his bat from the danger area.

There was a noise as the ball hurried through to wicketkeeper Murray, and the West Indies players appealed in unison. Umpire Darrell Hair raised his finger and pandemonium broke loose. The West Indies players were jubilant, while McDermott stood at the crease for a few moments looking stunned by the realisation Australia had lost by one run, the narrowest loss in Test match history.

McDermott had batted 88 minutes for his defiant 18 runs while Tim May's unconquered 42 had occupied 135 minutes. Together they had put on 40 runs for the last wicket and had come within two runs of getting Australia over the line for what would have been a famous victory. As May and McDermott trudged off Adelaide Oval that evening, the disappointment on their faces told the story.

Their unhappiness was compounded by the opinion of many observers, including some of the Australian players, that the noise which prompted umpire Hair to give McDermott out caught behind had come from the ball clipping his helmet on the way through to Murray.

Channel 9 television footage taken by a camera located behind the wicket supported that view. I have a copy of the videotape of McDermott's dismissal that I have replayed frame-by-frame dozens of times. It clearly shows the ball still climbing at head height when it reaches the batsman, who is desperately drawing his bat and gloves out of the way.

The ball then appears to hit the peak of McDermott's helmet, at which point it changes trajectory and starts suddenly to angle downwards. By this time McDermott has turned partly away from the umpire. Next you see is the ball very near McDermott's batting gloves, which are below head high as he continues to swing around to remove them from the firing line. After that the trajectory of the ball changes again; instead of angling down it balloons straight towards the wicketkeeper, who gleefully takes the catch.

When the delivery appeared to brush McDermott's gloves they were behind his body, giving the umpire no chance of seeing what had actually taken place. The only conclusion that I can draw from all of this is that Darrell Hair, a fine international umpire, got his decision right in giving McDermott out – but it seems to me to have been based on the helmet noise, not on contact with the gloves.

But all this makes not one jot of difference. Once the umpire gives a batsman out, he must accept the decision and depart for the dressing rooms. Sadly there have been far too many instances in recent times when batsmen have been reluctant to leave the field. Match referees need to be tougher on this in my view.

Furthermore, an umpire is not required to explain why he has given a player out in response to an appeal; his decision is final and covers any method of dismissal. Allan Border summed the situation up after the match when he said of McDermott's dismissal: 'He was technically out but it was a very brave decision.'

Craig McDermott preferred not to talk to the media when it was over, but he did send out a pointed message. Roughly translated, it said: 'Ask them if I backed away.' No one could ever doubt his courage again.

Several years after that historic Test match I spoke to Tim May about the part he played in it. May, now the Chief Executive of the Australian Cricketers' Association, gave me an insight into the high drama out in the middle:

> Actually being out there batting at the end was the best place to be as far as I was concerned. Every person in the rooms was on the edge of their seats before I went out to bat, including me. When I got out in the middle I was nervous but felt that I had some control over what was going on. The guys back in the rooms couldn't do anything about the situation. When we got somewhere near the score required I was

convinced that we were going to win – after all it was Australia's and also my birthday.

When 'Billy' got out I couldn't see what had happened but I heard a noise and just looked at the ground for about 10 or 15 seconds. Initially I couldn't accept the fact that we had lost – it was like a bad dream. When we got back into the rooms everyone was devastated. There was about 20 minutes of eerie silence, not a word was said. Eventually (Federal opposition leader) John Hewson came in and the ice was broken. I remember saying bad luck to 'Billy' and he muttered something about getting a glove to that final delivery.

I have to say that we really were lucky to get as close as we did. With about 25 runs to go a Courtney Walsh full toss hit Craig on the pad dead in front of middle and off stump but the lbw appeal was turned down.

Tim told me that not a week had gone by that he had not thought about the match in some way.

The Greatest Sheffield Shield Final

South Australia had earned the right to host the Sheffield Shield final in March 1996 by finishing on top of the points table. Under the rules of the competition, if the five-day match ended in a draw the home team would be declared the winner of the Shield. This meant that visitors Western Australia would need to win outright in order to take home Lord Sheffield's sterling silver trophy.

This was the first Sheffield Shield final to be staged at Adelaide Oval. Before the 1982/83 season the top team at the end of the home and away series was automatically awarded the Shield. South Australia had played in two away finals in that time, one in Perth in 1988/89 when a draw saw Western Australia retain the Shield, the other against Queensland in Brisbane in 1994/95 when the home team won convincingly to claim the trophy for the first time. I had been at both of those finals and was hoping that the one coming up would be a case of third time lucky for the Croweaters – among whose number I now included myself

As I went to work at Adelaide Oval in the days leading up to the final there was an air of confidence around the place – you could feel it. The evening before the game I had called it a day and went around to the workshop where Les Burdett and some of his ground staff were having a quiet drink. There was an esky of icy cold West End draught nearby so I opened one and started to chat with the boys. It had become something of a ritual before a big match to relax a bit and compare notes about how things were shaping up.

Our marketing department had put in a lot of effort promoting the final, including having some car stickers made that carried the message 'This aint no walk in the park'. There were a few of these stickers lying around so Les and I decided to attach some to the tractors, mowers, rollers and other equipment to be used on the oval over the next five days. We thought that the Western Australians might need reminding that they had a real battle on their hands.

It was a great feeling to me personally as CEO, and all the SACA staff, to know that at last we had a team genuinely capable of winning the Sheffield Shield. Adelaide Oval on that evening was, more than ever, a truly magical place to be – there was something indescribable in the air.

The South Australian team led by Jamie Siddons had learnt a lot from their humiliating loss at the Gabba 12 months earlier and the players were buoyed by the advantage of playing at home. Coach Jeff Hammond and Siddons knew that, man for man, SA had the players to win the Shield *provided* each performed to the high standards the team had maintained throughout the season.

Some tough decisions had to be made by the SA selectors. A player would need to make way for Siddons, who had missed the previous match with injury. All-rounder Ben Johnson was the unfortunate one despite recent runs. Desperately unlucky too was young left-arm fast bowler Mark Harrity; he was distraught when told that he had been overlooked for the experienced Shane George.

Western Australia's captain Tom Moody won the toss and batted on a pitch that looked full of runs. But the first day honours went to South Australia, which had the visitors worried at stumps with the score 6/255 and the top order back in the dressing room. The good news for WA was that in-form Adam Gilchrist was still at the crease on 25. The young former New South Welshman had already hinted in previous innings that he could tear an attack to pieces. Adelaide Oval spectators didn't have to wait long to see just how good he was.

After night watchman Jo Angel was out early next morning, Gilchrist launched one of the most astonishing assaults on a quality bowling attack that I have ever seen. He just kept hitting the SA bowlers for six in the direction of the Victor Richardson gates. Partnered by Brad Hogg, he set about the job of building Western Australia's moderate overnight total into a mammoth one.

At lunch WA was 7/365 with Gilchrist on 94. Soon after the resumption he brought up his century by pulling a ball from Jason Gillespie for a huge six over mid-wicket. That was the signal to up the tempo as the exciting wicketkeeper-batsman thrashed the South Australian attack, hitting boundaries effortlessly to all parts of the ground. Tom Moody put an end to the carnage when he declared the innings closed just before tea with the score at 9/520. Gilchrist remained not out on 189 from just 187 balls, having scored 164 in less than two sessions.

Western Australia could not possibly lose the match. But could they *win* it and thereby take the Sheffield Shield back home to Perth? South Australia's strong batting line-up and a beautiful batting strip suggested that was most unlikely. Still, the pressure was now on the SA batsmen.

It didn't take long for the going to get tough. Greg Blewett was out lbw to big Jo Angel for five then Darren Webber was caught in slips off Angel for a duck and SA were 2/8. Now it was time for the tough to get going.

Seasoned campaigners Paul Nobes and Darren Lehmann rallied to the cause and at stumps the home side was 2/100, still 420 runs adrift of the WA total and 221 short of the follow-on mark. During the day 365 runs had been scored for the loss of just five wickets.

Day three was a war of attrition between two equally determined teams. Lehmann and Nobes took their partnership to 123 before Lehmann, on 43, became Angel's third victim. Jamie Siddons joined Nobes who moved along steadily, reaching a typically gritty, but not pretty, century – his second in successive Sheffield Shield finals. Nobes was one of those players who looked to be doing everything wrong when he had a bat in his hand.

He'd use it like a baseball bat to slam the ball flat down the ground and square of the wicket from a stance that suggested if he crouched any lower, he'd surely fall on his face. But he was a very effective operator.

The stocky opener was dismissed for precisely a ton when he was bowled by Brendon Julian's first delivery with the second new ball. In the next over Julian removed Siddons, who had carried a hip injury into the match, for a restrained 38. From 3/208 South Australia had tumbled to 5/217, still more than 100 runs short of the follow-on target.

James Brayshaw and Tim Nielsen took the score to 291 when Nielsen was out for a patient 27, becoming lion-hearted Julian's third victim. Tim May followed soon after for five, leaving SA in bother at 7/296.

Jason Gillespie joined Brayshaw and they batted through until stumps, which were drawn with South Australia 7/330, just beyond the 321 it needed to avoid the follow-on. Brayshaw, playing against his old team, had toughed it out in an innings that would have given him more satisfaction than it did his father Ian, a former WA captain.

So far SA had survived four sessions, losing just seven batsmen in a situation where wickets in hand were critical. With two days to go, the outright win WA needed looked to be slipping away.

That situation changed dramatically the next morning. Julian dismissed Gillespie and Peter McIntyre in the third over of the day with the addition of only one run. When Brayshaw was run out for the dreaded 87, South Australia was all out for 347, leaving Western Australia with a lead of 173.

Tom Moody's tactics were now simple: score as many quick runs as possible then declare later in the day, allowing sufficient time and overs for the bowlers to dismiss South Australia.

The aggressive Damien Martyn was moved up the order to open the batting and Gilchrist was listed to come in at number four. Throwing caution to the wind, WA were quickly 3/18 with Martyn, Mark Lavender and Gilchrist all out. Two more quick wickets and it was 5/64 as the chase for quick runs continued.

Moody and Mike Hussey ended thoughts of a rout with a century partnership. The declaration finally came about 20 minutes after tea, leaving South Australia a target of 342 to win with nearly four sessions remaining. That worked out at about three runs an over. Of more relevance was the fact that there were at least 115 overs left for the home team to negotiate if it was to force a draw – which now seemed improbable. Western Australia only needed to pick up a wicket every 65 balls on a wearing, fifth-day pitch.

South Australia lost Nobes and Webber before stumps. Greg Blewett was looking rock solid on 22 and perennial night-watchman Jason Gillespie had hung in there for 13 minutes. SA would have to bat for at least another six hours without losing more than seven wickets to bring the Shield to Adelaide after 14 years. Big Tom Moody and his team must have been licking their lips.

I arrived at Adelaide Oval hours before play began on the last day, and immediately felt the tension. This was it – the whole season boils down to this one day, I thought to myself. The pitch, as you would expect after four days of heavy traffic, had footmarks that the bowlers could land the ball in, cracks that would only get wider as the day wore on. There were also a few loose pieces in the pitch about the size of a saucer. I didn't like our chances of surviving the day at all, especially as Siddons' hip injury had now become worse and he would only be able to bat with the help of pain-killing injections.

As soon as play got under way Julian was in the action and Gillespie was out of it, caught by Moody for five. Darren Lehmann walked out to join Blewett having been in tremendous touch for the whole season. Unfortunately for South Australia 'Boof's' tally of runs remained at 1237, lbw for a duck to a Julian in-swinger courtesy of umpire Steve Randell. Every South Australian at the ground, and the many thousands listening on the radio, must have given a groan of disappointment. If Lehmann had settled in perhaps SA could have scored at six-an-over and won the game. But now?

All of a sudden South Australia was four down with more than 90 overs to be bowled. Western Australia looked to have it all wrapped up.

Enter James Brayshaw. Rather than put up the shutters and play for the draw, Brayshaw went on the attack, blasting dangerous left-arm spinner Brad Hogg out of the attack.

As the balance of the game swung to and fro, so did my emotions. If we win the Sheffield Shield all the planning that had gone into developing this very competitive team over recent years would bear fruit. Spectators, sponsors, players, the board, staff, media, politicians and people in the street in SA would be happy. Lose? Don't even think about it – remain positive. This is *our* year.

Blewett and Brayshaw took the total to 4/140 at lunch. Now an SA win seemed possible again: 202 runs needed in four hours with six wickets in hand. But soon after the break Hogg took his revenge on Brayshaw and at 5/169 it was time for the injured captain Jamie Siddons to lead from the front. Normally Siddons would show the way with aggressive batting and fast running between the wickets. This time, however, the skipper – who could hardly walk, let alone run – made it clear that wickets in hand, not runs, were his priority.

In an innings that almost defies description, Jamie took just on an hour to get off the mark. Tom Moody had set a ring of close-in fielders in catching positions and switched his bowlers around who, in turn, tried bouncers, full tosses, long hops and just about every imaginable ploy in an attempt to remove the determined SA captain. But he was resolute.

I later asked Jamie what had caused the sudden rush of blood that made him thump his 58th delivery to the boundary. 'It was up there in the slot so I hit it through the gap before I knew what I had done,' he said with grin.

Siddons and Greg Blewett were using up valuable time and overs when, approaching the tea interval, Julian struck yet again, trapping Blewett lbw for a patient 72. Tim Nielsen and Siddons saw it through to tea with the Shield in the balance. WA needed four wickets; the home side needed only to endure

Nielsen was dismissed first ball after tea by a grubber from Jo Angel. A couple more of them and we could all go home – and there were still over 180 balls to be bowled on this exhausted pitch.

Tim May then joined his captain in a contest to see who could last the longest without scoring. The pair faced 16 overs without scoring a run off the bat. But there wasn't a slow hand clap to be heard – it was nail-biting stuff and the crowd was enthralled.

Eventually May was out for a truly magnificent duck. After 64 minutes at the crease he deflected a Julian faster ball from his gloves onto the stumps. Now only Peter McIntyre and Shane George were left to help the stationary Siddons bat out the remaining hour, or roughly 16 overs.

Jamie was having trouble playing forward defensively as the pain from his hip increased but, while he was still batting, we knew that one end was fairly safe. As for McIntyre and George – well, the captain had probably tossed a coin to determine which of these fine bowlers would bat at number 11.

McIntyre and Siddons took the score to 8/202 when, with 60 balls remaining, the brave Siddons was finally out after 107 minutes. He'd made brilliant centuries, but I reckon that Jamie would cherish his four-run vigil more than any of them. The captain departed to a standing ovation from a crowd that by now had swollen to well over 10,000 as the whisper spread around the city of the miracle at Adelaide Oval.

Could Peter McIntyre and Shane George survive 59 balls of Brendon Julian's speed and swing and Brag Hogg's sharp turn and bounce? Not bloody likely, you would think.

By now the crowd was counting down every ball, cheering each defensive prod. The batsmen had worked out a strategy: Macca would take the fast stuff from Julian and Georgey would handle the guile of Hogg.

At 30 balls to glory I started to think to myself that South Australia could pull this off. Not that I dared say it out loud to the staff up in the match office.

Faces were tense wherever you looked – out on the field, in the crowd and in the dressing rooms. Three overs to go, two and then just six balls more. Dog-tired Brendon Julian, who had given his all for his team, was asked by Moody to deliver his final over of the season.

His first ball beats the outside edge of the bat and goes through to the keeper. The next two are in-swinging yorkers that Macca somehow keeps out. Three balls to go and the tension is unbearable in the match office as big Brendon changes the line to leg stump from over the wicket. McIntyre turns it away to the on side but the batsmen ignore the easy single.

The fifth ball has a beam on middle stump but Mighty Macca keeps it out. The batsmen confer in mid-pitch to ease the pressure. What on earth are they talking about? Tom Moody gees up his tireless fast bowler, who is still running in hard at the end of his 29th over.

The crowd has stopped counting down the balls. All is dead quiet as Julian comes in to bowl. It's pitched up on the off stump but McIntyre gets right in behind it. The ball squirts away in front of him.

Mayhem breaks loose as McIntyre dances off the ground with George right behind. In the match office there are cheers and tears, hugs and handshakes – at last I am free to speak but I can't get a word out, it is all too much. Hundreds of excited spectators stream onto the ground. The Sheffield Shield has gone to South Australia in one of the greatest cricket matches of all time. The Western Australian players, bitterly disappointed, stay out on the ground and wait to congratulate the home team.

I make my way around to the South Australian dressing room. It is sheer chaos. The adrenalin is still pumping and the 'ghetto blaster' thumping as the players hug. The champagne and tears flow. Jamie Siddons embraces his wife, Deetha, in one of the most poignant cricketing moments I have witnessed.

Eventually SA coach 'Bomber' Hammond and I get the players out on to the ground for the presentation ceremony, which I have to conduct – somehow. Most of them were in the losing team in the Gabba final twelve months ago and they know how the gallant Western Australians are feeling. Out of respect they keep a lid on their emotions.

Denis Rogers, chairman of the Australian Cricket Board presents the Sheffield Shield to Jamie Siddons. Feeling no pain at all now, he hoists the heavy silver trophy over his head in triumph. The South Australian players come up one by one to receive their victory medals and then it is time to celebrate. And celebrate they did – for days and everywhere they went the Sheffield Shield went, with 'Boof' Lehmann as self appointed custodian of the silverware. He wouldn't let it out of his sight.

And all this for a draw! But it sure wasn't a walk in the park.

Looking back now on these three remarkable cricket matches and reflecting on my four decades of enjoyable involvement in the sport, I am reminded of some words I first read many years ago that encapsulate everything I love so dearly about the game.

I don't know the name of the author, nor how long ago it was written, as all my efforts over the years to find out who this wise person was have been fruitless. But it seems appropriate to share them here:

> Cricket is the most civilised sport devised by or for the human race.
>
> The health and fitness aspects are minor.
>
> Cricket is a means of our continuing to absorb, effortlessly, the lessons that the game has given us since we were children.
>
> Cricket is about competing interests accepting binding rules willingly; about taking victory and defeat; about the infinitely subtle quirks of nature, from the grass to the wind, and the limited feebleness of human endeavours in managing the physical world; about the use of guile and brain as much as muscle and fleetness; about caution and courage and stupidity; about the responsibilities that men have to each other in according dignity and fair-dealing; about the sad passage of youth in time.

INDEX

Wakefield Press has been publishing good Australian books
for over fifty years. For a catalogue of current and
forthcoming titles, or to add your name to our mailing list,
send your name and address to
Wakefield Press, Box 2266, Kent Town, South Australia 5071.

TELEPHONE (08) 8362 8800 FAX (08) 8362 7592
WEB www.wakefieldpress.com.au

Wakefield Press thanks Arts South Australia
for its continued support.